P9-CDK-294

THE THEATRE OF TENNESSEE WILLIAMS

Volume I

By TENNESSEE WILLIAMS

PLAYS

Baby Doll & Tiger Tail
Camino Real
Cat on a Hot Tin Roof
Clothes for a Summer Hotel
Dragon Country
The Glass Menagerie
A Lovely Sunday for Creve Coeur
Not About Nightingales
The Notebook of Trigorin
The Red Devil Battery Sign
Small Craft Warnings
Something Cloudy, Something Clear
Stopped Rocking and Other Screenplays
A Streetcar Named Desire
Sweet Bird of Youth
THE THEATRE OF TENNESSEE WILLIAMS, VOLUME I
Battle of Angels, A Streetcar Named Desire, The Glass Menagerie
THE THEATRE OF TENNESSEE WILLIAMS, VOLUME II
The Eccentricities of a Nightingale, Summer and Smoke, The Rose Tattoo, Camino Real
THE THEATRE OF TENNESSEE WILLIAMS, VOLUME III
Cat on a Hot Tin Roof, Orpheus Descending, Suddenly Last Summer
THE THEATRE OF TENNESSEE WILLIAMS, VOLUME IV
Sweet Bird of Youth, Period of Adjustment, The Night of the Iguana
THE THEATRE OF TENNESSEE WILLIAMS, VOLUME V
The Milk Train Doesn't Stop Here Anymore, Kingdom of Earth (The Seven Descents of Myrtle), Small Craft Warnings, The Two-Character Play
THE THEATRE OF TENNESSEE WILLIAMS, VOLUME VI
27 Wagons Full of Cotton and Other Short Plays
THE THEATRE OF TENNESSEE WILLIAMS, VOLUME VII
In the Bar of a Tokyo Hotel and Other Plays
THE THEATRE OF TENNESSEE WILLIAMS, VOLUME VIII
Vieux Carré, A Lovely Sunday for Creve Coeur, Clothes for a Summer Hotel, The Red Devil Battery Sign
27 Wagons Full of Cotton and Other Plays
The Two-Character Play
Vieux Carré

POETRY

Androgyne, Mon Amour
In the Winter of Cities

PROSE

Collected Stories
Eight Mortal Ladies Possessed
Hard Candy and Other Stories
One Arm and Other Stories
The Roman Spring of Mrs. Stone
Where I Live: Selected Essays

THE THEATRE OF TENNESSEE WILLIAMS

Volume I

Battle of Angels

The Glass Menagerie

A Streetcar Named Desire

A NEW DIRECTIONS BOOK

Manufactured in the United States of America.
New Directions Books are printed on acid-free paper.
First published clothbound in 1971 and as New Directions Paperbook 694 in 1990.
Published simultaneously in Canada by Penguin Books Canada Limited.

Library of Congress Cataloging-in-Publication Data

Williams, Tennessee, 1911-1983.
The theatre of Tennessee Williams.
p. cm.
Contents: v. 1. Battle of the angels. The glass menagerie. A streetcar named Desire —v. 2. The eccentricities of a nightingale. Summer and smoke. The rose tattoo. Camino Real —v. 5. The milk train doesn't stop here anymore. Kingdom of Earth (The seven descents of Myrtle). Small craft warnings. The two-character play.
ISBN 0-8112-1135-5 (v. 1: pbk.: alk. paper)
I. Title.
PS3545.I5365A19 1990
812'.54—dc20 90-5998
CIP

New Directions Books are published for James Laughlin
by New Directions Publishing Corporation,
80 Eighth Avenue, New York 10011

FIFTH PAPERBOUND PRINTING
SEVENTH CLOTHBOUND PRINTING

Contents

BATTLE OF ANGELS

Battle of Angels, a play in 2 acts and 3 scenes, was presented by the Theatre Guild, Inc., at the Wilbur Theatre, Boston, for two weeks, starting December 30, 1940, and ending January 11, 1941. Margaret Webster directed, the setting was by Cleon Throckmorton and the incidental music was by Colin McPhee, plus Negro spiritual recordings by H. F. Chalfin. No one is listed as lighting director in the program. *Orpheus Descending,* a later version of the play, is included in Volume III of *The Theatre of Tennessee Williams.*

The Cast:

DOLLY BLAND	DOROTHY PETERSON
BEULAH CARTWRIGHT	EDITH KING
PEE WEE BLAND	ROBERT EMHARDT
SHERIFF TALBOTT	CHARLES MCCLELLAND
CASSANDRA WHITESIDE	DORIS DUDLEY
VEE TALBOTT	KATHERINE RAHT
VALENTINE XAVIER	WESLEY ADDY
EVA TEMPLE	HAZEL HANNA
BLANCH TEMPLE	HELEN CAREWE
MYRA TORRANCE	MIRIAM HOPKINS
JOE	CLARENCE WASHINGTON
SMALL BOY	BERTRAM HOLMES
BENNIE	ICAN LEWIS
JABE TORRANCE	MARSHALL BRADFORD

Other characters: CONJURE MAN; a pair of middle-aged TOURISTS; three GIRLS; a Negro HUCKSTER; DAVID ANDERSON; LOON; three MEN; MRS. REGAN.

PROLOGUE

SCENE: *A "mercantile" store in a very small and old-fashioned town in the Deep South. It has large windows facing a tired dirt road, across which is a gasoline pump, a broken-down wagon and cotton fields which extend to a cypress brake and the levee. The windows are shielded from sunlight by a tin portico so that the interior is rather dusky. The ceiling is very high and has two or three ceiling fans and old-fashioned lighting fixtures. There are a good many vertical lines which contribute to a dramatic atmosphere in the setting. In the back wall of the store is a steep flight of stairs leading up to the living quarters above. Left of this stairway is an open arch revealing a further room, the store's confectionery department.*

At the time this Prologue takes place—a Sunday afternoon about a year after the culmination of the tragedy—the store is no longer being run as a store, but has been converted into a museum exhibiting souvenirs of the sensational events which had taken place there. Various articles connected with the tragedy are on display, such as the snakeskin jacket, which is suspended in a conspicuous position. All these articles are labeled with crude hand-lettered signs.

An ancient Negro, the CONJURE MAN, *is dozing in a chair in the archway. There is an awesome dignity in his appearance, despite the grotesque touches of his costume. He is small and cadaverous, a wizard-like figure, with a double strand of bleached chicken or hawk bones strung about his neck, tiny bells sewn to his sleeves so that he makes a slight tinkling sound when he moves, and various other odd tokens or charms scattered about his garments, which he sells to the superstitious.*

[*There is a knock at the door.*]

WOMAN'S VOICE: Uncle! Uncle! [*The old* NEGRO *starts up. He rises and shuffles leisurely across to the door, unbolts it and draws it open on the mellow afternoon sunlight.* EVA *and* BLANCH TEMPLE *step inside.*]

EVA: Goodness . . .

BLANCH: Gracious sakes alive! It takes you forever to move a couple of inches. Come on in, folks! This is the famous Torrance Mercantile Store of Two Rivers, Mississippi. [*They are followed by a pair of middle-aged tourists.*]

EVA: Some people think it's sort of commercial of us to turn it into what the newspapers refer to as a Tragic Museum —but after all . . .

BLANCH: There's nothing else we can do to pay the taxes. Nobody would use this building for any other purpose, knowing what all happened in here once.

EVA: Not that it's haunted, but . . .

BLANCH: It's full of shadows. Electric power's cut off. Needless expense.

EVA: Electric power was off at the time it happened.

BLANCH: The power always goes off when it rains real hard and that Good Friday was one of the heaviest rains we've had in Two Rivers County.

EVA: Miss Harkaway called it a cataclysm of nature.

BLANCH: She was that wonderful Memphis newspaperwoman who wrote it all up in the *Commercial Appeal.*

EVA: Everything's just as it was.

BLANCH: Except of course the merchandise was removed.

EVA: Nothing has been took out that had a connection.

BLANCH: Everything in the museum has a label on it. You all can just browse around and we'll explain everything.

EVA: How can they ask any questions, you talking so fast?

BLANCH: You get me all balled up with your interruptions! Now that over there is the famous Jesus picture!

EVA: Don't call it *that.*

BLANCH: That's what *everyone* calls it. He *was* good-looking.

EVA: I never noticed he was.

BLANCH: Don't be ridiculous. *Everyone* noticed he was.

EVA: Now that dress there is the dress that Myra was wearing. Beulah said to her, "What do they call that color?"

BLANCH: She smiled an' she said, "They call it ecstasy blue!" Then didn't Myra . . . ?

EVA: Myra went back upstairs. Jabe knocked on the ceiling. That was when Vee . . .

BLANCH: Never mind about that. We'll tell that later. There is the phone . . .

EVA: The receiver is still off the hook.

BLANCH: The cashbox drawer's still open.

EVA: The money has been removed.

BLANCH [*regretfully*]: There *wasn't* much.

EVA: Frightfully, frightfully *little.* We are the only surviving relations, of course.

BLANCH [*pointing to the floor*]: You see those stains?

EVA: They're fading out. We'll have to touch them up.

BLANCH: Across the floor? Toward the confectionery?

EVA: Let's go in there! [*She rushes eagerly forward.*] Uncle, the *lamp!*

BLANCH: You probably wonder why we put up with such a peculiar old man as the caretaker here. Well, it's like this...

EVA: He's part of the exhibition!

BLANCH: Don't call it that!

EVA: Oh, the memorial then! What's the difference? This Conjure Man, as they call him...

BLANCH: Comes from Blue Mountain. Myra gave him odd jobs.

EVA: He was on the place when everything happened that happened.

BLANCH: He claims he knows some things that he isn't telling.

EVA: He's kind of daft. Now this room here is the Torrance Confectionery. Myra had it all done over for spring.

BLANCH: Yes, redecorated. Somebody made a remark how lovely it was. "Yes," said Myra, "it's supposed to resemble the orchard across from Moon Lake!" Notice those imitations...

EVA: Dogwood blossoms. And that big Japanese lantern. It's dingy now but you all can just imagine how lovely it was.

BLANCH: Miss Harkaway put it in such a beautiful way. The mercantile store, she said, was reality, harsh and drab, but Myra's confectionery...

EVA: That was where she kept her dreams. Uncle, turn up that lamp. I want these people to see the place where she kept her dreams. [*The lamp is turned up higher. The confectionery blooms into a nostalgic radiance, as dim and soft as memory itself.*] Remind me, Blanch, to sprinkle a little roach powder on this floor.

EVA: Let's go upstairs.

BLANCH: I think we've left out something.

EVA: You can talk so fast I didn't keep track of it all.

BLANCH: It's you with your interruptions that ball things up. Watch out for these stairs, they're terrible, terrible steep.

EVA: We can't be responsible for an accident on them.

BLANCH: Goodness sakes alive, *no!* These terrible taxes . . .

EVA: Keep us poor as church mice! [*They lead the way up the stairs.*]

BLANCH: You keep awake, Uncle.

EVA: If anyone else stops in, just ring the bell.

BLANCH [*opening the door on the landing*]: Now these are the living quarters.

EVA: Myra's bedroom's on the right an' Jabe's on the left.

[*The light fades out as the door closes. The* CONJURE MAN *laughs to himself as the curtain falls.*]

ACT ONE

SCENE: *The same as for the Prologue, except that it is now a year earlier—in early February—and the store is in operation, stocked with merchandise. There are great bolts of pepperel and percale which stand upright on the counters. The black skeleton of a dressmaker's dummy stands meaninglessly in front of a thin white column. Along the wall at the left is the shoe department, with a ladder that slides along the shelves and two or three shoe-fitting chairs. Racks of dresses, marked "Spring Styles," line the right wall.*

DOLLY *and* BEULAH *are arranging candles and setting a buffet table in the general store. They are wives of small planters, about thirty and overdressed.* DOLLY'S *husband,* PEE WEE, *and the town* SHERIFF *are in the confectionery shooting pinball. A train whistles in the distance.*

DOLLY: Pee Wee! That's the Cannonball!

PEE WEE [*from the confectionery*]: Okay, Mama! [PEE WEE *enters: He is a heavy man. His vest comes midway down the white-shirted bulge of his belly; his laced boots are caked with mud.*] Ninety-five nickles an' no pay-off! What would you call that, Mama?

DOLLY: Outrageous! Not the machine, but you poor suckers that play it.

BEULAH: This meringue turned out real good.

SHERIFF [*entering from the confectionery, laughing*]: You got to mid-aisle it three times straight's the only way to crack that goddam pot.

PEE WEE: I'm gonna tell Jabe about it. Ninety-five nickels an' no pay-off. [*They go out.*]

DOLLY: I guess Jabe Torrance has got more to think about than that ole pinball game in the confectionery. Huh?

BEULAH: He ought to have. That meringue *is* nice and light. I put in two drops of almond. Yesterday I was talking to Dr. Bob. You know, young Dr. Bob?

DOLLY: Uh-huh. What did he say?

BEULAH: I ast him how Jabe was, what kind of condition he really seemed to be in. He's seen them X-ray pictures they took in the Memphis Hospital after the operation. Well . .

DOLLY: What did he say, Beulah?

BEULAH: He said the worst that a doctor can ever say.

DOLLY: What's that?

BEULAH: Nothing at all, not a spoken word did he utter; he simply looked at me with those big dark eyes and shook his haid—like this!

DOLLY [*speaking with doleful optimism*]: I guess he signed Jabe Torrance's death warrant with just that single motion of his haid.

BEULAH: Exackly what I thought. I understand that they cut him open . . .

DOLLY: An' sewed him right back up?

BEULAH [*struggling to speak and strangling on an olive*]: Mmm. Mmm. [*She points at her stuffed mouth.*] I didn't know these olives had seeds in them.

DOLLY: You thought they was stuffed?

BEULAH: Uh-huh.

DOLLY: Where's the Temple Sisters?

BEULAH: Snooping around upstairs.

DOLLY: Let Myra catch 'em at it, she'll lay 'em both out good. She never did invite nobody up there.

BEULAH: Well, I was surprised when I went up myself.

DOLLY: I know it.

BEULAH: Two separate bedrooms, too! Maybe it's just since Jabe's been sick.

DOLLY: Naw, it's permanent, honey. As a girl in Tupelo she certainly wasn't cold-blooded. We used to go double together me an' Pee Wee an' her and that Anderson boy. All of one spring we would go to the orchard across from Moon Lake ev'ry night. We was engaged, but they wasn't. Boll weevil and army-worm struck his cotton awful three times straight. He married into the Delta Planters' Bank and Myra married Jabe. Myra was Myra then. Since then she's just a woman that works in a mercantile store.

[CASSANDRA WHITESIDE *enters at the door on the right. She is dark and strikingly beautiful, of a type rather peculiar to the South—physically delicate with clear translucent skin and luminous eyes as though burnt thin by her intensity of feeling. With people she has a rather disdainful ease, not deliberate or conscious, but rooted in her class origin and the cynical candor with which she recognizes herself and the social contradictions and tragic falsity of the world she lives in.* SANDRA *is the only woman of aristocratic extraction in the group. Her family is the oldest in this part of the Delta and was once the richest, but their plantation has dwindled with each successive generation.* SANDRA *has been "going out" for ten years and is still unmarried, which is enough in itself to destroy a girl's reputation.*]

DOLLY: Sandra Whiteside! How are you?

SANDRA: Oh, I seem to be still living. God knows why. Where's Myra?

DOLLY: Gone to Memphis to bring Jabe back from the hospital.

BEULAH: The men folks just now went to the depot to meet them.

SANDRA: Oh. . . . I want some cartridges for this pistol of mine. [*She removes it from her bag.*] I thought I better carry one with me. I'm on the road so much you'd think I was making a political campaign tour, the number of places I've got to visit this weekend. Memphis, Jackson— Is this the hardware section? [*approaching the counter*] Aw, here's cartridges! [*She helps herself.*] Then on down to New Awleuns for the start of the carnival season. Tell Myra to charge these to me. I ought to buy an airplane. They say that you only crack up once in the air.

DOLLY: Well, you'd better stay out of airplanes, honey.

BEULAH: How many times have you cracked up on the highway?

SANDRA: Today was the seventh since New Year's.

DOLLY: No!

SANDRA: I fell asleep at the wheel an' ran into a fence.

BEULAH: Goodness!

DOLLY: Gracious!

BEULAH: Last week she had a collision with a mule.

DOLLY: My Lawd!

SANDRA: And just to show you the absolute lack of justice, the mule was killed and I was completely uninjured!

DOLLY [*with false concern*]: Darling, you'd better be careful!

SANDRA: Oh, I don't know. What else can you do when you live in Two River County but drive like hell! [*There is the sound of a car out in front.*]

BEULAH: 'S 'at them?

DOLLY [*sarcastically*]: Naw, it's the Sheriff's little fireside companion.

BEULAH: Vee Talbott! Who is that with her? A *man!* [*This word creates a visible stir among the three women.*]

DOLLY: Uh-huh! Yes, it is!

BEULAH: Who could it be I wonder?

DOLLY: I can't make out. Oh, my goodness! What an outfit he's got on! It looks like a snakeskin jacket.

BEULAH: *Wha-at?* Do you know him?

DOLLY: Naw, I don't know him a-tall. He looks like an absolute stranger. Poor Vee has got her skirt caught in the car door or something, it's hitched up over her knees and she's simply *frantic* about it! [*She utters a sharp laugh.*]

BEULAH: She's such a big clumsy thing. Who do you think the man is?

DOLLY: I told you I never have seen him, don't know him from Adam, darling. Maybe he's one of the Twelve Apostles that she's been painting on.

SANDRA: Is Vee painting the Twelve Apostles?

DOLLY: She's been painting them for twelve years, one each year. She says that she sees them in visions. But every one of them looks like some man around Two River County. She told Birdie Wilson that she was hoping she'd have a vision of Jesus next Passion Week so she could paint Him, too.

BEULAH: You better quit staring.

DOLLY: She's finally got her skirt loose. Oh, God, the hem's ripped out, it's trailing the ground! [*She laughs and crosses from the window.*]

[VEE *enters from the street. She is a heavy, middle-aged woman, about forty, whose personality, frustrated in its contact with externals, has turned deeply inward. She has found refuge in religion and primitive art and has become known as an eccentric. Although a religious fanatic, a mystic, she should not be made ridiculous. Her portrayal will contain certain incidents of humor, but not be devoid of all dignity or pathos. She wanders slowly about with a vague dreamy smile on her face. Her expression is often bewildered.*]

BEULAH [*with loud, false cordiality*]: Hello, Vee honey, how are you?

DOLLY: Hello, Vee.

VEE [*faintly*]: Hello. I got m' skirt caught in the lock of the Chevrolet door an' I think it's torn loose a little. I can't see behind me good. Does it look like it's torn to you? [*She peers awkwardly, ponderously, behind her at the hem which dangles across the floor, like a big heavy dog trying to catch its tail.*]

BEULAH: Just a little bit, honey.

DOLLY: Yes, it's scarcely noticeable even. [*She giggles.*]

VEE: I feel like something was dragging. Oh, it *has* been torn, the young man told me it wasn't!

DOLLY: Say, who is he?

VEE: I don't know who he is, but I think he's all right, though. He told me he'd been saved, doesn't smoke, doesn't drink. His parents are dead, both of them, but he's got an uncle who's a Catholic priest and he says that he stayed six years—I mean his uncle—in some leper colony on a South Sea island without ever catching any sign of disease. Isn't that wonderful, though?

DOLLY: Huh.

BEULAH: What's he doing here?

VEE: Says he's exploring the world an' ev'rything in it.

DOLLY: Laudamighty!

VEE: He come to the lockup las' night an' ast for a bed, but he couldn't stay in it, though, the bars made him nervous.

DOLLY: So what did you do with him then?

VEE: What do you mean? I was alone in the house so I give him a blanket; he went out to sleep in his car.

DOLLY: Sounds like a peculiar person.

BEULAH: Yeah.

VEE: Oh, no, he just isn't a type that you are used to seeing. I'm going to speak a good word for him to Myra, she said she might be needing some help around here. [VAL *appears in the front door. He is about twenty-five years old. He has a fresh and primitive quality, a virile grace and freedom of body, and a strong physical appeal.*] Come right on in, Mr. Xavier.

VAL: What shall I do with this here?

VEE: Jus' give me the sherbet. I thought Mr. Torrance might need somethin' light an' digestible so I brought sherbet.

BEULAH: What flavuh is it? Pineapple?

VEE: Pineapple.

BEULAH: Oh, goody, I love pineapple. Don't you-all? [*She hands* VEE *the napkin-wrapped bowl.*]

VEE: Mr. Xavier, I was just telling these ladies about your uncle that went to live with the lepers. Some people are doubtful about the power of faith but there's an example I think should convince anybody.

BEULAH: Isn't it, though? Let's put this right in the Frigidaire before it stahts t' melt.

DOLLY [*lifting the napkin*]: I'm afraid you're locking the stable after the hause is gone.

BEULAH: Wh-at? Is it melted awready?

DOLLY: Reduced to juice!

BEULAH: Oh foot!—Well, let's put it in anyhow, it might thicken up.

VEE: Where is the Frigidaire?

BEULAH: It's in the confectionery. [*The three women go back through the archway.* SANDRA *is left with* VAL. *She laughs in her throat and leans provocatively back.* VAL *stares at her with a touch of antagonism. This challenging silence continues for a marked pause. Then* SANDRA *laughs again, somewhat louder.*]

VAL [*sharply*]: Is something amusing you, lady?

SANDRA [*drawling*]: Yes, very much. I think it's that jacket you're wearing. What stuff is it made of?

VAL: Snakeskin.

SANDRA [*with a disgusted grimace*]: Ouuu!

VAL: I didn't ask your opinion.

SANDRA: I didn't express one, did I?

VAL: Yeah. You said "Ouuu!" [*He mocks her grimace.*]

SANDRA: You know what that was? It was fascinated revulsion. [*She goes into the confectionery and starts the juke box. It plays* "Custro Vidas."] Would you like to dance?

VAL: I don't know how to dance.

SANDRA: I'd love to teach you. We'll go out jooking some night.

VAL: Jooking? What's that?

SANDRA: That's where you get in a car and drink a little and drive a little and dance a little. Then you drink a little more and drive a little more and dance a little more. Then you stop dancing and just drink and drive. Then you stop driving and you just drink. And then, finally, you stop drinking.

VAL: Then what do you do?

SANDRA: That depends entirely on who you happen to be out jooking with. If you're out with me, and you're sufficiently attractive, you nearly always wind up on Cypress Hill.

VAL: What's that?

SANDRA: That's the graveyard, honey. It's situated, appropriately enough, on the highest point of land in Two River County, a beautiful windy bluff just west of the Sunflower River.

VAL: Why do you go out there?

SANDRA: Because dead people give such good advice.

VAL: What advice do they give?

SANDRA: Just one word—*live!* [BEULAH *rushes in with a bowl of something.*]

BEULAH: You're going to stay fo' the pahty, Mr. . . . ?

VAL: Xavier.

BEULAH: I know some Seviers in Blue Mountain. Any relation?

VAL: Spelt with an "S" or an "X"?

BEULAH: An "S," I believe.

VAL: No relation.

BEULAH [*sympathetically*]: Awwww. [*She rushes back out.*]

SANDRA: I have a great aunt who's laid away on Cypress Hill. Her name was Cassandra, the same as mine is, so I always empty my bottles on her grave. She loved to drink. She finally got so she just lay on the bed and drank and drank all night and all day. They asked her if she didn't get tired of it. She said, "No, I never get bored. I have moving pictures on my ceiling. They go on all the time, continuous performance. I'm the main actress," she said, "and I do the most mah-velous things!" That was Cassandra the second. I'm the third. The first was a little Greek girl who slept in the shrine of Apollo. Her ears were snake-bitten, like mine, so that she could understand the secret language of the birds. You know what they told her, Snakeskin? They contradicted everything that she'd been told before. They said it was all stuff an' nonsense, a pack of lies. They advised her to drive her car as fast as she wanted to drive it, to dance like she wanted to dance. Get drunk, they said, raise hell at Moon Lake casina, do bumps an' wiggle your fanny! [VEE TALBOT *enters; she stops short with an outraged look.* SANDRA *laughs and extends a pack of cigarettes toward* VAL.]

VEE: Mr. Xavier don't smoke. [*She sets the potato chips down and goes out.*]

DOLLY [*rushing through*]: Mr. Xavier, if you're looking for work, you might drop in on my husband, Pee Wee Bland. He runs that cotton gin right over the road there.

BEULAH: The marguerites! I smell them burning! [*She runs out.*]

SANDRA: How did you happen to come to this dark, wild river country of ours?

VAL: A broken axle stopped me here last night.

SANDRA: You'd better mend it quick and move along.

VAL: Why's that?

SANDRA: Why? Why? Don't you know what those women are suffering from: Sexual malnutrition! They look at you with eyes that scream "Eureka!" [*She laughs and saunters casually to the door. She raises her revolver and fires two shots into the sky.*]

VAL: For God's sake! [*The three women scream and come rushing back in. The* TEMPLE SISTERS *shriek upstairs and come scuttling down,* BLANCH *losing her footing and sliding down the last three steps. There is babble and confusion.*]

DOLLY: What are you *doing?* Oh, God, in my condition! I . . .

BEULAH: Sandra, for the love of . . .

BLANCH [*moaning*]: I've broke my laig in two!

EVA [*screaming*]: She's broken her laig! [VEE *goes over to her.*]

DOLLY: Oh, she has *not!* Sandra, what on earth did you fire that damn thing faw?

SANDRA [*laughs and comes unsteadily back into the store*]: I took a pot shot at a buzzard!

BEULAH: A what? [SANDRA *laughs wildly and looks at* VAL, *who crosses to her and takes the pistol roughly from her grasp.* MYRA *enters.* MYRA *is a slight, fair woman, about thirty-four years old. She is a woman who met emotional disaster in her girlhood and whose personality bears traces of the resulting trauma. Frequently sharp and suspicious, she verges on hysteria under slight strain. Her voice is often shrill and her body tense. But when in repose, a girlish softness emerges—evidence of her capacity for great tenderness.*]

MYRA: What in God's holy name has been going on here? Who fired those shots out the door? [*She sees* VAL *with the revolver in his hand; she gasps and starts toward the door.*] You! [*They stare at each other for a brief moment.*]

VAL [*slowly smiling*]: No ma'am, it wasn't me. It was this young lady here.

SANDRA: Yes, I fired it, darling.

MYRA: What at?

SANDRA: A bird of ill omen was circling over the store.

MYRA: Yeah? One of those imaginary things that people see in a certain condition. Hello, Beulah, Dolly. [*She flings off her hat.*] I'm evermore tired. I've never had such a trip. Jabe took a bad spell on the train. They carried him up the back way. How are yuh, Vee. Blanch Temple, what are you sitting on the floor faw?

EVA: She took a spill on the stairs when Sandra Whiteside fired the shots!

MYRA: On the stairs? You two were upstairs, were you?

EVA: Yes, we were straightening things up a little . . .

MYRA [*quickly*] I see. An investigation?

EVA: Yes. I mean . . .

BLANCH: No, no, no! We wanted to see that ev'rything was in order. I've got such awful weak ankles, I'm always tripping and falling. An' I've got to march in church with the choir if I got to go on crutches. [*She rises painfully with* BEULAH'S *and* EVA'S *assistance.*]

MYRA: Oh, look what you all have done, that beautiful table! Candles an' ev'rything sweet that goes to make a nice party! Some of your lovely floating island, Beulah? Sweet! The spirit is willing but the flesh is completely exhausted. [*A Negro enters, crosses to* MYRA *carrying a tower of pastel-colored hatboxes and a big gay placard reading* "Welcome Sweet Springtime."] Oh, Joe, bring me those cards. Welcome sweet springtime! I've bought a pile of spring hats. [*She extricates one of the cards.*] This one here is the nicest—"In the spring, a young maid's fancy lightly turns to new chapeaux."

BEULAH [*reading the rest of it*]: "Mary Lou and Jane and Frances wear new hats to please their beaux!"

DOLLY: Oh, that's perfectly dahling. It seems so eahly, though, to think about spring.

EVA: I don't know. Somebody tole me that carps have been seen in Yazoo Pass. That always indicates that flood season's 'bout to start.

BLANCH: Myra . . .

MYRA: Yes?

BLANCH: I don't suppose you feel like talkin' about it right now, but I do hope Jabe's operation was completely successful.

MYRA: No.

BLANCH: It wasn't? [*All the women stare greedily at* MYRA.]

MYRA: No. It *wasn't.*

BLANCH: Oh!

EVA: My! My!

BEULAH: I'm so sorry to hear it.

DOLLY: If there's anything I can do . . . I—? [JABE *is heard knocking on the ceiling from his room above.* MYRA'S *face becomes suddenly listless and tired.*]

EVA: What's that knocking upstairs?

MYRA: Jabe.

SHERIFF [*calling from above*]: Myra, Jabe wants you.

MYRA: Excuse me, I'll have to go up. [*She crosses wearily toward the stairs, her hat dangling from one hand, pauses be-*

fore the "Welcome Sweet Springtime" *sign, with its bluebirds, flutes and gilded scrolls and cherubim, gravely lifts it and places it in a higher position.*] Dolly, look at this hat! I think it must have been created just for you! [*She smiles and goes on upstairs.*]

SANDRA [*who has engaged* VAL *in low conversation since* MYRA'S *entrance*]: Speaking of knocks, I've got one in my engine. A very mysterious noise. I can't decide whether I'm in communication with one of my dead ancestors or whether the carburetor or something is just about to drop out an' leave me stranded, probably at midnight in the middle of some lonesome black forest! [*She smiles at* VAL.] I don't suppose you'd have any knowledge of mechanics?

VAL: I dunno. I might. [DOLLY *is trying on the hat but is watchful of this exchange—also the other women who are opening hatboxes.*]

SANDRA: Would you be willing to undertake a kind of exploratory operation on it?

VAL: Well, I might if it didn't take too long.

SANDRA [*drawling*]: Oh, with your expert knowledge it shouldn't take lo-ong at-all! [DOLLY *giggles.*]

DOLLY: This hat! Isn't it the strangest thing?

BEULAH: Them things on the brim—what are they—carrots an' peas? I think they'd be much better *creamed*—with chicken croquettes! [VAL *has slid slowly off the counter. He moves past* SANDRA *and the secret looks of the women, toward the door.*]

VEE: Mr. Xavier . . . [*She crosses as if to stop him but they have already disappeared.*] Oh, I was going to ask Myra if she would give him a job.

BEULAH: Well . . .

DOLLY: It looks like he's *got* one now!

EVA: What did she say? A knock . . . ?

BLANCH: In her engine! [*innocently*] Whatever that is.

DOLLY [*with a peal of laughter*]: Did you *evuh* see such a puh-faum-ance! *Nevuh* in all my . . .

BEULAH: Bawn days? *Neither* did I! You see how she looked at the boy? An' the tone of huh voice. Corrupt? Absolutely—de-*grad-ed!*

DOLLY: Hank says her father got drunk one time at the Elks an' told him that she was kicked out of both of those girls' schools. Had to send her out East where morals don't matter. She's got two degrees or something in *lit*-era-*chure.*

BEULAH: Six degrees of fever if you ask me!

VEE [*who has been silently brooding over the situation*]: I certainly hope she doesn't get him to drink.

DOLLY: Vee, honey, you might as well face it, this is one candidate fo' salvation that you have *lost* to the opposition!

VEE: I don't believe it. He told me that he'd been saved already. [*She fixes her resentment on* DOLLY.] If some of the older women in Two River County would set a better example there'd be more justice in their talk about girls!

DOLLY [*with asperity*]: What do you mean by that remark?

VEE: I mean that people who give drinkin' pahties an' get so drunk they don't know which is *their husband* an' which is somebody else's an' people who serve on the altar guild an still play cards on Sundays . . .

DOLLY: Just stop right there! Now I've discovered the source of that dirty gossip!

VEE: I'm only repeating what I've been told by others! I certainly never have been entertained at such affairs as that!

DOLLY: No, an' you never will be; you're a public killjoy, a professional hypocrite!

BEULAH: Dolly!

DOLLY: She spends her time re-fauming tramps that her husband puts in the *lockup!* Brings them here in Myra's store an' tries to get them jobs here when God knows what kind of vicious ideas they've probably got in their heads!

VEE: I try to build up characters! You an' your drinkin' pahties are only concerned with tearin' characters down! I'm goin' upstairs with Myra. [*She goes out.*]

DOLLY: Well, you know what brought on that tantrum? She's jealous of Sandra Whiteside's running off with that strange boy. She hasn't lived as a natural wife for ten years or more [*to* EVA] so her husband has got to pick up with some bright-skinned nigger.

BEULAH: Oh, Dolly, you're awful. Sometimes I think you ought to wear a backhouse on your haid instead of a hat.

DOLLY: I've got no earthly patience with that sort of hypocriticism. Beulah, let's put all this perishable stuff in the Frigidaire and get out of here. I've never been so thoroughly disgusted.

BEULAH: Oh, my Lawd! [*They go into the confectionery.*]

EVA: Both of those two women are as common as dirt.

BLANCH: Dolly's folks in Blue Mountain are nothin' at all but the poorest kind of white trash. Why, Lollie Tucker told me the old man sits on the porch with his shoes off drinkin' beer out of a bucket! Nobody wants these marguerites. [*She goes to the hardware counter and gets her bag.*] Let's take 'em, huh?

EVA [*looking at the flowers*]: I was just wondering what we'd use to decorate the altar with tomorrow. The Bishop

Adjutant's comin'. As far's I know nobody's offered flowers. We can give Myra credit in the Parish notes.

BLANCH: Put the olive-nut sandwiches in here with the marguerites. Be careful you tote them so they won't get squashed.

EVA: They'll come in very nicely for the Bishop's tea. [DOLLY *and* BEULAH *re-enter from the confectionery.*]

DOLLY: We still have time to make the second show.

BEULAH: Dolly, you still have on that awful hat!

DOLLY: Oh, Lawd! [*She tosses it on the counter.* DOLLY *and* BEULAH *go out quickly together.*]

EVA [*when they are out*]: Sits on the po'ch with his shoes off?

BLANCH: Yes! Drinkin' *beer* from a *bucket!* [EVA *and* BLANCH *go out. The* SHERIFF *comes downstairs, grunting and puffing, followed by* PEE WEE.]

PEE WEE: Took one dose at noon. When that didn't work, I took a double one about five o'clock. Jabe sure looks bad.

SHERIFF: Looks no better 'n no worse 'n he always looked, but if what they say is correct, he'll more'n likely go under before the cotton comes up! See that there? [*He indicates his bandaged knuckle.*] Broke my knuckle! Never hit a buck-tooth nigger in the mouf! That's *the moral of it.* [PEE WEE *laughs.*] Oh, Vee! . . . Them fool wimmin got in a ruckus down here, I don't know what it's about. [VEE *comes down-stairs.*]

VEE: Hush that bawling will yuh! I wanted to speak with Myra about that young man who needs work but I couldn't in front of Jabe. He thinks he's gonna be able to go back to work himself.

SHERIFF: Well, come awn here, quit foolin'!

VEE: I think I ought to wait 'till that young man gets back.

SHERIFF: Mama, you come awn. Aw else stay here, an' *walk* when you git ready. [*He strides out after* PEE WEE. *The car engine roars.* VEE *looks troubled and follows them slowly out. There is a slight pause. The* NEGRO *enters from the confectionery. He looks about him and laughs with a gentle, quiet laughter at something secret, opens the soft drink cooler and takes a coke out. He laughs again, softly, secretly, and goes out the front door of the store, leaving the door open. A hound bays in the distance. After a moment* VAL *comes back in, and shuts the door behind him. He goes to the table, picks up a paper napkin and scrubs lipstick off his mouth. He settles himself on the counter. After a moment or two* MYRA *comes downstairs bearing an oil lamp. She has on a cheap Japanese kimono of shiny black satin with large scarlet poppies on it. She appears to be very distraught and doesn't notice* VAL. *She crosses directly to the phone and turns the crank.*]

MYRA: Get me the drugstore, please. Mr. Dubinsky? This is Myra Torrance. Were you asleep? I'm sorry. I'm in a bad situation. I left my Luminal tablets in the Memphis hotel and I can't sleep without them. . . . I know your store's closed up. So's mine. I know the lights are out, they're out over here. But you don't need a thousand watt bulb to put a few Luminal tablets in a little cardboard box or paper bag. . . . Now look here, Mr. Dubinsky, if you want to keep my trade, you send your nigger right over with that box of tablets. Gone? Then bring 'em yourself! I'm absolutely desperate from lack of sleep. My nerves are all on edge. If I don't get a good sleep tonight, I'll go all to pieces. I've got a sick man to take care of. . . . Yes, I just brought him home from the Memphis hospital. The operation was not at all successful. Will you do that? I'll be very much obliged. Thank you, Mr. Dubinsky. Excuse me for speaking so sharply. Thank you, Mr. Dubinsky. I appreciate that, Mr. Dubinsky. Goodbye, Mr. Dubinsky. [*She hangs up the phone and leans exhaustedly against the wall.*] Oh, oh, oh, I wish I was dead—dead—dead.

VAL [*quietly*]: No, you don't, Mrs. Torrance.

MYRA: My God! [*She gasps and clutches her wrapper about her throat.*]

VAL: I didn't mean to scare you.

MYRA: *What is this?* What are you still doing here? Who *are you?* My God, you got eyes that shine in the dark like a dog's. Get out or I'll call for the Sheriff!

VAL: Lady . . .

MYRA: Well?

VAL: I've been to the Sheriff's already.

MYRA: Aw. Escaped from the lockup?

VAL: Naw. The Sheriff's wife took me in there last night.

MYRA: She did, uh?

VAL: She give me a night's flop there but I didn't stay.

MYRA: Naw?

VAL: It made me uneasy being locked up. I got to have space around me.

MYRA: Look here, that's interesting, but this store's closed and I'll thank you to please get out. I've got a sick man upstairs that requires a lot of attention. If you're hungry . .

VAL: I'm not.

MYRA: There's lots of fancy stuff they put in the Frigidaire, you might as well eat it, I can't.

VAL: No, thanks, but I'd be mighty obliged if you would give me a job.

MYRA: There's no work here.

VAL: Excuse the contradiction but there is. Mizz Talbott told me so.

MYRA: Vee Talbott? I'll thank her to let me decide such things for myself. I'm in the mercantile business, she's a painter of very peculiar pictures she calls the Apostles but look like men around town. She took you in, did she? Well!

VAL: Whatever it is you're suggesting is incorrect. I've met one bitch in this town but it wasn't her.

MYRA [*furiously*]: How—how—*dare* you say that!

VAL: It wasn't you neither, ma'am! It was one that picked me up in here before you come in. Said she had engine trouble and would I fix it. She took me for a stud—and I slapped her face!

MYRA: You *what?*

VAL: I said I slapped her face. She wasn't a bad piece neither but I didn't like the way she went about it, like she was something special and I was trash!

MYRA: You . . . Cassandra Whiteside? *Slapped?* [*She bursts into wild laughter.*] I've never heard anything so beautiful in all my life! Have a drink and get out; I've got to go up.

VAL [*stubbornly*]: You'll need help here with your husband sick upstairs.

MYRA: You think so, uh? Well, if I do it'll have to be local help. I couldn't hire no stranger. 'Specially one that slapped the face of one of the richest girls in the Mississippi Delta. [*She laughs again.*] You had sales experience?

VAL: I've had all kinds of experience.

MYRA: That's not what I ast you. I ast you if you've had experience in the mercantile line. I want to know if you would be able to sell?

VAL: Sell?

MYRA: Yes!

VAL: Lots in hell to preachers!

MYRA [*utters again that sharp startled laugh, her fingers tightly clutching a magazine and nervously turning through it*]: I guess you got character ref'rence?

VAL: Sure.

MYRA: Where was the last place you worked?

VAL: Garage in Oakley.

MYRA: Tennessee?

VAL: Yeah.

MYRA: Grease-monkey, was you?

VAL [*stiffly*]: I wouldn't call myself that.

MYRA: Excuse me. Why did you quit that job?

VAL: If I told you, you'd think I was crazy.

MYRA: I think ev'rybody is crazy, including myself. Why did you quit it?

VAL: The place next door burnt down.

MYRA: What's that got to do with it?

VAL: I don't like fire. I dreamed about it three nights straight so I quit. I was burnt as a kid and ever since then it's been something I can't forget. [*He offers her a paper.*] Here's a letter he wrote:

MYRA: Who?

VAL: Garage manager.

MYRA [*reading aloud*]: "This here boy's peculiar but he sure does work real hard and he's honest as daylight." What does he mean "peculiar"?

VAL: Unusual is what he means.

MYRA: Why don't he say unusual?

VAL: He's not exactly an expert in the use of the language.

MYRA: Oh, but you are?

VAL [*removing a small book from his pocket*]: See this?

MYRA: Funk and Wagnall's Pocket Dictionary.

VAL: I carry that along with me wherever I go.

MYRA: What for?

VAL: You ever seen a coal-miner's cap? [MYRA *shakes her head.*] I wore one once when I was mining in the Red Hills of Alabama. It had a little lamp in front so you could see what your pick was digging into. Well—I'm still digging.

MYRA: Digging?

VAL: I don't claim to know very much, but I am writing a *book.*

MYRA: Well—you don't have to spit in my face to convince me of it!

VAL [*grinning*]: Excuse me.

MYRA: What's your book about?

VAL: Life.

MYRA: Sorry, but I can't use you.

VAL: Why not?

MYRA: Other people ain't as charitable as that garage manager is. They wouldn't say "peculiar," they'd say "nuts!" Also your appearance is much against you.

VAL: What's wrong with that.

MYRA: I don't know exactly. If you're hungry, eat. But otherwise . . . [*She is interrupted by knocking on the ceiling.*] Otherwise . . . get out. I'm too bone-tired to carry on conversation.

VAL: If you'll excuse me for telling you so, you're just about the rudest talking woman I've ever met.

MYRA: Yes, I'm mean inside. You heard me cussing when I come downstairs? Inside I cuss like that all the time. I hate ev'rybody; I wish this town would be bombarded tomorrow and everyone daid. Because—

VAL: Because?

MYRA: I got to live in it when I'd rather be daid in it—an' buried. [*She takes a drink of wine.*] What I meant about your appearance is you're too good-looking. Can you read shoe sizes?

VAL: Yeah.

MYRA: What does 75 David mean? [VAL *is stymied.*] You see how you lie? You lie like a dawg in summer! [*She laughs, not unkindly.*] 75 means 7½ in length and David means D wide. For flat-footed wimmin. You would either scare trade out of this store completely or else you'd bring it in so thick the floor would collapse. I can't decide which it would be.

VAL: I'd bring it in, lady.

MYRA: Gosh—[*There is a knock at the front door.* MYRA *crosses to it.*] A new floor would be an awful expense! [*She opens the door and steps outside.*] Thank you, Mr. Dubinsky. [*coming back in*] That was the sandman with my Luminal tablets. Suppose you—[*She opens the box and places a tablet on her tongue, washing it down with wine.*]

VAL: Huh?

MYRA: Suppose you try to sell me a pair of white kid pumps out of that new stock there. Imagine me a customer hard to please and you the clerk. Go on. . . . Naw, them over there is Red Goose shoes for kiddies. Them're men's shoes. Growing girls', misses'. Them on the end of the shelves are women's; sizes range down from the top. [*He pulls out a pair.*] You call them kid? That's suede, young man; 'snot a pump, neither, 's a blucher oxford; I don't believe you've ever tried to sell a thing in your life. Go on, roll your hoop, you're worse than useless to me! [*As he moves slowly toward the door,* MYRA *says softly:*] Sure you're not hungry? You're walking kind of unsteady.

VAL: What's that to you? I've got dog's eyes—you don't like me!

MYRA: I didn't say that.

VAL: I can't read shoe sizes. I don't know suede from kid. You can't use me; I'm worse than useless! What does it matter whether I'm hungry or not? [*He shakes with fury.*]

MYRA [*very softly, gently, with a slight mournful, tender shake of her head*]: Lawd, child, come back in the mawning and I'll give you a job. [*She moves slowly over to the candles and blows them out.* VAL *stares at her dumbly.*]

VAL: God, I—! Lady, you—!

MYRA [*laughing a little*]: God you an' lady me, huh. I think you are kind of exaggerating a little in both cases. [*They laugh. She blows out more of the candles leaving two lighted.*] You never have any trouble getting to sleep?

VAL: No. I know how to relax.

MYRA: How do you relax?

VAL: Imagine yourself a loose piece of string.

MYRA: A loose piece of string. That's lovely! I'm a loose piece of string. [*There is a knock on the ceiling.*]

VAL: What's that knocking upstairs?

MYRA: Jabe. [*She averts her face.*]

VAL: Who?

MYRA: My husband.

VAL: It scared me for a minute.

MYRA: Why?

VAL: Clump. Clump. Clump. Sounds like a skeleton walking around upstairs.

MYRA: Maybe you're gifted with too much imagination. [*She bends over to blow out the last candle.*]

VAL: Uh-huh. That's always been one of my biggest troubles. [*The candles gutter out. A dog is heard baying in the distance; the sound has a peculiar, passionate clarity.*]

MYRA [*softly*]: Hear that houn' dawg? . . . He's bayin' at th' moon. . . . Sky's cleared off? . . . Yes, it's clean as a whistle. . . . Isn't that nice?

VAL [*hoarsely*]: Yes, Ma'am.

MYRA: Well. . . . [*It grows rapidly darker as they stand hesitantly apart, looking at each other.* MYRA *turns slowly back toward the stairs.*] Well . . . the door locks itself when you slam it. Good night.

VAL [*speaking in a low, hoarse whisper*]: G'night. [*She starts up the stairs, slowly. He opens the door. Once more the dog is heard baying. They both stop short as though caught by the magic of the sound and face each other again from the stairway and the door.* VAL *speaks again, still more hoarsely.*] G'night.

MYRA [*in a whisper*]: Good night.

CURTAIN

ACT TWO

SCENE ONE

It is about a week later. VAL *is seated on the counter of the store leaning dreamily against a shelf. In his hand is a pencil and a shoebox lid. He is raptly composing an idyllic passage in his book. The juke box is playing as he speaks aloud.* MYRA *appears in the confectionery archway with a couple of boxes. She overhears his soliloquy and stops short to listen.*

VAL: Day used to come up slow through the long white curtains.

MYRA: Val! [VAL *starts.*] Who are you talking to?

VAL: Myself, I suppose.

MYRA: Isn't that kind of peculiar, talking to yourself?

VAL: No, ma'am. That's just a habit that lonesome people get into.

MYRA: Please don't do it when anyone's in the store. I don't want it spread around town that a lunatic's been employed here. That sunshine's *terrific*—you better let down the awnings. [VAL *moves slowly from the counter.*] Slew-foot!

VAL: Huh?

MYRA: Slew-foot, slew-foot! You walk like you're on fly-papers! Pick up your feet when you walk and get a *move* on! [VAL *laughs and saunters leisurely out the door.*] Talks to himself, writing poems on shoeboxes! What a mess. [*She stares through the window as* VAL *lowers the awning. Three young girls follow* VAL *as he comes back in.*]

A GIRL: Hello!

VAL [*amiably*]: Hello there.

THE GIRL: Jane wants to look at some kickies.

SECOND GIRL [*giggling*]: No— you do.

THIRD GIRL: I'd like to try on some. Can you dance in kickies?

VAL: Sure you can dance in kickies. Sit down there. Let's measure your little foot.

THE GIRL [*beating her to the chair*]: Me first, me first.

VAL: Okay. First come, first serve. [*He pulls her shoe off. She giggles spasmodically.*]

VAL: Five and one half, Bennie. [*He goes to the shelf.*]

THE GIRL: Isn't he *cute?*

SECOND GIRL: Say, do you dance?

THIRD GIRL: Would you like to go out jooking?

MYRA: Val! I'll wait on these girls. You take these empty boxes out of here. [*As soon as* VAL *leaves, the girls giggle and run out of the store.* MYRA *looks very annoyed as* EVA TEMPLE *enters.*]

EVA: Mr. Xa-*vier?*

MYRA [*sharply*]: Our popular young shoe clerk is in the basement. What do you want?

EVA: A pair of bedroom slippers.

MYRA: Sit down and I'll show you some.

EVA: I'll wait till Mr. Xavier comes back upstairs. He seems to understand my feet so well. How's Cousin Jabe this mawning?

MYRA: Just the same.

EVA: Dear me. [VAL *reappears.*] Mr. Xa-*vier!*

VAL: How are you this mawning?

EVA: I seem to be comin' down with th' most abominable earache.

MYRA [*sympathetically*]: Aww! Let me give you a little laudanum faw it.

EVA: No, thanks. I put some in already. I think Birdie Wilson was partially responsible faw it.

VAL: Why? Is earache contagious?

EVA: No, but Birdie was singing right next to me at choir practice, which did it absolutely no good. [*She titters a little.*] What'm I sittin' here faw?

VAL: T' look at some shoes.

EVA: Aw. Well, I guess I might. Haven't you all noticed about Birdie? Her voice always cracks on that *Te Deum*. She can hit "A" pretty good but she always flats on "B." You'd think she'd have better sense than to even attempt to make "C" because it's completely out of her range, but I'll say this for Birdie, she's got the courage of her convictions.

VAL: These are the new wine shades.

EVA: Oh! Pretty! Yes, she goes right on up there and I'm telling you all, it's a perfect imitation of the Cannonball Express. [*She giggles.*] Oh, my goodness, these *pinch!*

VAL: Do they?

EVA: They certainly do. [*She giggles archly.*]

VAL: Well, let's try a David on that.

EVA: What's David?

VAL: Next size broader!

EVA: Oh, my goodness, no! There must be some mistake!

VAL [*climbing the shelf ladder*]: Don't you know what a broad foot's a sign of, Miss Temple? Imagination! And also of . . .

EVA: Of *what?* [CASSANDRA WHITESIDE *enters the front door.*]

MYRA: Hello, Sandra!

SANDRA: Hello, Myra. I just drove home from New Awleuns fo' the Delta Planters' Cotillion. And do you know I neglected to bring a single decent pair of evenin' slippers back with me.

MYRA: Oh, honey, we don't keep evenin' slippers in stock, we don't get any calls fo' them here.

SANDRA [*noticing* VAL]: I didn't suppose you would.

MYRA: Oh, wait! Val, reach me down that old Queen Quality box up there! [DOLLY *and* BEULAH *enter.*]

BEULAH: Well, it is exasperating to have your table broke up at the very last . . . *Sandra!*

DOLLY: Sandra Whiteside! I thought you were gonna stay in New Awleuns till after Mardi Gras.

SANDRA: I just drove home for the Delta Planters' Cotillion.

MYRA [*wistfully*]: How is Mardi Gras this yeah?

SANDRA: As mahvelously mad as usual. If I were refawming the world I'd make it last forever.

MYRA: I went to it once a long, long time ago. I remembuh they danced in the streets.

SANDRA: They do ev'rything in the streets!

MYRA: I was just fourteen, I had on my first long dress an' a marcel wave an' some perfume called *Baiser d'Amour* that I bought at the Maison Blanche. Something wonderful happened.

SANDRA: What was it?

MYRA: A boy in a Pierrot suit.

SANDRA: How lovely! What did he do?

MYRA: Caught me around the waist, whirled me till I was dizzy—then kissed me and—*disappeared!*

SANDRA: Disappeared?

MYRA: Completely. In the crowd. The music stopped. I ran straight back to my room and lay on the bed an' stared an' stared at a big yellow spot on the ceiling.

SANDRA: Oh, my Lawd, how tragic.

MYRA: It *was.* [*She smiles.*] I still can feel it whenever the carnival's mentioned.

SANDRA: Your first heartbreak!

MYRA: Uh-huh. [*She laughs.*]

VAL [*bringing a shoebox*]: This one?

MYRA: *Yes, that's it.* [to Sandra:] I hope you're not superstitious!

SANDRA [*lighting a cigarette*]: Why?

MYRA: Because this box contains some silver and white satin slippers that were intended for Rosemary Wildberger...

DOLLY: Rosemary!

BEULAH: Wildberger!

MYRA: . . . To wear at her wedding exactly three years ago this Valentine's Day. [*She lifts one of the slippers.*] She had such a tiny foot.

BEULAH: Such a tiny, delicate girl. Rosemary...

DOLLY: Wildberger!

SANDRA [*laughing lightly*]: Well, what happened? Did she fall dead at the altar?

BEULAH: Oh, no.

DOLLY: Worse than that!

BEULAH: Much worse. The man stood her up.

MYRA: Where did Rosemary go, does anyone know?

BEULAH: Some people say she went crazy an' some people say she went to Cincinnati to study voice.

SANDRA [*carelessly*]: Which was it?

EVA [*piping up resentfully, having been ignored*]: Neither. She went into Chinese missionary work.

DOLLY [*sarcastically*]: Trust Eva Temple to have complete information.

BEULAH: Oh, yes.

SANDRA: And these are the fabulous Rosemary's little silver and white wedding slippers. How lovely.

MYRA: I ordered 'em from St. Louis for her but, of course, I never had the heart to mention them to her parents after she disappeared. What size do you wear, honey?

SANDRA: Four, triple A.

MYRA: Gracious. These are four B. Val, see how they fit Miss Whiteside. [*She turns to* DOLLY.] Oh, Dolly, I wanted you to see this; soon as I unpacked it I had a vision of you! [*She removes an outlandish red dress with brass trimming from the racks; it looks like a bareback rider's outfit.*]

DOLLY [*rushing to it*]: Oh, my God, ain't it lovely! But you know, honey, I won't be able to wear anything one piece this spring.

MYRA: Really?

DOLLY: Oh, for the usual reason. Y'know there's absolutely no justice in nature. I mean the way she ties some women down while others can run hog wild. Look at Myra, for instance. Not one kid an' me turning out the seventh.

MYRA [*averting her face*]: Bring your measurements—I'll order you some maternity garments from Memphis.

DOLLY: Measurements? Fifteen square yards. How long'll it take?

MYRA: Probably two or three weeks. [DOLLY *shrieks and throws up her hands.*] Can't you wait that long?

DOLLY: I can, but my figure can't. [BLANCH TEMPLE *enters, and trips over the rubber mat at the door. She utters a shrill cry.*]

EVA [*jumping up*]: Blanch, that might have *thrown* you!

MYRA: Val, you must tack that down.

VAL: Get the nigger to do it.

BLANCH: My ankle is twisted. I can't even step on that foot.

EVA: Oh, my Lawd, she'll have to have it treated again. Cost us five or six dollars. I simply can't pay for these shoes.

MYRA: All right, you don't have to, Eva, we'll just call it square. Val! Wrap these up for Miss Temple. [*She turns to* SANDRA.] How did they fit? [VAL *picks up the shoes and goes to the cash register.*]

SANDRA: I couldn't wear them. Let me see a pair of plain white pumps.

MYRA: Surely.

DOLLY: We must be goin', Beulah, bye, bye, you all. [DOLLY *and* BEULAH *go out.*]

BEULAH [*Her voice is heard off stage*]: I just been thinkin'. Lulu Belle don't play contract at all. She just plays auction.

MYRA: Hurry back! [*She gets some other shoes down; sits on the stool; opens the box for* SANDRA.]

BLANCH [*peeking among the valentines on the counter*]: Here's where she must've bought it 'cause here's another just like it.

VAL: What's that?

BLANCH: Somebody sent us a comic valentine. It wasn't funny at all, it was simply malicious. Old maids. There's no such thing as an old maid anymore.

EVA: No, they're bachelor girls.

VAL [*suppressing a smile*]: Here's your shoes, Miss Temple.

EVA: Oh, thanks, aw'fly. Miss DeQuincy was telling me you'd been to Yellowstone Park.

VAL: I've traveled all over, not only Yellowstone Park, but Yosemite, Gran' Canyon . . .

BLANCH: How marvelous. Why don't we get him to give us a little descriptive talk at our next auxiliary meeting?

EVA: Oh, would you do that, Mr. . . .

VAL: Xavier.

EVA: Mr. Xavier. You won't fo'get the meeting?

BLANCH: It's Saturday at four-fifteen.

MYRA: Val couldn't take the time off. We're too rushed on Saturday afternoon.

EVA: Aw, what a shame. I meant to ask you, how's Cousin Jabe?

MYRA: No better.

EVA: Aw. What exactly resulted from the operation in Memphis?

BLANCH: Is it true that . . .

EVA: It was too late for surgical interference?

MYRA: Yes, it is true.

BLANCH: Goodness gracious.

EVA: They cut him open and sewed him right back up?

MYRA [*turning away in distaste*]: Excuse me.

BLANCH: Eva.

EVA: What did I say?

BLANCH: Goodbye, Mr. Xavier. [*They go out.*]

SANDRA: Aren't they delightful. The little white doves of the Lord. [*With a sidelong glance at* VAL.] Do you suppose I'll get like that if I remain a virgin?

MYRA: Well, I don't believe I'd worry about it, Sandra. [JABE *knocks overhead.*]

SANDRA: Ouuu! What's that noise?

MYRA: Jabe's knocking. [*Her face darkens.*]

SANDRA: Oh.

MYRA: I'll have to run up for a minute. [*She goes quickly upstairs.*]

SANDRA [*lighting a cigarette, with a quizzical look at* VAL]: I didn't come in here for evening slippers.

VAL: No. I figured you didn't.

SANDRA: I didn't come home for the Delta Planters' Cotillion. I came back here to see you. I haven't been able to get you off my mind. I woke up thinking about you last night in the Hotel Monteleone. I went downstairs to the bar at three o'clock in the morning. I thought I might forget if I got drunk. They must've poured my whiskey out of the wrong bottle, though. At half-past three I was on the highway, headed back to Two Rivers—seventy, eighty, ninety miles an hour—scared that you'd be gone before I got here. What do you think about that?

VAL: I think you'd better go back to the Mardi Gras.

SANDRA: You don't like me very much, do you?

VAL: I want to keep this job. Every place I've gone to it's been some woman I finally had to leave on account of.

SANDRA: I believe that. You're the center of much discussion in Two River County—among the women. That snakeskin jacket, those eyes; that special technique you use in fitting on shoes.

VAL: I don't use any special technique.

SANDRA: Maybe they just imagine that you do. I can understand why. You're beautiful, you're wild. I have a feeling we'll come together some night.

VAL: Yeah?

SANDRA [*rhapsodically*]: In the dark of the moon, beside a broken fence rail in some big rolling meadow. [VAL *turns away.*] We won't even say hello.

VAL: Let's quit this!

SANDRA: This what?

VAL: Double talk.

SANDRA: All right. [*She removes her dark glasses and arches her body in a provocative pose. She speaks childishly.*] Why did you slap me, Val?

VAL: Because.

SANDRA: Just because?

VAL: I didn't want to be interfered with by you. You think I've got a sign "Male at Stud" hung on me?

SANDRA: Yes, I think you have. Nobody could possibly make a mistake about it.

VAL: You made a mistake about it. I'm not in your class. I'm the kind of fellow you get to wash your car or chop the cotton. That night you drove me up to Cypress Hill, I wasn't nothing to you. It was like you had hired me to give you a little amusement.

SANDRA: That's what you thought? You were wrong about that. I felt a resemblance between us.

VAL: There's none that I know of, lady.

SANDRA: You must be blind. You—savage. And me—aristocrat. Both of us things whose license has been revoked in the civilized world. Both of us equally damned and for the same good reason. Because we both want freedom. Of course, I knew you were really better than me. A whole lot better. I'm rotten. Neurotic. Our blood's gone bad from too much interbreeding. They've set up the guillotine, not in the Place de Concorde, but here, inside our own bodies!

VAL: Double talk, smart double talk.

SANDRA: No. Look at my wrists. They're too thin. You could snap them like twigs. You can see through my skin. It's transparent like tissue paper. I'm lovely, aren't I? But I'm not any good. I wear dark glasses over my eyes because I've got secrets in them. Too much of something that makes me rather disgusting. Yes, you were right when you slapped me, Val. You should have killed me, before I kill myself. I will some day. I have an instinct for self-destruction. I'm running away from it all the time. Too fast. New Orleans, Vicksburg, Mobile. All over the goddam country with something after me every inch of the way! But the poison I've got in my blood isn't the kind that makes me fatal to kiss! Why don't you kiss me, Val? [VAL *moves away from her but she follows him.*] Scaredy cat! *Scaredy cat!* [VAL *catches his breath and starts to embrace her. She suddenly jabs him in the middle with her knee and bites his hand. She laughs wildly.*] There! There now! That's what I came back for! Nobody's ever slapped me and gotten away with it, Snakeskin! Goodbye! [*She runs out the door.*]

VAL: Goddam little bitch! [MYRA *appears on the stairway.*]

MYRA: What did she do?

VAL: She dared me to kiss her.

MYRA: Did you oblige her this time or did you slap her again?

VAL: I would've done it if she hadn't kicked me.

MYRA: Well, I'm glad that she kicked you. You can find some other place to do your carrying on.

VAL: I wasn't carrying on.

MYRA: You just admitted you would have if she'd let you. [*She goes to the shelves.*] Oh, lights of delirium, look where you put the kids!

VAL: You didn't say where to put them.

MYRA: In six days time I thought you might've caught on to where some things belong in this store.

VAL: Look here, if I was a mind reader, lady, I'd put up a tent on the commons and tell your fate by the stars at fifty cents a disaster!

MYRA: Disaster is right! I wish you'd use your noggin for something beside sweet looks at the women! Anybody with the brain of a newborn calf should know better'n to put a bunch of kids in here with—look at that, will you? [*She tosses a box furiously to the floor.*] Those Queen Quality evening slippers stuck in here, too. Why don't you fill up the rest of the space with cigar boxes and candy bars? Why do you wanta show so little imagination that you don't put nothing but shoes in the Shoe Department? You're writing a book? Surely you can think of some fancy new ideas like hanging dresses from the ceiling fans!

VAL: Look here, Myra.

MYRA: Since when am I Myra to you? My name is Mrs. Torrance!

VAL: You call me Val.

MYRA: That's different. I'm the employer here, you work in my store!

VAL: You mean I *worked* in your goddam store! [*He tears off his white clerk's jacket and flings it to the floor. There is a shocked silence.*]

MYRA: I was going to give you your notice tonight, anyhow.

VAL: You don't have to give it to me, I've already took it.

MYRA: Well, you can't walk out in the middle of the day like this.

VAL: Why not? I'm no help to you.

MYRA: I didn't say that . . .

VAL: Oh, no? Actions speak louder than words, Mrs. Torrance! [MYRA *looks at him, stunned, as he puts on his snakeskin jacket. A Negro huckster passes along the street singing his wares.*] You are a very difficult, hardheaded woman—and much as I wanted a job I got to admit that working for you is no pleasure. When you tell me to do things, how can I understand you, the way you talk?

MYRA: The way I talk?

VAL: You talk to the *wall.* You talk to the *ceiling.* You never talk straight to *me!* You never even look in my face when you say something to me! I just have to guess what you said 'cause you talk so fast an' hard an' keep your face turned away . . . I've had the feeling ever since I come here that everything I do has displeased you!

MYRA [*averting her face*]: I didn't mean to give you that impression. As a matter of fact I was pretty well satisfied with the way you were coming along.

VAL: You certainly kept your satisfaction a secret.

MYRA: I know, I know. I'm nervous, I'm cross, I'm jumpy. [*pathetically*] I thought that you understood my nervous condition and made some allowance for it!

VAL: Being nervous is no excuse for acting like a nine-tailed catawampus!

MYRA: What is a nine-tailed catawampus?

VAL: I don't know. But I sure would hate to meet one.

MYRA [*she is hurt*]: Oh! [*She raises a handkerchief to her eyes.*] How should I act with you—you carrying on with people like Sandra Whiteside—right here in the store!

VAL: So that's why you flew off the handle.

MYRA: Not just that. You know why those high school girls keep flocking in here?

VAL: Sure. To buy spring shoes.

MYRA: Spring shoes nothing! They come in here for a *thrill!*

VAL: A *what?*

MYRA: A *thrill.* You know what that is, don't you?

VAL [*laughing*]: Can I help it?

MYRA: Yes! You don't have to *give* them one.

VAL: How do I give them a thrill?

MYRA: Don't ask *me* how. You don't have to manipulate their knees to get shoes on them.

VAL: Manipulate their . . . I never *touch* their knees!

MYRA: I've got eyes in my head!

HUCKSTER [*chanting out in the street*]: Ahhhh ahhhh. Turnip greens, new potatoes, rutibagas. Ahhh-ahhh. Carrots, string beans, onions!

MYRA: Also your attitude is very suggestive.

VAL: Suggestive of what, Mrs. Torrance?

MYRA: Bedrooms, if you want to know.

VAL: Bedrooms!

MYRA: Yes!

VAL: That sure is peculiar. How do I do *that?*

MYRA: Everything that you do. The way you talk, the way you walk, every single motion of you. Slew-footing this way and that way like one of those awful, disgustin', carnival dancers! [*The huckster is heard calling further away.* VAL *stares at* MYRA *with a long troubled look.*]

MYRA: Quit looking at me like that! [*She sobs.*] I know how awful I look.

VAL [*gently*]: You don't look awful, Myra.

MYRA: Yes, I do—my hair all stringing down—my face always turns so red when I get worked up. [*She sobs and turns away.*]

VAL [*very gently*]: Myra—I mean, Mrs. Torrance. I wanted to keep this job. I was tired of moving around and being lonesome and only meeting with strangers. I wanted to feel like I belonged somewhere and lived like regular people. Instead of like a fox that's chased by hounds!

MYRA: Maybe I haven't understood you exactly.

VAL: No. You haven't.

MYRA: How could I though? You're still a stranger to me.

VAL: My name is Val Xavier.

MYRA: And mine is Myra Torrance. Now do you feel like you know me any better?

VAL: No.

MYRA [*still sobbing a little*]: Well, I don't feel much better acquainted with *you.* Give me one of them tissue paper things. [*She blows her nose.*]

VAL: How do you get to know people? I used to think you did it by touching them with your hands. But later I found out that only made you more of a stranger than ever. Now I know that *nobody* ever gets to *know* anybody.

MYRA: Nobody ever gets to *know* anybody?

VAL: No. Don't you see how it is? We're all of us locked up tight inside our own bodies. Sentenced—you might say—to solitary confinement inside our own skins.

MYRA [*giving him a long, puzzled look*]: Is that something out of The Book?

VAL [*grinning*]: No. That goes into The Book.

MYRA: You're a queer one. A lot of people have dropped in off the road since I've been here, but nobody quite like you. I can't figure out what you *belong* to, exactly.

VAL: Me? Belong to? Nothing.

MYRA: Don't you have folks anywhere?

VAL: I used to.

MYRA: What become of them?

VAL: I lost track of 'em after they lost their land.

MYRA: They worked on shares?

VAL: No, not shares—but leavings, scraps, tidbits! They never owned a single inch of the earth, but all their lives they gave to working on it. The land got poor, it wouldn't produce no more, and so my folks were thrown off it.

MYRA: Where did they go?

VAL: I don't know where. They were loose chicken feathers blown around by the wind.

MYRA: You didn't go with 'em?

VAL: No. No, I made up my mind about something and I've stuck to it ever since.

MYRA: What's that?

VAL: To live by myself. So when the others left, I stayed on Witches' Bayou. It was a good place to hide in. Big cypress trees all covered with long gray moss the sun couldn't hardly shine through. Not in chinks, though, not in squares but all spread out . . .

MYRA: Misty-like.

VAL: Yeah.

MYRA: How old were you? How did you live?

VAL: Fourteen. I lived like a fox. I hunted and fished but most of the time I was hungry. I guess it must've made me a little lightheaded, because I know I had some peculiar notions . . . I used to lay out naked in a flatboat with the sun on me.

MYRA: What did you do that for?

VAL: I had a feeling that something *important* was going to come *in* to me.

MYRA: In? Through your skin?

VAL: Kind of. Most people don't expect nothing important to come *in* to them. They just expect to get up early—plow—rest—go turtle-eggin' an' then back to bed. They never look up at the sky, dark—or with stars—or blazing yellow with sunlight—and ask it, "Why? why? why?"

MYRA: Did you ask it, "Why"?

VAL: That was the first word I learned to spell out at school. And I expected some answer. I felt there was something secret that I would find out and then it would all make sense.

MYRA: How would you find it out?

VAL: It would come *in* to me. Through my eyes—see? Through my ears, through my skin. Like a net—see? If you don't spread it out, you won't catch nothing in it. But if you do, you *might*. Mine I used to spread it out, wide-open, those afternoons on the bayous—ears pricked, eyes peeled—watchin', waitin', listenin' for it to come!

MYRA: Did it ever?

VAL: No. Never quite. It would of though, if I hadn't gotten thrown off the track by the girl.

MYRA: There was a girl. What girl?

VAL: A girl I met on the bayou.

MYRA: Oh, what about her?

VAL: She was the first one, yeah. That day I was real excited. I had a feeling that if I just kept polin' on a little bit further I'd come bang on whatever it was I was after!

MYRA: And she was it?

VAL [*violently*]: Naw, she *wasn't*. But she made me *think* she was.

MYRA: How did she do that?

VAL: How? By standin' naked on the dogtrot, in the door of the cabin, without a stitch on.

MYRA: What was she like?

VAL: J'ya ever notice the inside of a shell? How white that is?

MYRA: She was young I suppose. Very young?

VAL: Her shape up here, it wasn't no bigger than this [*slightly cupping his palm*]. I hadn't noticed before the special diff'rence in women.

MYRA: But you did then?

VAL: Yes, I did then.

MYRA: Was she . . . ?

VAL: What?

MYRA: More attractive than—anyone since?

VAL: She was—th' first.

MYRA: What did you do? What happened?

VAL: I poled th' boat up closer. An' she came out on the dogtrot an' stood there a while with the daylight burnin' around her as bright as heaven as far as I could see! Oh, God, I remember a bird flown out of the moss and its wings made a shadow on her! [*He bows his head.*] An' then it sang a single high clear note. An' as though she was waitin' for that as a kind of a signal—to *trap* me— she turned and smiled an' walked on back in the cabin!

MYRA: And you followed, of course? What was it like inside?

VAL: Inside it was—empty inside.

MYRA: It couldn't have been!

VAL: Well, maybe it wasn't, but all I remember's the bed.

MYRA: Only the bed?

VAL: Made out of cypress an' covered with heaps of moss.

MYRA: Doesn't sound nice.

VAL: Well, it was. She'd been lonesome.

MYRA: How did you know? Did she tell you?

VAL: She didn't have to. She had it carved in her body.

MYRA: Carved? Is lonesomeness carved in people's bodies? [*She unconsciously touches her own.*]

VAL: Kind of. Anyhow you can see it.

MYRA: Could you see it in anybody's?

VAL: Sure. You could see it. Or feel it.

MYRA [*softly*]: What did she say to you?

VAL: She couldn't talk much except in some Cajun language. I taught her some words.

MYRA: Such as what?

VAL: Such as *love.*

MYRA: You taught her that?

VAL: It was then I thought I discovered what it was that I'd been hankerin' after all those times I used to go off on the bayou.

MYRA: You thought it was that? [*She turns to the shelves.*] You mean she answered "me"?

VAL: Her! Me! Us together! Then afterwards—afterwards I thought that wasn't it. I couldn't make up my mind. When I was with her, I quit thinking because I was satisfied with just that; that sweetness between us, them long afternoons on the moss. But when I'd left her, the satisfaction would leave me an' I'd be . . . like this. [*He clenches his fist.*] Right on the edge of something tremendous. It wasn't her. She was just a woman, not even a woman quite, and what I wanted was . . .

MYRA: Was *what?*

VAL: Christ, I don't know. I gotta find out!

MYRA: I guess your love for her didn't amount to so much after all. What did you do after that?

VAL: I made some money cane-grindin', sold a bunch of 'gator an' diamondback skins. And bought myself a jalopy. I took to moving around. I thought I might track it down, whatever it was I was after. It always kept one jump ahead of me. That went on for ten years. Then I settled down for a spell in Texas. Seemed like the restlessness had worn off and I might get connected with something. But things went wrong. Something happened.

MYRA: What?

VAL: Never mind what. But everything was different after that. I wasn't free anymore. I was followed by something I couldn't get off my mind. Till I came here . . .

MYRA: Well, now that you've come here and got a good job, you can live a regular life and forget all of that.

VAL: I don't forget as easy as you, Mrs. Torrance. You don't even remember that I've lost my job.

MYRA: You haven't lost your job.

VAL: I'm not fired, huh?

MYRA [*smiling and shaking her head*]: We both got a little upset but that's over.

VAL: God, I . . .

MYRA: God you and lady me? [*She laughs.*] What is this place, a funeral parlor? Let's have some lights, some music. Put something on the Victrola.

VAL: What would you like?

MYRA: I like that Hawaiian number with the steel guitars.

VAL: Yeah, that one! [*He crosses to the confectionery and starts the music; then he comes back.*] Myra, you know the earth turns.

MYRA: Yes.

VAL: It's turning that way. East. And if a man turned west, no matter how fast, he'd still be going the other way, really, because the earth turns so much faster. It's no use to struggle, to try to move against it. You go the way the earth pulls you whether you want to or not. I don't want to touch you, Myra.

MYRA: No, I don't want you to.

VAL: It wouldn't be right for me to.

MYRA [*half questioning*]: On account of Jabe?

VAL: No, on account of you. You been good to me. I don't want nothing to hurt you. Let's shake hands with each other, huh?

MYRA: That's not necessary! [*Without knowing why, she is suddenly angry. She crosses to the foot of the stairs.*] Take off that horrible jacket and get back to work. I have to fix Jabe's lunch. [*He follows her to the stairs.*]

VAL: Why wouldn't you shake hands with me? You're not still afraid of me, are you? [MYRA *starts quickly upstairs.*] Mrs. Torrance! Myra! [MYRA *pauses a moment on the landing, looking down at him with nervous hesitation.*]

VAL [*in an intense whisper*]: Myra! [*She disappears through the door and slams it shut.* VAL *stares in bewilderment.*]

SLOW CURTAIN

SCENE TWO

It is several hours later on the same day. The mellow afternoon sunlight is muted. There is the puff-puff of the cotton gin. VAL *stands in the confectionery archway with his back to the audience. He is staring intently up at a large Coca-Cola ad through the arch. In conjunction with the beverage, this ad forcefully expounds the charms of a "Petty Girl" in a one-piece lemon-yellow bathing suit. She and* VAL *appear to be experiencing a long and silent spiritual communion. In his hand* VAL *has a Coke. Slowly, dreamily, he elevates the bottle to his mouth. Outside, at some distance, a rooster crows longingly at the sun. A man enters the front door in boots and riding breeches, bearing a shotgun. He coughs twice to divert* VAL'S *attention from the seductive picture.*

VAL [*turning*]: Sorry, I was dreaming. Beautiful afternoon, huh?

MAN: I'd like to see Mrs. Torrance.

VAL: She's gone upstairs with her husband. He's not so well.

MAN: Tell her that David Anderson is here.

VAL: Just press that buzzer on the counter and she'll be down.

ANDERSON: Thank you. [*Hesitantly he follows this suggestion. The buzzer is heard above. After a moment, the door on the landing opens and* MYRA *appears. She descends a few steps. Then seeing* ANDERSON, *she stops short.*]

MYRA [*sharply, involuntarily*]: David! [*They exchange a long, wordless stare. Then* MYRA *recovers herself and comes down.*]

MYRA [*to* VAL]: Will you go to the drugstore for me?

VAL: What do you want?

MYRA: Nothing. I mean some ice cream.

VAL: A pint of vanilla? [MYRA *says nothing.* VAL *looks curiously at them both and goes out.*]

MYRA: Well.

DAVID: How are you, Myra?

MYRA: Very well, thanks. How are you?

DAVID [*staring at her*]: All right. [*There is an awkward pause.*]

MYRA: You came in here once before and I ordered you out.

DAVID: That was six years ago.

MYRA: No. Eight.

DAVID: Right after your marriage.

MYRA: Not so long after yours.

DAVID: You can't hold a grudge that long.

MYRA: Oh yes I can. I think I can hold one forever. What do you want?

DAVID: Cartridges.

MYRA: You're going out shooting wild birds? I don't have to wish you luck. I haven't forgotten what a good marksman you were. Here's your cartridges. Is there anything else?

DAVID: It seems odd to see you in here, like this.

MYRA: Waiting on trade? Does that seem *common* to you?

DAVID: No. You never were practical, though. You were always such a . . .

MYRA: *Fool? Yes!* But I've changed since then.

DAVID: You haven't changed in appearance.

MYRA: Some women are like green things. They're kept on ice. I guess I'm one of that kind. You've changed a good deal. I wouldn't have known you at all except for your walk. You still move around like you were the lord of creation. I should think you might have found out by this time that your ten thousand acres don't make up the whole universe. Other people have got some property, too. I have this store, for instance. I don't have to *clerk* in it either. I *have* a clerk. [*Her voice trembles.*] I haven't come down so terribly far in the world.

DAVID [*embarrassed*]: Of course you haven't.

MYRA: No, I've gone *up*. And I'm going to go up still *higher*.

DAVID: I'm glad of that, Myra. People have told me about your husband's sickness. I . . .

MYRA [*feverishly*]: Yes. He's dying. After his death I'm planning to sell the store. Thirty or thirty-five thousand it ought to be worth. I'm planning to leave Two River and travel around. Florida, California, New York. I've been an object for pity for a little too long around here. "Poor Myra, she's hopeless, she's crushed!" That isn't exactly the truth and I'm tired of having it whispered behind my back. My life isn't over, my life is only *commencing*. A dollar ten for the cartridges, please.

DAVID [*extending the money*]: Here, Myra.

MYRA: Just put it down on the counter. Now get out. Don't ever come back here again.

DAVID [*quietly*]: All right, Myra. [*He goes slowly out.* MYRA *looks after him. A rooster crows mournfully in the distance.* MYRA *raises her hand to her lips. She looks stunned.* VAL *enters. He grins at her.*]

VAL: Finished your talk?

MYRA [*vaguely*]: Yes, David.

VAL: David?

MYRA [*starting*]: Excuse me, I mean "Val." [*bitterly*] I made a fool of myself.

VAL: Huh?

MYRA [*evasively*]: That rooster always crows about sundown. Sounds like he's remembering something. [JABE *knocks on the ceiling.*] I wonder if he *is.* [*She goes back upstairs.* VAL *opens the ice cream, dips it out with his fingers.* VEE TALBOTT *enters, stops short in the doorway as though dazed. The rooster crows.*]

VAL: Oh, hello, Mrs. Talbott.

VEE: Something's gone wrong with my eyes. I can't see nothing.

VAL: Here, let me help you. You probably drove up here with that setting sun in your face.

VEE: What? Yes. That must be it.

VAL: There now. Sit down right here.

VEE: Oh, thank you so much.

VAL: I haven't seen you since that night you let me sleep in the lockup.

VEE: Has the minister called on you yet? Reverend Tooker? I made him promise he would. I told him that you were new in the community and that you weren't affiliated with any church yet. I want you to visit ours.

VAL: Well, that's mighty gracious of you, Mrs. Talbott.

VEE: The Church of the Resurrection! Episcopal, you know. Some people, especially Catholics, think our church was founded by Henry the Eighth, that horrible, lecherous old man who had as many wives as a cat has lives! There's not a word of truth in it. We have direct Apostolic Succession through St. Paul, who converted the early Angles. Angles is what they called the original English.

VAL: Angles, huh?

VEE: Yes, Angles. Our church is sometimes known as the Anglican Church.

VAL: Well, now, that's right int'restin', Mrs. Talbott. What's that picture you got? Something to put on display?

VEE: I thought that Myra might put it up with the Easter decorations.

VAL: I tell you what. We'll put it on display in the confectionery. Myra is going to do it over for spring. What's this picture of?

VEE: The Church of the Resurrection!

VAL: I didn't recognize it.

VEE: Well, I give it a sort of imaginative treatment.

VAL: Aw. What's this?

VEE: The steeple.

VAL: Is the church steeple red?

VEE: Naw.

VAL: Why did you paint it red then?

VEE: I felt it that way. I always paint a thing the way that it strikes me instead of always the way that it actually is. That's why the New Awleuns artists took an in'rest in my work. They say that it shows a lot of imagination. Primitive is what they call it an' one of my pictures they've hung on *ex*-hibition in the Audubon Park museum! [*Her voice shakes with pride as she states this.*]

VAL: Aw. [*He crouches slowly in front of her with a faint smile.*] You need some new shoes.

VEE: Do I?

VAL: Yes. I'll sell you a pair of beautiful wine-colored slippers. [*He clambers quickly up the ladder and jerks out a box.*]

VEE: I don't know.

VAL: Come on. Sit down there. Give me your foot. [*He grasps it roughly and jerks the shoe off. He clasps her foot in both hands and rubs it.*] You got a bad circulation.

VEE: What?

VAL: Your feet are cold. Know why? These here elastic garters are too tight on you. Why don't you leave 'em off and roll your stockings like the other girls do?

VEE: Uh?

VAL: Skittish?

VEE: It's late; I got to be going!

VAL: With one shoe off and one shoe on? "Hey diddle, diddle, my son Tom!" Here, I'll put it back on for you. Just lean on my shoulder a minute!

VEE: No, I . . . [*She sways precariously.*]

VAL: Watch out. [*He clutches her about the thighs and looks up at her, grinning.*] There now! Got your balance?

VEE [*catching her breath sharply*]: Oh, I got to be *going!*

VAL [*jumps away from her, clambers up the ladder and places the picture on the shelf*]: How's that, Mrs. Talbott? Okay? [VEE, *still too startled to speak, turns vaguely and barges out of the door.* VAL *looks after her, then suddenly breaks into lighthearted laughter.* MYRA *comes back downstairs slowly with a tense, concentrated expression.* VAL *smiles.*]

VAL: Myra, did you ever see a red church steeple?

MYRA [*absently*]: No.

VAL [*chuckling*]: Neither did I.

MYRA: Jabe's took a turn for the worse. I had to give him morphine.

VAL: So?

MYRA: He must be out of his mind; he says such awful things to me. Accuses me of wanting him to die.

VAL: Don't you?

MYRA: No! Death's terrible, Val. You're alive and everything's open and free, and you can go this way or that way, whichever direction you choose. And then all at once the doors start closing on you, the walls creep in, till finally there's just one way you can go—the dark way. Everything else is shut off.

VAL: Yes . . . [*then abruptly*] You got the sun at the back of your head. It brings the gold out in your hair!

MYRA [*diverted*]: Does it?

VAL: Yes, it looks pretty, Myra. [*They stand close together. She moves suddenly away with a slight, nervous smile.*]

MYRA: It's closing time.

VAL: Uh-huh. I'll put these back on the shelves. [*He picks up the wedding slippers.*] She had a small foot.

MYRA: Rosemary Wildberger?

VAL: Naw, naw, that Whiteside bitch.

MYRA: I could wear these slippers.

VAL: They'd be too small.

MYRA: You want to bet? Try them on me.

VAL [*laughing*]: Okay! [*He slips the shoes on her feet.*] Pinch, don't they?

MYRA: No, they feel marvelous on me!

VAL [*doubting*]: Aw!

MYRA: They do! [*She looks down at them.*] Silver and white. Why isn't everything made out of silver and white?

VAL: Wouldn't be practical, Myra.

MYRA: Practical? What's that? I never heard of practical before. I wasn't cut out for the mercantile business, Val.

VAL: What was you cut out for? [*A derelict Negro,* LOON, *stops outside the door and begins to play his guitar in the fading warmth of the afternoon sun. At first the music is uncertain and sad; then it lifts suddenly into a gay waltz.*] What *was* you cut out for, Myra?

MYRA [*enrapt with the music*]: Me cut out for? Silver and white! Music! Dancing! The orchard across from Moon Lake! You don't believe me, do you? Well, look at this. You know where I am? I'm on the Peabody Roof! I'm dancing to music! My dress is made out of *mousseline de soie!* Yes, with silver stars on it! And in my hair I've got lovely Cape jasmine blossoms! I'm whirling; I'm dancing faster and faster! A Hollywood talent scout, a Broadway producer: "Isn't she lovely!" Photographers taking my pictures for the *Commercial Appeal* and for the *Times-Picayune,* for all the society columns and for the rotogravure! I'm surrounded by people. Autograph seekers, they want me to sign my name! But I keep on laughing and dancing and scattering stars and lovely Cape jasmine blossoms! [*Her rhapsodic speech is suddenly interrupted by* JABE'S *furious knocking on the ceiling. Her elation is instantly crushed out. She stops dancing.*] I thought he had enough to go to sleep . . .

VAL: Why don't you give him enough to . . .?

MYRA: Val! I'm a decent woman.

VAL: What's decent? I never heard of that word. I've written a book full of words but I never used that one. Why? Because it's disgusting. Decent is something that's scared like a little white rabbit. I'll give you a better word, Myra.

MYRA: What word is that? [*The guitar changes back to its original slow melody.*]

VAL: Love, Myra. The one I taught the little girl on the bayou.

MYRA: That's an old one.

VAL: You've never heard it before.

MYRA: You're wrong about that, my dear. I heard it mentioned quite often the spring before I got married.

VAL: Who was it mentioned by—Jabe?

MYRA: No! By a boy named David.

VAL: Oh. David.

MYRA: We used to go every night to the orchard across from Moon Lake. He used to say, "Love! Love! Love!" And so did I, and both of us meant it, I thought. But he quit me that summer for some aristocratic girl, a girl like Cassandra Whiteside! I seen a picture of them dancing together on the Peabody Roof in Memphis. Prominent planter's son and the debutante daughter of. . . . Of course, after that, what I really wanted was death. But Jabe was the next best thing. A man who could take care of me, although there wasn't much talk about love between us.

VAL: No. There was nothing but hate.

MYRA: No!

VAL: Nothing but hate. Like the cancer, you wish you could kill him.

MYRA: Don't! You scare me. Don't talk that way. [*She crosses slowly to the door and* LOON *sings as the scene dims out.*]

SCENE THREE

Immediately following, without a break in the music. LOON *stops playing, retreats inside the store, and* SHERIFF TALBOTT *follows.*

SHERIFF: Hey, Loon! Didn't I see you on Front Street this mawnin' an' tell you to clear out of town?

LOON [*entering store*]: I thought you was jokin', Cap'n.

SHERIFF: Well, you made a big mistake. We don't allow no unemployed white transients in this town an' I'll be dogged if I'm gonna put up with colored ones.

LOON: I ain't transient, Cap'n.

SHERIFF: Where you livin'?

LOON: Nowhere, right this minute. Slep' on the levee las' night.

SHERIFF: Where you workin'?

LOON: Nowhere, Cap'n. I'se dispossessed.

SHERIFF: Aw, you'se dispossessed! Where'd you pick up all that fancy langwidge? You mean that Mr. Henley got fed up with your no-'countness an' turned you offen his property?

LOON: He turned me off but not fo' no-'countness. I wukked *hard.*

SHERIFF: If you work hard, you oughta make the state a good road-hand. Come on, you're under arrest.

LOON: What fo', Cap'n.

SHERIFF: Vagrancy. Ten dollar fine or thirty days hard labor.

LOON: Cap'n Talbott, I likes nine-fifty of bein' able to pay that fine.

SHERIFF: Come along.

VAL: Just a minute. I owe this boy ten dollars on his guitar.

SHERIFF: Huh?

VAL: I just bought his musical instrument off him. Here's the money. [LOON *starts to turn it over to the* SHERIFF.] Just a minute. Put that in your pocket. You can't fine a man for vagrancy when he's got ten dollars, can you, Sheriff? Not if I'm acquainted with the law.

SHERIFF: Huh?

VAL: He's also got a job. Hey, Loon, you drop back in tonight an' give me a *lesson* on this thing. Okay?

LOON: Yes, suh! Okay! [*He shuffles hurriedly out. The* SHERIFF *stares hard and silently at* VAL. VAL *casually strums a chord on the guitar.* DEPUTY SHERIFF PEE WEE BLAND *wobbles ponderously into the doorway laughing heartily, having just delivered some witticism to the men on the porch. He notices the tension and beckons the others to enter. They have all been drinking.*]

MYRA [*re-entering; nervously*]: Val, take these boxes . . .

SHERIFF [*interrupting*]: Just a minute. [*He catches* VAL'S *arm as* VAL *starts to move past him.* VAL *jerks his arm free. All this happens very rapidly.*] You beat the county out of a good road-hand.

VAL: I thought he might be better as a musician.

SHERIFF: Musician, hell! That worthless no'count nigger?

VAL: A man's not worthless because he's dispossessed.

PEE WEE: Hear, hear! *Dispossessed!*

FIRST MAN: Where'd he pick up that Nawthun radical lingo?

SECOND MAN: Who's he talkin' about?

FIRST MAN: That nigger, Loon.

SECOND MAN: Come down here to organize our niggers?

FIRST MAN: Make them bosses, huh? Us chop their cotton for 'em?

PEE WEE: It's talk like that that's back of all our colored tenant trouble. [*He wobbles up to* VAL.] Dispossessed? Did you say *dispossessed?*

VAL: Yes, I *did.*

PEE WEE: How yuh figure a man can be dispossessed from somethin' that never was his'n.

VAL: The land belongs to the man that works the land!

PEE WEE: Hear, hear!

FIRST MAN: That's red talk!

SECOND MAN: Yeah, go back to Rooshuh!

FIRST MAN: Anybody don't like this guvement oughta go back to Rooshuh!

SECOND MAN: Pack 'em all off togethuh, Jews, and radicals, and niggers! Ship 'em all back to *Rooshuh!*

FIRST MAN: Back to Africa with 'em!

MYRA [*frightened*]: Sheriff, stop this disturbance! My husband is sick upstairs!

SHERIFF: Quiet down, you boys!

PEE WEE [*very drunk and sententious, he talks like a Southern orator of the old school*]: Yeh, you all hush up. I'm talkin' to this young fellow. Now, looky here: a nigger works on a white man's property, don't he? White man houses him an' feeds him an' pays him livin' wages as long as he *produces.*

But when he *don't,* it's like my daddy said, he's gotta be blasted out a th' ground like a *daid tree stump* befo' you can run a *plow* th'ough it! [*A third man enters; he is a huge lout.*]

THIRD MAN: What's this here?

FIRST MAN: Some red-neck peckerwood with a Nawthun edjication's tellin' us how we oughta run our niggers!

MYRA: Sheriff, make them stop right now!

PEE WEE: That nigger, Loon, got dispossessed from nothin'. The land wasn't his.

VAL: No, nothin' was his. Nothin' but his own black skin and that was his damnation!

FIRST MAN: Listen to that!

SECOND MAN: The carpetbaggers are comin' back agin!

THIRD MAN [*going up to* VAL]: You know what I do when I see a snake?

VAL: No, what?

MYRA: Val!

THIRD MAN: I get me a good fork stick to pin it down with. Then I scotch it under the heel of my boot—I scotch its goddam yellow gizzards out!

SECOND MAN: Go *on!*

FIRST MAN: *Show* him, Pinkie.

MYRA: Sheriff! *Please!*

[*The* THIRD MAN *spits at* VAL'S *shoe.*]

VAL: You spit on my shoe! *Wipe it off!* [*He spits again.* VAL *knocks him down. The men close in about* VAL *like a pack of hounds. There is a near riot for a few moments. Then the* SHERIFF *disperses them.*]

SHERIFF: Come on, you all! Clear out! *Clear* out! Pee Wee, you're Deputy. Git these men out of here! [*The men are shoved out, grumbling.*]

MYRA: Those drunken stave-mill workers make nothing but trouble!

SHERIFF [*to* VAL]: Who are you? What's your name?

VAL: Val Xavier.

MYRA: Val didn't mean anything; he's just a talker.

SHERIFF: Where do you come from?

VAL: Any number of places! [*He picks up the guitar again.*]

MYRA: Down state—Witches' Bayou.

SHERIFF: Let him answer for himself, Mizz Torrance.

MYRA: Well, don't snap questions at him like he was up on trial. I know everything about this boy.

SHERIFF: You do, huh?

MYRA: Yes, I do. He come to me with the highest recommendations.

SHERIFF: Who from?

MYRA: Friends, relatives. He likes to talk. He's done some writing, but he's no more a radical than you or me! I give you my trusted word on it.

SHERIFF: It ain't a question of doubtin' your word, Mizz Torrance.

MYRA: All right. Goodbye. I'm closin' up the store.

SHERIFF: Just one more question, please. What's your draft number, buddy? [VAL *stares at him and strikes a chord on the guitar.*] *What's your draft number?*

MYRA [*quickly*]: Eight thousand an' something. Val, take those empty shoeboxes out to the incinerator! [VAL *goes out with the boxes.*]

SHERIFF: How do you happen to know his draft number?

MYRA: He happened to tell me this mawning. Is there anything else that I can do for you, Sheriff?

SHERIFF: Yes, ma'am. You can do yourself a favor an' get a new clerk. That impudent young peckerwood won't bring yuh nothin' but trouble. G'night. [*The* SHERIFF *goes out.* MYRA *leans exhaustedly against the door.* VAL *re-enters slowly.*]

MYRA: Oh, Val, Val, Val, why didn't you keep your head? Why didn't you hold your tongue?

VAL: A man has got to stick up for his own kind of people.

MYRA: Your kind of people? That old colored beggar, Loon?

VAL: We're both of us dispossessed. Just give me my wages an' I'll be moving along.

MYRA: Where?

VAL: Where I was headed when I broke that axle. [MYRA *stares at him speechlessly.*]

MYRA: Val, I don't want you to go.

VAL: I'd ruin your business for you.

MYRA: Never mind that.

VAL: Besides I'm under suspicion now, and it wouldn't be safe.

MYRA: Just wait. This'll all blow over.

VAL: No. There's something I didn't mention about me this mawning.

MYRA: What happened in Texas?

VAL: Yes. I'm *wanted,* Myra.

MYRA: Wanted? You're *wanted?* [VAL *gravely picks up the guitar, without looking at* MYRA, *and strikes a slow chord on it.*] What are you *wanted* for, Val?

VAL [*quietly, without looking up*]: For rape.

MYRA: What?

VAL: Rape!

MYRA: Shhh! I don't believe it. That's something *nigguhs* are lynched for—not *you,* Val.

VAL: Yes, me. [*He strikes a chord on the guitar.*]

MYRA: When did it happen?

VAL: About two years ago.

MYRA: Who was the woman? [VAL *punctuates his speech with strumming on the guitar which he never puts down till the end of the scene. He avoids* MYRA'S *eyes.*]

VAL: A woman from Waco, Texas. Wife of an oil-field superintendent. I boarded with them while I was working down there. A plain sort of woman; I never noticed her much. One night her husband got drunk. Passed out in the car. This woman from Waco come to my room that night. Well, I was drunk. What happened was accidental. Afterwards, I was disgusted with her and with me, I said to her, "Listen, I don't want nothing like this; I'm getting away!" "I'm goin' with yuh," she said. "Oh, no you're not," I told her, "I travel alone." She started to scream. She run to the phone and screamed that she'd been raped. I lost my head for a minute and struck her in the mouth. Then I left. I drove clean out of Texas before daybreak. But not long afterwards, though, I begun to see my name and my description in public buildings—"Wanted for Rape in Texas."

MYRA: You've changed your name.

VAL: Yes, but not my description.

MYRA: That's why you're quitting this job. You're scared she'll track you down?

VAL: Not just for that reason. I have another reason.

MYRA: What's that?

VAL: *You.* Like I told you this morning, I oughtn't to touch you, but I keep *wanting* to, Myra.

MYRA: Oh.

VAL: You don't get rid of something by holding it in. It gathers, it grows, it gets to be *enormous.*

MYRA: Yes.

VAL: You said this morning I touched the women too much when I tried shoes on them. Maybe I do. My hands—I'm afraid of my hands. I hold them in so hard the muscles ache. [*He strikes a chord sharply.*] You know what it's like? A herd of elephants, straining at a rope. How do I know the rope won't break sometime? With you or with somebody else?

MYRA [*going slowly to the door*]: You don't have to leave on account of a reason like that. [*She touches her forehead.*] My head's still whirling from all that excitement in here. I don't seem able to *think.* The cotton gin bothers me, too. It makes a sound like your heart was pounding a lot too fast.

VAL: Mine does sometimes. [*strumming.*]

MYRA: Everyone's does sometimes.

VAL: Your belt's untied in the back.

MYRA: Is it? Fix it for me.

VAL [*slowly he sets down the guitar on the counter; crossing slowly to her, he touches her waist*]: You come way in at the middle.

MYRA: I haven't let go of my figure like some women do. I've kept it.

VAL: For what?

MYRA: What for? Maybe because I don't feel everything's done for me yet.

VAL: Why should you?

MYRA: Some women do about my age. They have babies.

VAL: You never?

MYRA: No. I lived in a state of—what do they call it?—artificial respiration. Something that pumps the breath in and out of your body when otherwise you'd be dead. Dead as a rock is, Val! [*She turns abruptly to him.*] Oh, Val, I don't want you to go. I'll make it all right. I'll fix things up so nobody's going to suspicion. I'll make up all kinds of stories if you'll stay here! Huh? Huh, Val?

VAL [*hoarsely*]: Myra. . . .

MYRA: Yes?

VAL: Let's—let's—go in the back room a minute. [*The cotton gin can be heard in the distance.*]

MYRA: That room's locked, Val.

VAL: Where's the key?

MYRA: I took it an' thrown it away.

VAL: What did you do that for?

MYRA: Because I known you would ask me to go in there sometime an' I was scared I might be weak enough to do it. So I took the key and I thrown it away so far I don't think you could find it. [*He releases her and goes quickly out through the confectionery. The gin seems to pump even louder. After a moment Val returns to the room.*]

VAL [*in a hoarse whisper*]: That lock was no good, Myra.

MYRA: You broke it open?

VAL: Yes.

MYRA: Christ! I was scared that you would. [*For a long moment they stare at each other, then rush together in a convulsive embrace.*]

CURTAIN

ACT THREE

SCENE: *The same, but the room in the rear through the arch has been redecorated. The walls have been painted pale blue and have been copiously hung with imitation dogwood blossoms to achieve a striking effect of an orchard in full bloom. The room is almost subjective, a mood or a haunting memory beyond the drab actuality of the drygoods department. Its lighting fixtures have been covered with Japanese lanterns so that, when lighted, they give the room a soft, rosy glow. It is a rainy spring afternoon about two months after the preceding scene. The old-fashioned lights of the store cannot entirely dispel the silvery gloom. The Gothic features of the room are accentuated by this shadowy effect.* VAL *is alone in the store. He is working on his book, the loose pages of which he keeps in a battered old tin box. He writes with a stub pencil which he chews reflectively; then scribbles with rapt expression. The juke box is playing a number with steel guitars. He looks very simple and lonely, a little faunlike, seated on one of the low shoe-fitting stools, absorbed in his creative labor. There is a faint whisper of rain, and of wind.* MYRA *enters from the street in a transparent white raincoat, very glowing and warm and happy.* VAL *quickly stuffs the script back in the box and pushes it out of sight.*

MYRA: Hello, hello, hello! What are you hiding from me? Is it the book? Ah, the mysterious book. I never was quite sure that it existed.

VAL: What d'ja think it was?

MYRA: Something you dreamed those afternoons on the bayou! Let me look at it.

VAL: No.

MYRA: Let me just hold it.

VAL: Don't be silly.

MYRA: Please! [*He surrenders the bundle of papers grudgingly.*] It's like holding a baby! Such a big book, too; so good an' solid.

VAL: It's got life in it, Myra. When people read it, they're going to be frightened. They'll say it's crazy because it tells the truth! Now, give it back to me, Myra. It's not finished yet.

MYRA: I wish that I had something to do with it, too. Wouldn't it make it kind of more legitimate like if it had two parents, Val? [*She laughs tenderly, and hands it back to him.*] I had a wonderful time this afternoon. After I got Jabe's new prescription, I drove over to Tunica to get my hair done. I knew it would be my last chance before Easter. How does it look, Val?

VAL: Swell.

MYRA: How're things going?

VAL: Slow. I haven't rung up a single cash-sale since noon.

MYRA: Rain, rain. You certainly kill our trade. I was stuck on th' road coming home for nearly an hour before I got pulled out. [*She takes off her raincape and puts on a bright smock.*] I kind of enjoyed it, though. The air was so fresh, an' when the bells started ringing . . .

VAL: What're they ringing for?

MYRA: Good Friday church service. Dr. Hector is preaching the Seven Last Words from the Cross. Just as they started to ring, a big white moth flew in the car window. Val, I hate most bugs, but this one I felt a kind of a sympathy for. He was terribly young.

VAL: How do you know he was young? Did you ask him his age?

MYRA: No, but he had that surprised, inexperienced look about him that young things have. It was easy to see he had just come from the cocoon, and was *sooo* disappointed. Of cou'se he expected th' world t' be bright an' gold, but what he found was a nasty, cold spring rain. His two long whiskers were covered with strings of pearls. He sat on the steering wheel an' shook them off. I asked him, "Why?" An' he said, "Don'tcha know? It's in bad taste to put on pearls before dark!"

VAL: You're talking foolishness, Myra.

MYRA: Am I? Fo'give me, da'ling. I'm in that kind of a humor. My God, you got eyes that shine in th' dark like a dawg's. [*She starts humming a tune.*] Remember that? Such a long time ago. Before Columbus discovered America even. Oh, beautiful fo' spacious skies, for amber fields of grain. . . . Greta Garbo is at the Delta Brilliant. . . . Fo' purple mountain majesties, above the fruited. . . . Lemme up on that ladder. I want to be on a high, high place in the sun! What's these here?

VAL: Women's soft sole slippers. They just come in. [*Impulsively she gathers them up like an armful of plushy red flowers and tosses them into the air.*]

MYRA [*ecstatically*]: Wake me early, Mother, fo' I shall be Queen of the May!

VAL: For Chrissakes, Myra, what did'ja do that for?

MYRA: Oh, soft sole slippers. Women's soft sole slippers! They seem t' be so damned unnecessary!

VAL: What's the matter with you this afternoon?

MYRA: When people have dreams, unusually good dreams, they get up singing, they go to the beauty parlor, and act like fools all day! When serious-minded people who write big books say, "What's th' matter with you?" they simply smile an' say, "We have our secrets." [VAL *opens the door.*] The rain's slacked up?

VAL: Yeah, a little.

MYRA: That's good. Maybe we'll have a nice bright Easter, Val. We'll go to church an' look so lovely the Lawd will have to fo'give us for all our sins!

VAL [*in the doorway*]: River's way up over flood-stage at Friar's Point Landing. They say sometimes this place is cut off by water.

MYRA: They say! They say! What of it? Ten thousand years from today we'll just be little telltale marks on the sides of rocks which people refer to as fossils. [*There is the sound of slow tolling bells across the wide, rainy fields.*] That's all will be left of our big tremendous adventures! [*She smiles with amazement at this thought.*] Teeny-weeny little pencil-scratches, things like pigeon tracks will be what's left of Myra—what's left of Val! Then old Mr. Important Scientific Professor will pick up his microscope—"Humph!" he'll say, "This girl had remarkable legs." Or, "Goodness, this young man lost a rib somewhere." That will be all they'll ever find out about us! Were we in love? Were we happy? Did white moths fly in our windows? How do they know? They can't tell. History isn't written about *little* people. All that little people ever get to be is marks on rocks called *fossils.*

VAL: Yes, unless they write books or something.

MYRA: Oh, yes, of course, unless they write books or something! Then they're remembered *always!* [*She jumps down from the ladder and hugs him tenderly against her.*] You will be, da'ling! Don't worry!

VAL: Sarcasm?

MYRA: No, not a bit! [*She laughs gently.*] You're such a wonderful, wonderful baby! When I'm a fossil, even if it makes Mr. Science Professor blush, I hope he discovers my scratches are all scrambled up with yours. [*She laughs gaily. A small* NEGRO BOY *enters the store.*] Wipe yo' feet off, sonny, don't track th' floor.

BOY: Yes, ma'am.

MYRA: What do you want? Peanuts?

BOY: I wan' peanuts, but granny wan' a nickel's worth a snuff.

MYRA: Aw. Well, Granny's got to have her snuff, now, don't she? How is Granny feelin'?

BOY: She been laid up in bed with breakbone fever.

MYRA: Aw, now, that's a shame. You tell 'er Mizz Torrance say to get well quick, quick, quick, cause we can't do without 'er. [*A young* NEGRO *enters in overalls.*]

BOY: Yes, ma'am.

NEGRO: Howdy, Mizz Torr'nce.

MYRA: Hello, Bennie. Val, give the little boy a bag full a goobers, will yuh? They're on th' house.

NEGRO [*admiringly*]: You sho' are gracious, ma'am. I wunder if you would take my note for somethin'?

MYRA: Bennie, I've got enough notes from you to paper th' store with already. What do you want?

NEGRO: A little plug tobacco.

MYRA: Well, put your cross on this.

NEGRO: Thanks, ma'am. [*The* NEGRO BOY *comes back out with the peanuts and goes out the front door. There is a sound of shouting.*]

MYRA: Oh, they're shouting up over there at the big Lent meeting. Sounds like they might be hitting the sawdust trail.

NEGRO: Will be before sundown.

MYRA: How 'bout you, Bennie?

NEGRO: Me hit it? Naw, I guess I glories too much in the flesh for that. Good afternoon, Mizz Torrance.

MYRA [*to the* NEGRO]: Good afternoon. Where you takin' that load of sandbags to?

NEGRO: Down river t' Mr. Sikeses.

MYRA: You think there's a chance the levee might go out?

NEGRO: Ah reckon not unless th' Lawd intends it to. G'by, ma'am.

MYRA: Goodbye. [*The* NEGRO *starts the mules. His wagon wheels are heard.*] Val? [*There is no answer. She switches on the lights in the confectionery. Spring blooms with a soft radiance for an instant and then dies out as she releases the switch.*] Val! [*She turns smiling slightly, her lips moving as she whispers, excitedly, to herself. With a sudden, rapturous awareness she draws her hands up the front of her body and clasps them over her breasts.*] Oh . . . [*In the archway there is suspended a string of Chinese glass pendants with a tiny gong. With an impulse of childish gaiety, she sets the pendants tinkling, softly, musically, in the store's greenish gloom and she laughs to herself with a child's quick, delicate laughter. While her back is turned, the* CONJURE MAN *glides noiselessly into the store. Now, for the first time, there is a low muttering of thunder. The lights in the confectionery flicker a little. Still unaware of the* CONJURE MAN'S *presence,* MYRA *shivers slightly and a bewildered, uncertain look appears on her face and she raises a hand to touch her cheek and her forehead. As though with a disturbing prescience of something unnatural, she turns about slowly and meets the* NEGRO'S *gaze. She catches her breath in a sudden, sharp gasp. The* CONJURE MAN *smiles and makes a slight obeisance. He stretches out his small clawlike hand, in the hollow of which he is presenting some object.*]

MYRA [*breathlessly*]: What—what do you want? [*The* CONJURE MAN *mumbles something which cannot be heard.*] What? No! No, I don't want it. [*then, smiling defiantly*] I don't need holy stones to bring me luck. [*The* CONJURE MAN *makes another slight bow, then starts to turn away.*] If you want to make an honest dollar, though, you can go out back and wash the Mississippi Delta off my car. You'll find a sponge, a bucket, and a bunch of old chamois hanging in the garage. [*The* CONJURE MAN *mumbles some eager words of thanks and starts to enter the confectionery.* MYRA *looks after him, troubled, not knowing why. In the archway he stops and looks back over his shoulder to meet her gaze. There is a moment of curiously tense stillness. Then he grins and makes another slight bow and disappears. There is the sound of low thunder again. The front door opens and* DOLLY *comes in.*]

DOLLY: Has he gone?

MYRA: Who?

DOLLY: That *awful* lookin' ole darky.

MYRA: He's gone out back. Who is he?

DOLLY: They call him the Conjure Man—from Blue Mountain. When I first caught a sight of him out there, I swear to goodness I neahly had a conniption! I was scared to death that he would *mark* my *baby!* Which reminds me to ask you! Have those maternity garments got here yet?

MYRA: No, they haven't come yet.

DOLLY: What? I ordered 'em two months ago.

MYRA: I know, and I can't understand what's causin' the delay.

DOLLY: Neither can I. My God, what am I going to do?

MYRA: I'm sorry.

DOLLY: I guess I'll have to hang out a sign, "Excuse me, people." [MYRA *turns away in distaste.* BEULAH *rushes in.*]

BEULAH: Excitement! Cassandra Whiteside's come in town drunk as a lord.

DOLLY: No.

BEULAH: I just seen her on Front Street. Wearin' a white satin evenin' dress. She's been in another wreck; the side of the car's bashed in.

DOLLY: I thought they revoked her license.

BEULAH: She's got her a nigger chauffeur. At least I *hope* he's a chauffeur.

DOLLY: Beulah.

BEULAH: Well, there has been a great deal of speculation about 'em that's not very pleasant. They say that she's been ostracized in Memphis, asked to leave sev'ral parties; and her father has actually received a warning note from the Klan.

DOLLY: Goodness. She'll be worse than ostracized if she keeps up at this rate.

BEULAH: Myra, what will you do if she comes in here and starts to make a disturbance?

MYRA [*shortly*]: Put her out.

BEULAH: You think you could? They say she fights like a tiger.

MYRA [*as* VAL *enters*]: I think Val would be able to handle her for me.

VAL [*setting the boxes down*]: What did you call me for, Myra?

MYRA [*confused*]: Call you? Oh, yes, I—I can't remember just now.

BEULAH: That sounds extremely suspicious. [*She winks.*]

DOLLY: Don't it, though? Look, they're blushing.

BEULAH: Both of them. Oh, I think it's marvelous to see a man who can blush.

MYRA [*with nervous haste*]: Val, are those the new Keds?

VAL: No, women's rubbers.

MYRA: Just in time for the rain; how very lucky.

DOLLY [*meaningfully*]: How's Jabe?

MYRA [*still confused*]: Jabe?

DOLLY: Yes, your husband, honey. Jabe Torrance.

MYRA: Jabe's no better.

DOLLY: Ain't that turr'ble!

BEULAH: I don't guess you *could* look for much improvement.

MYRA: No. All we can do is try to relieve the pain. Val, bring up the rest of those boxes and stack them up there. [VAL *is glad to get out.*]

DOLLY: Myra, that green is your color!

BEULAH: Don't it look sweet on her, though? I had my eye on that dress; it's the nices' thing you had in stock, Myra Torrance.

MYRA: It's more of a blue than a green.

BEULAH: What do they call it?

MYRA [*with a slight, suppressed smile*]: They call it "ecstasy blue."

DOLLY: I swan. [*She exchanges a significant look with* BEULAH.]

BEULAH: But don't it become her, though? It brings the gold out in her hair.

DOLLY: *It does.*

MYRA: I just had it washed. That always brightens the color.

DOLLY: What with? Goldenfoam?

MYRA: No, with a few drops of lemon. That's all I use.

DOLLY: Honestly? Well, she's took on more *sparkle* this spring.

BEULAH: I think it's wonderful that you can be so brave.

MYRA: What do you mean?

BEULAH: Why, I mean about Jabe's condition.

MYRA: Oh, excuse me a minute. I gotta take Jabe his medicine. He's been so restless today. [*She goes back upstairs.* BEULAH *looks at* DOLLY *and giggles.* DOLLY *looks at* BEULAH *and giggles an octave higher. They both cover their mouths* as the TEMPLE SISTERS *enter.*]

BLANCH: I want you to know . . .

EVA: Dr. Hector had just finished preaching the Seven Last Words from the Cross . . .

BLANCH: When who should we run into . . .

EVA: Yes! on Front Street.

BEULAH: Sandra Whiteside?

EVA and BLANCH: Yes!

DOLLY: I know. We just been talking.

EVA [*catching her breath*]: Did you know she was just put out of the Cross Roads Inn?

BLANCH: Literally thrown out. They tried to get her father on the phone. Useless!

EVA: He's drunker than she is. We passed her just now up there on the Sunflower Bridge. She seemed to be having d.t.'s. What's that she was shouting, Blanch?

BLANCH: "Behold Cassandra! Shouting doom at the gates!"

EVA: Yes. An' some bright-skin nigger was in the car with her. It's really created a perfeckly terrible stir.

BLANCH: Imagine—on Good Friday!

EVA: Utterly shameless! Where's that nice-lookin' young man?

BLANCH: I got to return those shoes. I went to a very expensive obstetrician in Memphis. He said they'd ruined my feet. Why, Palm Sunday mawning I couldn't hardly march in church with the choir. [*She calls out.*] Mr. Xavier? Oh, they've closed the confectionery.

EVA: Yes. The noise was disturbing to Jabe.

BLANCH: She's had it redecorated.

EVA: All done over. She says it's supposed to resemble the orchard across from Moon Lake. [VEE *enters. She wears black, nunlike garments for Good Friday, and her look is exalted.*] Vee! How are you, honey?

VEE [*almost sobbing*]: I've waited and prayed so long. Now it's finally come.

BEULAH: *What's* come?

VEE: The vision. I seen him early this mawning. I painted the picture.

BEULAH: Picture of what?

VEE: Of Jesus!

DOLLY: I thought you said you'd never paint the Lawd until you'd actually seen Him face to face.

VEE [*simply*]: I have. This mawning. On the way to church, by the cottonwood tree, where the road branches off toward the levee. I been on a fast since Ash Wednesday to clear my sight. Veils seemed to drop off my eyes. Light—light! I never have seen such brilliance. Like needles it was in my eyes; they actually ached when I stepped out in it.

BEULAH: In what?

VEE: The sun this mawning, before the Passion began.

DOLLY: Weakness from fasting. You're such an excitable nature.

VEE: No, no. I've had other signs. Look at my palms.

BEULAH: What about them?

VEE: Can't you see the red marks?

BEULAH: They do look so't of inflamed.

BLANCH: Ain't that remarkable, though?

BEULAH: What happened?

VEE: I been tormented. He took all the torment off me.

DOLLY: Tormented by what?

VEE: Evil thoughts. Those men in the lockup, they write nasty words on the walls. At night I can see them. They keep coming up in my mind. He took that cross off me when he touched me.

BEULAH: Touched you?

DOLLY: Where? [VEE *lifts her hand reverently and touches her bosom.*] Aw. [*She giggles.*] He made a pass at you? [*She giggles.*] He made a pass at you?

BEULAH: Dolly, you're awful!

DOLLY: I couldn't help it; it just popped out of my mouth.

BEULAH: Vee, can't we see the picture?

BLANCH: Yes, let's *see* it.

VEE: I brung it here for Myra t' put on display. [*She starts to unwrap the canvas. There is the sound of an angry outburst and the simultaneous crash of glass on the floor above.*]

BEULAH: What's that? [*The women congregate quickly at the foot of the stairs in listening attitudes.*]

VEE [*at the right of* DOLLY]: No, I've had other manifestations. When I was seven years old, my little sister, Rose, got typhoid fever.

MYRA [*upstairs*]: Jabe.

BEULAH: What's that?

DOLLY: Can you make it out?

MYRA: Jabe!

BEULAH [*going to the foot of the steps*]: What's that shouting upstairs?

VEE: She hadn't been baptized yet an' the doctor said she was dyin'. So Reverend Dabney come over at midnight.

JABE: No, I won't take it.

MYRA: The doctor prescribed it for you. It helps the pain.

JABE: I know what you're trying to do. You're trying to kill me.

DOLLY: What?

BEULAH: What?

MYRA: You're out of your head.

DOLLY: What's that?

BLANCH: Sssh.

EVA: Sssh.

VEE: Afterwards, he give me the bowl of Holy water an' told me to empty it outside on the bare ground. But I didn't. I poured it out in the kitchen sink.

MYRA: Jabe, you don't know what you're saying. [*The door bangs open.*] I'll call for the doctor.

BLANCH: Delirious!

EVA: Yes, out of his haid!

VEE [*slowly*]: The kitchen sink turned *black. Black*—absolutely *black!* [*The door above is suddenly thrown open and* MYRA *calls out wildly.*]

MYRA: Val! Val!

DOLLY: I'll get him for yuh, Myra! Mr. Xavier. [*There is great excitement.* VAL *comes in.*]

VAL: What's the matter?

BLANCH: Oh, something's goin' on, I don't know what...

EVA: But it's awful! [MYRA *appears above.*]

MYRA: *Val?*

VAL: Yeah?

MYRA: Phone Dr. Bob, and tell him to come right over! [*She slams the door.*]

EVA: Where's Dr. Bob?

BLANCH: Ain't he in Jackson Springs?

VAL: Howdy, Mizz Talbott.

EVA: I'm very much afraid the wires are down! [*As* VAL *crosses in front of* VEE, *she slowly rises, following him with her eyes, her lower jaw sagging open slowly with a stricken expression.*]

VAL [*lifting the phone*]: Get me Jackson Springs. [VEE *utters a stifled cry.* VAL *is struck by her shocked gaze.*] What's the matter, Mizz Talbott? [*into the phone*] Jackson Springs?

VEE: No, no!

DOLLY: What's the matter with Vee? She's white as goat's milk.

BEULAH: Seems to me like she's tooken some kind of a spell.

DOLLY [*grasping her shoulders roughly*]: Vee!

VEE: Le' me go! Leave me be!

BLANCH: That vision she had has probably got her wrought up.

EVA: Passion Week always upsets her. Get a wet cloth, somebody!

VAL: The wires are down.

BEULAH: Don't Myra keep some kind of a stimulant on the place?

VAL: There's some rum in the back. I'll get it.

VEE [*struggling up, panting*]: Naw, I can't stay, le' me go!

DOLLY: Nobody's holding you, honey.

VEE [*her eyes follow* VAL *as he crosses to the confectionery*]: Where's he going *to?*

BEULAH: Get you a little something to pull you together. [DOLLY *picks up the picture.*]

VEE [*crying out wildly*]: You take your hands off my picture! [*She wrests it from* DOLLY *before she can see it.*]

BEULAH: Well!

VEE: It's not t' be touched by you, you foul-minded thing!

DOLLY: I thought that you brung it here to put on dis*play.*

VEE: I never.

DOLLY: Just let me take one look!

VEE: No! [DOLLY *makes a move toward the canvas.* BEULAH *crosses to the right of the steps.* VEE *cries out and thrusts her away.* MYRA *appears on the stairs.*]

MYRA: Oh, for God's sake, will you all please hush up? I've got to get in touch with Dr. Bob! [*Her hair is disarranged, and her dress torn open as though she had been in a struggle.*] Jabe's delirious. He wouldn't take the morphine. Did you hear him? He said I was trying to kill him! [*She picks up the receiver, jiggles it.*]

EVA: Val tried to phone.

BLANCH: They told him the wires were down.

MYRA: Then I'll just have to drive over.

BLANCH: Oh, but they say there's danger of the bridge collapsing.

MYRA: What else can I do?

EVA: Blanch, if you were married and your husband was desperately ill, wouldn't you take a chance on the bridge collapsing?

BLANCH: No, I certainly wouldn't. No, I certainly. . . . Oh, before you go, Myra—about these shoes . . .

MYRA [*snatching a raincoat from the closet*]: Oh, I'm distracted, I—Val, tell the nigger to put the chains on the tires!

VAL: I can't do six things at once. Miss Eva here wants some money back on a pair of shoes.

MYRA: Money back? What money? You got the shoes for nothing!

BLANCH: Oh, horrors, don't you remember how I tripped over that rubber mat an' practickly broke my ankle?

EVA: Two trips to the doctor it cost us!

BLANCH: Six dollars!

EVA: But we'll take five since Myra has been so . . .

MYRA: Thanks. Val, give the ladies five dollars out of the cashbox. Now if you'll excuse me . . .

BEULAH: Myra, if there's anything I can do.

DOLLY: Don't hesitate to call on me if they is. [MYRA *has already disappeared through the confectionery.*]

BLANCH: Gracious . . .

EVA: Sakes alive! What excitement! Blanch, you go up an' sit with Cousin Jabe.

BLANCH: Oh, I couldn't. I'm having palpitations!

VEE: I . . . I . . . have to leave, too. [*She retreats toward the door.*]

DOLLY: Not without showin' the picture!

VEE: Dolly, get out of my way!

BEULAH [*snatches the picture held behind her back and tears the paper wrapping off; she gasps and shrieks with laughter*]: Mr. Xavier!

DOLLY: Mr. *Xavier?*

VAL: What?

BEULAH: Vee Talbott here has just conferred a wonderful honor on you.

DOLLY: Oh, so it *is,* I *suspected!*

BEULAH: You're going to sit at the head of the table with all of the Twelve Apostles sitting around'ja!

DOLLY: You even have a silver dishpan sort of on top of your haid. [*They both shriek with laughter.*]

VEE [*wildly*]: No, no, no! Let go of my picture!

BEULAH: Ain't it a wonderful likeness?

DOLLY: From memory, too. Or did you pose for it, Val?

BEULAH: He didn't *have to.* She seen him in the cottonwood tree. The *lynching* tree, as they call it!

DOLLY: I hope that don't make you *nervous,* Val!

VEE: No! You're all of you cooking up something without no excuse!

DOLLY: No? No excuse? That's why you nearly collapsed when Mr. Xavier came up an' said hello to yuh!

BEULAH: Your spiritual nature an' all, what a big joke it is!

DOLLY: Carping at other people, criticizing their morals . . .

BEULAH: Stirring up all that card-playing rumpus here in the congregation.

DOLLY: Declaring in public that I wasn't fit to associate with because I had drinking parties.

BLANCH: Dolly!

EVA: Don't you all go on like this!

DOLLY: She's got to have her eyes opened, now, once an' for all. A vision of Jesus? No, but of Val Xavier, the shoe clerk who sold 'er them shoes.

VAL: Mrs. Bland!

DOLLY: And where did she have this vision? Where? Under the cottonwood tree where the road turns off toward the levee. Exactly where time an' time again you see couples parked in cars with all of the shades pulled down! And what did he do? He stretched out his hand and *touched* yuh! [*She thrusts her hand against* VEE'S *bosom.* VEE *cries aloud as though the hand were a knife thrust into her, and, turning awkwardly, runs out of the store.*]

VAL: You all better go or you'll get bogged down on th' road.

BLANCH: Dolly, you shouldn't have done that.

EVA: So unnecessary!

BEULAH: I don't know. She's always held herself so high.

DOLLY: Yes, superior to us all. I guess after this she won't have so much to say on the subjeck of bridge during Lent! Come on, Beulah, let's go! Blanch, you an' Eva comin'?

BLANCH: Yes, just a minute! What happened to those old shoes? You see 'em, Mr. Xavier?

VAL: I thrown 'em in the trash bin. You want 'em back?

BLANCH: Please.

EVA: We couldn't wear 'em, of course, but it's no use throwin' 'em away.

BLANCH: No. Willful waste makes woeful want, they say. [*She giggles as they back skittishly out of the door.*] Don't you feel it? The atmosphere is simply *charged* with electric disturbance! [VAL *is left alone. He picks up the canvas* VEE *left, places it on the counter and stares at it for several seconds. The* CONJURE MAN *comes back into the archway, gliding noiselessly as before. He stares inscrutably at* VAL'S *back.* VAL *turns, as* MYRA *had turned, with the same air of troubled presentiment, and catches the* NEGRO'S *gaze. Unconsciously he raises his hands to draw his shirt closer about his throat as though the air had turned colder.*]

VAL: What—what do you want? [*The* CONJURE MAN *mumbles almost indistinguishably.*] Oh. Sure. You can stay back there all night, if it don't stop raining! [*The* CONJURE MAN *grins and bows, then extends his palm with the lucky token.*] Huh? Naw, naw, naw, I don't want it! Sorry but I don't truck with that conjure stuff. [*The* CONJURE MAN *bows once more and disappears as noiselessly as he came. There is a low muttering of thunder.* VAL *looks uneasy. He takes off his working jacket. There is a wild burst of drunken laughter outside. The door is thrown open and* SANDRA *enters, a flash of lightning behind her. Her hair hangs loose and she wears a rain-spattered, grass-stained white satin evening gown.*]

SANDRA: Behold Cassandra, shouting doom at the gates!

VAL: What do you want?

SANDRA: Oh. It's you. Snakeskin. Remember we're even now.

VAL: What do you want in here?

SANDRA: Protection. I'm in danger.

VAL: Danger of what?

SANDRA: Immolation at the hands of the outraged citizens of Two Rivers County. They've confiscated the nigger that drove my car and ordered me out of Two Rivers.

VAL: You must've given 'em some provocation.

SANDRA: Plenty of provocation. They say that I run around wild and stir up trouble—and neither parental nor civil law is able to restrain me. Why, only this afternoon I was on Cypress Hill with that bright-skinned nigger. They suspect me of having improper relations with him.

VAL: Did you?

SANDRA: No. I poured a libation of rum on my great-aunt's grave. But they don't believe me. The vigilantes decided that I was *persona non grata* and warned me to leave before something bad happened to me. How about you?

VAL: Huh?

SANDRA: Why don't you come along with me? You an' me, we belong to the fugitive kind. We live on motion. Think of it, Val. Nothing but motion, motion, mile after mile, keeping up with the wind, or even faster! Doesn't that make you hungry for what you live on? [VAL *shakes his head.*] Maybe we'll find something new, something never discovered. We'll stake out our claim before the others get to it. What do you say? [VAL *turns away.*] Where's Myra?

VAL: She's gone to Jackson Springs to get a doctor.

SANDRA: Good! We're alone together.

VAL: What's good about it?

SANDRA: Why do you hate me, Val?

VAL: I don't want trouble.

SANDRA: Am I trouble?

VAL: Yeah. As fine a piece of trouble as ever I've seen.

SANDRA: Is Myra trouble?

VAL: Leave her out of it.

SANDRA: Don't you think I know what's going on?

VAL: What are you talking about?

SANDRA: I saw her in Tupelo this morning, having her hair fixed up! What radiance! What joy!

VAL: Shut up about Myra.

SANDRA: Oh, you'd better watch out. It isn't kiss and good-bye with a woman like that! She'll want to keep you forever. I'm not like that.

VAL: Aw, leave me alone. [*He takes his jacket from a hook.*]

SANDRA: Women will never leave you alone. Not as long as you wear that marvelous jacket.

VAL: I want to close up.

SANDRA: I'll go in a minute.

VAL: Make it *this* minute, will you? [SANDRA *crosses to him. She loosens her red velvet cape and drops it to the floor at her feet. The white evening gown clings nakedly to her body.*]

VAL: Don't stand there in front of me like that!

SANDRA: Why not? I'm just looking at you. You know what I feel when I look at you, Val? Always the weight of your body bearing me down.

VAL: *Christ!*

SANDRA: You think I ought to be ashamed to say that? Well, I'm not. I think that passion is something to be proud of. It's the only one of the little alphabet blocks they give us to play with that seems to stand for anything of importance. Val . . . [*She touches his shoulder. He shoves her roughly away. The door opens and* MYRA *enters.*]

MYRA: Oh!

SANDRA [*casually*]: Hello, there. I thought you'd gone for the doctor.

MYRA: I couldn't get over the river. The bridge is out. What are *you* doing here?

SANDRA: I came here to give you a warning.

MYRA: A warning? Warning of what?

SANDRA: They've passed a law against passion. Our license has been revoked. We have to give it up or else be ostracized by Memphis society. Jackson and Vicksburg, too. Whoever has too much passion, we're going to be burned like witches because we know too much.

MYRA: What are you talking about?

SANDRA: Damnation! You see my lips have been touched by prophetic fire.

MYRA: I think they've also been touched by too much liquor. The store is closed.

SANDRA: I want to talk to you, Myra.

MYRA: Come back in the morning.

SANDRA: What morning? There isn't going to be any.

MYRA: I think there is.

SANDRA: That's just a case of unwarranted optimism. I have it on the very best of authority that time is all used up.

There's no more time. Can't you see it? Feel it? [*with drunken exultation*] The atmosphere is pregnant with disaster! [*She laughs and suddenly clasps the palms of her hands to her ears.*] Now, I can even *hear* it!

VAL: What?

SANDRA: A battle in heaven. A battle of *angels* above us! And *thunder!* And *storm!* [*She laughs wildly.*]

MYRA: Sandra, I've had too much. I can't stand anything more. You go home now before I do something I shouldn't.

SANDRA: I believe you *would.* You'd fight like a *tiger* for him.

MYRA: Be careful, Sandra.

SANDRA: Yes, I can tell by looking at you in that mad dress with your eyes spitting fire like the Devil's, you've learned what I've learned, that there's nothing on earth you can do. No, nothing! But catch at whatever comes near you with both your hands, until your fingers are broken! [SANDRA *flings herself upon* VAL *and kisses him with abandon.* MYRA *springs at her like a tiger and slaps her fiercely across the face.*]

MYRA: Leave him be, damn you, or I'll . . . [SANDRA *whimpers and staggers to the counter. Her head lolls forward and the dark hair slides over her face; she slips to her knees on the floor.*] Take her upstairs to my room. When dogs go mad, they ought to be locked and chained. [VAL *picks* SANDRA *up and carries her up the stairs. The storm increases in violence; rain beats loud on the tin portico outside. There is a terribly loud thunder clap.* MYRA *gasps. The electric current is disrupted and the lights dim out. Someone bangs at the door.* MYRA *calls—*] The store's closed up!

MAN: It's me, Mrs. Torrance. Jim Talbott!

MYRA: Oh, Sheriff Talbott. [*She opens the door.*] Is something the matter?

SHERIFF: Yes. [*He enters, followed by a woman. There is something remarkably sinister about the woman's appearance. She is a hard, dyed blonde in a dark suit. Her body is short and heavy but her face appears to have been burned thin by some consuming fever accentuated by the masklike makeup she wears and the falsely glittering gems on her fingers which are knotted tight around her purse.*] This is Mrs. Regan from Waco, Texas.

WOMAN: Never mind about that. Where is the man that clerks here?

MYRA: Val?

WOMAN: Is that what he calls himself? In Waco he was known as Jonathan West.

MYRA [*to the* SHERIFF]: What does this woman want here?

WOMAN: I want that man.

SHERIFF: That clerk of yours is wanted for rape in Texas.

MYRA: I'm sure you're mistaken.

WOMAN: Oh, no, I don't think I am. I've sent out descriptions of him to every town in the country. Canada, Mexico, even. The minute I got news of this shoe clerk I hopped a plane out of Waco. I feel pretty sure that I've finally tracked him down. Where is he? Where does he keep himself?

MYRA: I don't know.

WOMAN: Surely you . . .

MYRA: I don't have any idea!

WOMAN: You—you *must,* Mrs. Torrance!

MYRA: *No!* No, I don't. Oh, yes, he—he drove into Memphis.

WOMAN: Two days before Easter? He suddenly drove into Memphis and left you without any help? That certainly does sound peculiar.

MYRA: I gave him his notice. He's gone.

WOMAN: I don't believe you.

MYRA [*to the* SHERIFF]: This woman has got a pistol in her purse.

WOMAN: What if I have? You don't go hunting a dangerous animal down without any weapons. [*She suddenly starts forward.*] Wait! Look here! This picture! [*She crosses to* VEE'S *portrait.*]

SHERIFF: It's one of my wife's.

WOMAN: Now I'm convinced. It's *him.* I'd recognize it hanging on the moon. Come along, Sheriff, we're wasting time with this woman. She's telling us lies to protect him. The place to look is them sporting houses on Front Street. [*She rushes from the store.*]

SHERIFF: Don't play with fire, Mrs. Torrance. [*He follows her out.* MYRA *gasps and crosses to the door, bolting it shut.* VAL *steps noiselessly out upon the upstairs landing and stares down at* MYRA. *He descends a few steps with caution.*]

VAL [*on the stairs*]: Who was it?

MYRA: Sheriff Talbott.

VAL [*descending two steps*]: Who was the woman? [MYRA *stares up at him dumbly.*] *Who was the woman with him?*

MYRA: Val, don't act so excited.

VAL: Oh. It was her then.

MYRA: Yes. The woman from Waco.

VAL: Christ! I heard her voice but I thought I must be dreaming. [*He suddenly catches his breath and darts down the stairs and toward the front door.*]

MYRA: Where do you think you're goin'?

VAL: *Out!*

MYRA: Don't be a fool. You can't leave now. Those drunken stave-mill workers are on the street.

VAL: They know, already? She's *told* 'em?

MYRA: Val, will you please . . .

VAL: Lock up that door!

MYRA: It's locked.

VAL: The door in the confectionery?

MYRA: That's locked, too.

VAL: What happened to the lights?

MYRA: Went out in the storm. I'll turn on a lamp . . .

VAL: No. *Don't!*

MYRA: In the confectionery. They can't see in.

VAL: What did you tell her?

MYRA: That you'd gone into Memphis.

VAL: Did she believe you?

MYRA: No.

VAL: Where did they go to look for me?

MYRA: Sporting houses on Front Street.

VAL: Yeah. She'd think of that. Oh, God, Myra, I've washed myself in melted snow on mountains trying to get the touch of her off my body. It's no good.

MYRA: Keep *hold* of yourself.

VAL: You can't understand what it is to be hounded by somebody's hate.

MYRA: I looked in her face. What I saw wasn't hate.

VAL: What was it then?

MYRA: A terrible, hopeless, twisted kind of *love.*

VAL: That's worse than hate.

MYRA: I *know.* [*She picks up a lamp.*] Dry as a bone. Give me the other one, Val. [VAL *stares at nothing.*] Never mind, I'll get it. You're safe in here. They looked here once; they won't come back until morning.

VAL: *Safe?* She mentioned it in her description.

MYRA: Mentioned what?

VAL: Scars from burns on his legs. Afraid of fire. She'll have them *burn* me, Myra.

MYRA: Oh, Val, darling, don't act like a scared little boy.

VAL: I'm not so scared. I'm sick.

MYRA: I know how you feel.

VAL: Like something was crawling on me. Something that crawled up out of the basement of my brain. How did she look?

MYRA: A vicious, pitiful, artificial blonde.

VAL: She had on black?

MYRA: Yes.

VAL: All loaded down with imitation diamonds. That's how I see her. Leaning against a wall and screaming, "You can't get away! Anywhere that yuh go I'll track yuh down!" And now she has—She's *here!*

MYRA [*pityingly*]: Oh, Val, stay there on the stairs. I'm going to fix you a drink. The rain has made the air colder. Don't you feel it?

VAL: No.

MYRA: I do. I seem to be shaking a little. I guess my blood's too thin. Of course, you'll have to get away from Two River.

VAL: Get away? Yes, if I'm lucky!

MYRA: Oh, you'll be lucky, darling. I was just thinking, thinking about *myself*. Val . . .

VAL: What?

MYRA: I haven't traveled much. I've never been west of the Mississippi. Never much east of it either. I think it's time I took a trip somewhere.

VAL: What are you talking about?

MYRA: I'm leaving here with you tonight!

VAL: No.

MYRA: Oh, yes, I *am*. I've *got* to. We'll run off *together* as soon as the storm slacks up.

VAL [*rising*]: Myra . . .

MYRA: Give me a nickel; I want to play the Victrola.

VAL: Myra, you're . . .

MYRA: No. Never mind. I've got some change in my pocket. Wait just a minute. [*She goes to the juke box and starts the music.*]

VAL: Myra, you've got to . . .

MYRA: *Shhh!* [*She comes back in.*] When I was a girl, I was always expecting something tremendous to happen. Maybe not this time but next time. I used to dance all night, come home drunk at daybreak and tiptoe barefooted up the back stairs. The sky used to be so white in the early mornings. You know it's been a long time since I've even noticed what color the sky is at daybreak. Traveling on a lonely road all night in an open car I guess you'd notice such things. I'd enjoy that. I could point them out to you while you were driving the car. I'd say, "Look, Val, here's something to put in the book!" "What is it?" I'd say, "It's white!" "What is?" "The sky is!" "Oh," you'd say, "is it?" "Yes," I'd say, "it is, it is, it *is!*" And you would have to believe me! [*She clings to him;* VAL *breaks away from her.*]

VAL: I got to go by myself. I couldn't take anyone with me.

MYRA: That's where you're mistaken. You're dreadfully mistaken if you think that I'm going to stay on here by myself in a store full of bottles and boxes while you go traipsing around through all the world's dark corners without me having a forwarding address even.

VAL: I'll give you a forwarding address.

MYRA: That's not enough. What could I do with a forwarding address, Val? Take it into the backroom with me at night? Oh, my darling, darling forwarding address! A wonderful companion *that* would be. So sweet. And satisfying!

VAL: Myra! Don't talk so loud!

MYRA [*breathlessly*]: Excuse me. I'll get your drink. [*She goes to the confectionery and comes back out with a bottle.*] How much do you want? Three fingers? What was I . . . ?

Oh, oh, yes, I wanted to tell you [*she pours the rum*] we had a fig tree in the back of our yard that never bore any fruit. We thought that it never would. I'd always pitied it so because they said it was barren. But it surprised us one spring. I was the one that discovered the first little fig. Oh, my God, I was so excited. I ran in the house; I was screaming, "Daddy, daddy, it isn't barren, it isn't barren, daddy! The little fig tree . . ." I told him, "It's going to have figs this year!" It seemed such a marvelous thing, it needed a big celebration, so I took out Christmas ornaments. Yes, little colored glass bells and tinsel and artificial snow! [*She laughs breathlessly.*] And I put them all over the fig tree, there, in the middle of April, because it was going to bear fruit! Here, Val, step up to the bar and take your drink! [VAL *crosses to her.*] Oh, darling, haven't we any Christmas ornaments to hang on me? [VAL *stops short.*]

VAL [*sharply*]: What do you mean?

MYRA: I mean that I'm not barren. Not anymore!

VAL: You're making this up!

MYRA: No, Val! You see, being clever, Val, isn't enough when you're up against something as big as life is. Sure, you can make keys for a door. That's clever, Val, but somebody comes along and breaks the door down. That's life! And that's what happened to me. Oh, God, I knew that I wouldn't be barren when we went together that first time. I felt it already, stirring up inside me, beginning to live! The first little fig on the tree they said wouldn't bear. What a mistake they made! Here. Here's your drink. [*He stares at her dumbly.*] Take it! [*She thrusts it into his hand.*] So now you see we can't be separated! We're bound together, Val!

VAL: Bound? No! I'm not bound to nothing! Never could be, Myra!

MYRA: Oh, yes, you could!

VAL: What do you mean by that?

MYRA: In one respect I'm like that woman from Waco. I'll never let you get away from me, Val. I want you to understand that.

VAL: There's one thing you don't understand good, Myra.

MYRA: No? What's that?

VAL: I travel by myself. I don't take anything with me but my skin.

MYRA: Then I'm your skin. Skin yourself and you'll be rid of me!

VAL: Listen, Myra, there's one thing safe for me to do. Go back to New Mexico and live by myself.

MYRA: On the desert?

VAL: Yes.

MYRA: Would I make the desert crowded?

VAL: Yes, you would. You'd make it crowded, Myra.

MYRA: Oh, my God, I thought a desert was *big.*

VAL: It is big, Myra. It stretches clean out 'til tomorrow. Over here is the Labos Mountains, and over there, that's Sangre de Cristo. And way up there, that's the sky! And there ain't nothing else in between, not you, not anybody, or nothing.

MYRA: I see.

VAL: Why, my God, it seems like sometimes when you're out there alone by yourself (not with nobody else!) that your brain is stretched out so far, it's pushing right up against the edges of the stars!

MYRA: Uh, huh! Maybe, that's what happened! [*She laughs harshly.*] That's why you act so peculiar; you scrambled your brains on the stars so you can't think straight!

VAL: Shut up, God damn you!

MYRA: Val! [*Rain falls in a gust on the tin portico. There is a silence between them.*]

VAL: I'm sorry, Myra.

MYRA: So what are you planning to do? Drive west by yourself?

VAL: Yes. [*He moves to the wall and takes his book out.*]

MYRA: You can't leave yet. Those stave-mill workers are still across the street.

VAL: In two or three more years she may forget . . .

MYRA: The woman from Waco?

VAL: Yes.

MYRA: I don't think so. I don't think she ever will.

VAL: Well, anyway, when I've finished this book I'm going to send for you.

MYRA: Are you? Why?

VAL: Because I do love you, Myra.

MYRA: Love? You're too selfish for love. You're just like a well full of water without any rope, without any bucket, without any tin cup even. God pity the fool that comes to you with a dry tongue!

VAL: I promise I'll send for you, Myra.

MYRA: Thanks. Thanks. And what'll I do in the meantime? Stay on here with our lucky little. . . . What shall I call it? Myra's little Miracle from Heaven? [*She laughs wildly.* JABE *knocks on the ceiling.*]

VAL: Jabe's knocking.

MYRA: Don't you think that I hear him? Knock, knock, knock! It sounds like bones, like death, and that's what it is. Ask me how it feels to be coupled with death up there. His face was always so thin, so yellow, so drawn. I swear to you, Val, his face on the pillow at night, it resembled a skull. He wore a nightshirt like a shroud, and when he got up in the dark, you know what I said to myself? "It's walking," I said to myself, "the ghost is walking!" And I—I had to endure him! Ahh, my flesh always crawled when he touched me. Yes, but I stood it, though. I guess I knew in my heart that it wouldn't go on forever, the way I suppose the fig tree knew in spite of those ten useless springs it wouldn't be barren always. When you come in off the road and asked for a job, I said to myself "This is it, this is what you been waiting for, Myra!" So I said with my eyes, "Stay here, stay here, for the love of God, stay here." And you did, you stayed. And just about at that time, as though for that special purpose, he started dying upstairs, when I started coming to life. It was like a battle had gone on between us those ten years, and I, the living, had beaten him, the dead one, back to the grave he climbed out of! Oh, for a while I tried to fight myself but it was no use. It was like I was standing down there at the foot of the levee and watched it break and known it was no use running. I tried to get rid of the key but that didn't work. Since then all decency's left me, I've stood like a woman naked with nothing but love—love, love. [*She clings to him fiercely.*]

VAL: Let go of me, Myra. [*He shoves her roughly away.*] You're like the woman from Waco. The way you . . .

MYRA [*slowly*]: You know what I've done? I've smashed myself against a rock. [*She crosses to the door.*] If you try to leave here without me, I'll call for the Sheriff!

VAL: That's what she did.

MYRA: *I'll* do it, *too.* Strike me in the face so I can scream. [*She catches at him again, he breaks loose, she utters a choked cry. The door slams open on the landing. At this instant a flickering match light appears on the stairs and spills down them and across the floor. Heavy dragging footsteps and hoarse breathing are heard.*]

MYRA [*whispering*]: Christ in Heaven, what's that? [*The ghastly, phantomlike effect of this entrance is dramatically underlined.* JABE'S *shadow precedes him down the stairs and his approach has the slow, clumping fatality of the traditional spook's. He is a living symbol of death, as* MYRA *has described him. He wears a purple bathrobe which hangs shroudlike about his figure and his face is a virtual death mask. Just as he appears in full view in the stairwell, the match which he holds under his face flickers out and disappears from view, swallowed in darkness like a vanished apparition.*]

MYRA [*horrified, incredulous*]: Jabe.

JABE [*hoarsely*]: Yes, it's me! [*He strikes another match and this time his face wears a grotesque, grinning expression.*] I didn't have much luck at knocking on the floor.

MYRA [*dazed*]: I didn't hear you.

JABE: Naw?

MYRA: The storm made too much noise.

JABE: Aw, absorbed in the storm.

MYRA: Yes.

JABE: Lamp light, huh?

MYRA: Yes, the lights went out when that awful lightning struck.

JABE: Your dress is torn open.

MYRA: You did that, Jabe, when I tried to give you morphine.

JABE: I thought you might give me too much.

MYRA: How did you get out of bed?

JABE: The usual way. Why? Does that seem remarkable to you?

MYRA: Yes. I didn't know you was able to.

JABE: You always been too optimistic about my condition. [MYRA *gasps involuntarily with loathing.* JABE *laughs hoarsely.*] I'm okay now. I'm not going to cash my chips in yet for a while. [VAL *coughs uneasily and clears his throat.*]

MYRA: Jabe—Jabe, this is Val Xavier.

JABE: You don't need to introduce me. I know him; I'm payin' his wages. [to VAL:] Myra here seems to think I had a tumor on the brain and they cut the brain out an' left the tumor. [*He laughs again and Myra repeats her involuntary gasp of loathing.*] Gimme that lamp; I wanta look at the stock.

MYRA: Here. We finished straightening up.

JABE: Aw, is that what you was doing?

MYRA: Yes. Val couldn't go home in the storm so we took advantage of the extra time.

JABE: Uh-huh. [*He takes the candle and goes unsteadily toward the confectionery. He passes through the archway;*

the pale walls hung with artificial blossoms have an eery effect in candlelight. The confectionery has a misty, flickering unreal pallor like a region of death, and JABE, *in his long dark robe, stands at the entrance like the very Prince of Darkness. He hesitates as though he senses that deathlike quality himself.*] Hell. It looks like a goddam honky-tonk since you done it over! [*He moves resolutely on into the room.*]

MYRA [*under her breath*]: Oh, God, I can't stand it, Val. I'm going to scream! Say something to him. Don't stand there doing nothing!

VAL: What should I say to him?

MYRA: Oh, I don't know—anything! [*She speaks in a loud, false tone.*] It seems miraculous, don't it, to see him downstairs?

VAL [*uncertainly*]: Yes. [JABE *laughs mockingly in the next room. Very softly:*] Death's in the orchard, Myra!

MYRA: Val.

JABE: How about a little pinball game? Would you like to play one, Mr. Whatsit?

MYRA: Answer him!

VAL [*inaudibly*]: No.

JABE: Huh? Can't you talk out loud in there?

VAL [*shouting*]: No! No!

MYRA: Shhh!

JABE: I think I'll shoot a few.

VAL: Give me my wages. Let me get out. [VAL *moves toward the counter, but* MYRA *blocks him.*]

MYRA: You can't leave me alone with him, would you?

JABE: Hot damn. I clicked on three.

MYRA: You couldn't be such a coward.

VAL: Let go of my arm.

JABE: Twenty-five hundred, Myra.

VAL: This place is shrinking; the walls are closing in!

JABE: Thirty-five. Forty-five.

MYRA: Give me time, darling. A little more time. [VAL *tears loose.*]

JABE: Fifty!

MYRA: I swear to God, I won't let you.

JABE: Right down the middle aisle, twice straight.

VAL: Let go!

JABE: Sixty-five, seventy.

MYRA: You've got to stick with me, Val.

VAL: Don't have to do nothing. I'm going!

JABE: Buzzards! Buzzards!!!! I hear you croaking in there. You think you've got a corpse to feed on, but you ain't! I'm going to live, Myra. [MYRA'S *hysteria is released. She laughs wildly and rushes to the doorway.*]

MYRA: Oh, no, you're not; no, you're not! You're going to die, Jabe. You're rotten with death already!

JABE [*shouting*]: Die, am I?

MYRA: Yes, and I'm glad, I'm *glad,* I'm planning a celebration! I'm going to wear Christmas ornaments in my hair!

Why? Because I'm not barren. I've gotten death out of me and now I've taken life in! Yes, oh, yes, I've got *life* in me—in *here!* [*She clasps her hands over her stomach.*] Do you see what I've got my hands on? Well, that's where it *is,* you see! I'm way, way, way up *high!* And you can't drag me *down!* Not any more, *Mr. Death!* We're through with each other. [*She laughs in wild exultance; then suddenly covers her face and runs sobbing back to* VAL. *She is terrified.*] Val! [*She clutches his arm. He breaks away and crosses toward the front door of the store.*]

VAL: It's finished! [*He goes to the cash register, rings it open.* JABE *creeps in with the lantern, unseen by them, and steals towards the hardware counter.*]

MYRA [*screaming at him wildly, completely distracted*]: What are you doing? You're robbing the store!

VAL: I'm taking my wages out.

MYRA: You're robbing the store; I won't let you! [*She rushes to the phone and shouts into it.* JABE *is loading a revolver.*] Give me the Sheriff's house. The store's being robbed!

VAL: Go on, you little bitch.

MYRA: The store's being robbed, the clerk is robbing the store. He's running off with the money; you got to stop him! [JABE'S *face is livid with hatred and he holds the revolver, which he levels carefully at* MYRA, *holding the candle above him to give a light.*]

JABE: Buzzards! [*He fires. The first shot strikes* MYRA. *She utters a smothered cry and clutches at the wall.* VAL *springs at him and wrests the revolver from his grasp.*]

VAL: You shot her.

JABE [*slowly, panting*]: Naw. *You* shot her. Didn'tja hear her shouting your name on the phone? She said you was robbing the store! They'll come here an' burn you for it! Buzzards! [*He turns slowly and staggers out the front door. His voice is heard shouting wildly against the wind.* VAL *gasps, slams the door, and bolts it, the revolver still in his grasp.* MYRA *moves out from the shadow of the wall with a slight, sobbing breath.*]

VAL: Myra! You're hurt!

MYRA: Yes.

VAL: How bad?

MYRA: I don't know. I don't feel nothing at all. It struck me here, where I would have carried the child. There's nothing but death in me now.

VAL: I'll call for the doctor!

MYRA: There's no way to get any doctor. Go on, look out for yourself, get away! I don't need anyone now. . . . [*She staggers out from the wall.*] Isn't it funny that I should just now remember what happened to the fig tree? It was struck down in a storm, the very spring that I hung those ornaments on it. Why? Why? For what reason? Because some things are enemies of light and there is a battle between them in which some fall! [*The confectionery suddenly blooms into soft springlike radiance as the electric current resumes.*] Oh, look! The lights have come on in the confectionery! [*She staggers through the archway.*] That's what I wanted! Not death, but David—the orchard across from Moon Lake! [*She advances a few more steps and disappears from sight. Her body is heard falling.* VAL *crosses to the archway.*]

VAL: Myra! Myra! [*The lights flicker and go out. Now the clamor of the crowd is heard distantly. Under his breath:*]

Fire! [*He looks frenziedly about him for a moment, then plunges out through the confectionery. A door opens at the top of the stairs and* SANDRA *appears, aroused by the clamor. At first she descends the steps fearfully, then with a sort of exultation, appearing like a priestess in her long, sculptural white dress. When she has reached the bottom of the stairs, the front door is opened and the* WOMAN FROM WACO *enters, the crowd crying out behind her and the pine torches glaring through the windows.*]

WOMAN [*to* SANDRA]: You—where is he?

SHERIFF: Watch out, Mrs. Regan! He's armed!

MRS. REGAN: So am I! Where is he?

SHERIFF [*advancing not too bravely*]: Xavier! [*A flickering light appears in the confectionery.*]

MAN: In back!

VOICES: In the confectionery! Get him! Git him outta there! Kill him! Burn the son of a bitch! Burn him!

WOMAN FROM WACO: What are you waiting fo'? Scared—scared? [*She plunges toward the archway with drawn revolver. The* CONJURE MAN *suddenly appears, bearing a lantern. The shocking apparitional effect of his entrance stuns them for a second. The* WOMAN FROM WACO *stops short with a stifled cry.*]

VOICE: Christ! Who's that? The Conjure Man! The Conjure Man from Blue Mountain!

WOMAN: Git out of my way! Make him git outta my way!

SHERIFF [*stepping up beside her*]: Where is Xavier, you niggah? [*Slowly, tremblingly, the* NEGRO *elevates something in his hand. He holds it above his head. There is a momentary hush as all eyes are centered upon this lividly mottled object, which, though inanimate, still keeps about it the hard, immaculate challenge of things untamed.*]

A VOICE: His jacket!

ANOTHER: *The Snakeskin Jacket!* [*The* WOMAN FROM WACO *screams and covers her face. A gong is struck and the stage is drowned in instant and utter blackness.*]

CURTAIN

EPILOGUE

After a few seconds the curtain is raised again, and we are returned to the Sunday afternoon a year later. The scene is the same as for the Prologue. The stage is empty and sinister with its testimony of past violence. Faintly, as from some distance, there comes the sound of chanting from a Negro church. The store itself is like a pillaged temple with the late afternoon sunlight thrown obliquely through the high Gothic windows in the wall at the left. The CONJURE MAN *sits with immobile dignity upon his stool near the archway like the Spirit of the Dead Watching. The door at the top of the stairs opens and the* TEMPLE SISTERS *emerge with their customers.*

BLANCH: Watch out for these stairs; they're awful, awful steep! Eva, you better go first with the lamp.

EVA [*descending first*]: Uncle! Uncle!

BLANCH: He's deaf as a post! [*The* CONJURE MAN *rises.*]

EVA: Oh, there you are, Uncle. Bring us Cassandra's things from that shelf over there. [*The* CONJURE MAN *complies with slow dignity.*]

BLANCH: We only have two things that belonged to Cassandra Whiteside on display in the museum.

EVA [*displaying the articles*]: This pair of dark sunglasses and this bright red cape.

BLANCH: Cassandra's body was never recovered from the Sunflower River.

EVA: Some people say that she didn't know the bridge was washed out.

BLANCH: But we know better, however. She deliberately drove her car into the river and drowned because she knew that *decent* people were done with her.

EVA: Absolutely. The Vigilantes had warned her to get out of town.

BLANCH: Now, Uncle, the *Snakeskin Jacket.*

EVA: He's already got it.

BLANCH: That is one article in the museum that me an' Eva won't lay our bare hands on.

EVA: I don't know what, but it simply terrifies me.

BLANCH: Uncle, hold it up there in the archway like you did when you reported his capture. [*The* CONJURE MAN *unfolds the jacket which he had held in his lap and elevates it above his head as he did at the end of the preceding scene.*]

EVA: It's marvelous how fresh and clean it stays.

BLANCH: Other things get dusty. But not the jacket. What was it that Memphis newspaper-woman called it? "A souvenir of the jungle!"

EVA: "A shameless, flaunting symbol of the Beast Untamed!"

BLANCH: Put it down, Uncle. Uncle was washing the car in back of the store when the murderer tried to escape by that back door.

EVA: He fell right in the hands of the stave-mill workers.

BLANCH: They torn off his clothes an' thrown him into a car.

EVA: Drove him right down the road to the lynching tree . . .

BLANCH: That big cottonwood where the road turned off toward th' levee.

EVA: Exackly where Vee Talbott seen him that day in her vision.

BLANCH: We showed you the Jesus picture? That was the last thing she painted before she lost her mind.

EVA: Which makes five lives, as they said in one of the papers . . .

BLANCH: "Tied together in one fatal knot of passion."

EVA: Not counting the woman from Waco, who disappeared.

BLANCH: Nobody knows what ever become of her. [*She crosses to the wall and takes something down.*]

EVA [*with relish*]: Oh, the blow-tawch!

BLANCH: It's not the original one but it's one just like it. Look! [*She presses a valve and a fierce blue jet of flame stabs into the dark atmosphere. The woman tourist utters a sharp, involuntary cry and sways slightly forward, covering her eyes.*]

WOMAN: Oliver, take me out! [*The man hastily assists her to the door.*]

BLANCH [*to* EVA]: They haven't paid yet!

EVA: *Fifty cents, please! That will be fifty cents!*

BLANCH: To keep up the museum!

EVA: Yes, to preserve the memorial—twenty-five cents each.

[*They go out, following the tourists. The door remains open. Sunlight flows serenely, warmly, through it, a golden contradiction of all that is past. The* CONJURE MAN *glides toward the door. His face assumes a venomous, mocking look. He crouches forward, and spits out the open door with dry crackling laughter, then turns, and, unfolding the brilliant snakeskin jacket once more, he goes to the back wall and hangs it above his head in the shaft of sunlight through the door. He seems to make a slight obesiance before it. The religious chant from across the wide cotton fields now swells in exaltation as the curtain falls.*]

THE GLASS MENAGERIE

Nobody, not even the rain, has such small hands.

E. E. CUMMINGS

The Glass Menagerie was first produced by Eddie Dowling and Louis J. Singer at the Civic Theatre, Chicago, Ill., on December 26, 1944, and at the Playhouse Theatre, New York City, on March 31, 1945. The setting was designed and lighted by Jo Mielziner; original music was composed by Paul Bowles; the play was staged by Eddie Dowling and Margo Jones. The cast was as follows:

THE MOTHER	LAURETTE TAYLOR
HER SON	EDDIE DOWLING
HER DAUGHTER	JULIE HAYDON
THE GENTLEMAN CALLER	ANTHONY ROSS

SCENE: *An Alley in St. Louis*

Part I. Preparation for a Gentleman Caller.
Part II. The Gentleman calls.

Time: Now and the Past.

THE CHARACTERS

AMANDA WINGFIELD (*the mother*)

A little woman of great but confused vitality clinging frantically to another time and place. Her characterization must be carefully created, not copied from type. She is not paranoiac, but her life is paranoia. There is much to admire in Amanda, and as much to love and pity as there is to laugh at. Certainly she has endurance and a kind of heroism, and though her foolishness makes her unwittingly cruel at times, there is tenderness in her slight person.

LAURA WINGFIELD (*her daughter*)

Amanda, having failed to establish contact with reality, continues to live vitally in her illusions, but Laura's situation is even graver. A childhood illness has left her crippled, one leg slightly shorter than the other, and held in a brace. This defect need not be more than suggested on the stage. Stemming from this, Laura's separation increases till she is like a piece of her own glass collection, too exquisitely fragile to move from the shelf.

TOM WINGFIELD (*her son*)

And the narrator of the play. A poet with a job in a warehouse. His nature is not remorseless, but to escape from a trap he has to act without pity.

JIM O'CONNOR (*the gentleman caller*)

A nice, ordinary, young man.

PRODUCTION NOTES

Being a "memory play," *The Glass Menagerie* can be presented with unusual freedom of convention. Because of its considerably delicate or tenuous material, atmospheric touches and subtleties of direction play a particularly important part. Expressionism and all other unconventional techniques in drama have only one valid aim, and that is a closer approach to truth. When a play employs unconventional techniques, it is not, or certainly shouldn't be, trying to escape its responsibility of dealing with reality, or interpreting experience, but is actually or should be attempting to find a closer approach, a more penetrating and vivid expression of things as they are. The straight realistic play with its genuine Frigidaire and authentic ice-cubes, its characters who speak exactly as its audience speaks, corresponds to the academic landscape and has the same virtue of a photographic likeness. Everyone should know nowadays the unimportance of the photographic in art: that truth, life, or reality is an organic thing which the poetic imagination can represent or suggest, in essence, only through transformation, through changing into other forms than those which were merely present in appearance.

These remarks are not meant as a preface only to this particular play. They have to do with a conception of a new, plastic theatre which must take the place of the exhausted theatre of realistic conventions if the theatre is to resume vitality as a part of our culture.

THE SCREEN DEVICE: There is *only one important difference between the original and the acting version of the play* and that is the *omission* in the latter of the device that I tentatively included in my *original* script. This device was the use of a screen on which were projected magic-lantern slides bearing images or titles. I do not regret the omission of this device from the original Broadway production. The extraordinary power of Miss Taylor's performance made it suitable to have the utmost simplicity in the physical production. But I think it may be interesting to some readers to see how this device was conceived. So I am putting it into the published manuscript. These images and legends, projected from behind, were cast on a section of wall between the front-room and dining-room areas, which should be indistinguishable from the rest when not in use.

The purpose of this will probably be apparent. It is to give accent to certain values in each scene. Each scene contains a particular point (or several) which is structurally the most important. In an episodic play, such as this, the basic structure or narrative line may be obscured from the audience; the effect may seem fragmentary rather than architectural. This may not be the fault of the play so much as a lack of attention in the audience. The legend or image upon the screen will strengthen the effect of what is merely allusion in the writing and allow the primary point to be made more simply and lightly than if the entire responsibility were on the spoken lines. Aside from this structural value, I think the screen will have a definite emotional appeal, less definable but just as important. An imaginative producer or director may invent many other uses for this device than those indicated in the present script. In fact the possibilities of the device seem much larger to me than the instance of this play can possibly utilize.

THE MUSIC: Another extra-literary accent in this play is provided by the use of music. A single recurring tune, "The Glass Menagerie," is used to give emotional emphasis to suitable passages. This tune is like circus music, not when you are on the grounds or in the immediate vicinity of the parade, but when you are at some distance and very likely thinking of something else. It seems under those circumstances to continue almost interminably and it weaves in and out of your preoccupied consciousness; then it is the lightest, most delicate music in the world and perhaps the saddest. It expresses the surface vivacity of life with the underlying strain of immutable and inexpressible sorrow. When you look at a piece of delicately spun glass you think of two things: how beautiful it is and how easily it can be broken. Both of those ideas should be woven into the recurring tune, which dips in and out of the play as if it were carried on a wind that changes. It serves as a thread of connection and allusion between the narrator with his separate point in time and space and the subject of his story. Between each episode it returns as reference to the emotion, nostalgia, which is the first condition of the play. It is primarily Laura's music and therefore comes out most clearly when the play focuses upon her and the lovely fragility of glass which is her image.

THE LIGHTING: The lighting in the play is not realistic. In keeping with the atmosphere of memory, the stage is dim. Shafts of light are focused on selected areas or actors, sometimes in contradistinction to what is the apparent center. For instance, in the quarrel scene between Tom and Amanda, in which Laura has no active part, the clearest pool of light is on her figure. This is also true of the supper scene, when her silent figure on the sofa should remain the visual center. The light upon Laura should be distinct from the others, having a peculiar pristine clarity such as light used in early religious

THE CATASTROPHE OF SUCCESS

[This essay was first published in "The New York Times," later reprinted in "Story," and is now included, as an introduction, in The New Classics edition of this play.]

This winter marked the third anniversary of the Chicago opening of "The Glass Menagerie," an event that terminated one part of my life and began another about as different in all external circumstances as could well be imagined. I was snatched out of virtual oblivion and thrust into sudden prominence, and from the precarious tenancy of furnished rooms about the country I was removed to a suite in a first-class Manhattan hotel. My experience was not unique. Success has often come that abruptly into the lives of Americans. The Cinderella story is our favorite national myth, the cornerstone of the film industry if not of the Democracy itself. I have seen it enacted on the screen so often that I was now inclined to yawn at it, not with disbelief but with an attitude of Who Cares! Anyone with such beautiful teeth and hair as the screen protagonist of such a story was bound to have a good time one way or another, and you could bet your bottom dollar and all the tea in China that that one would not be caught dead or alive at any meeting involving a social conscience.

No, my experience was not exceptional, but neither was it quite ordinary, and if you are willing to accept the somewhat eclectic proposition that I had not been writing with such an experience in mind—and many people are not willing to believe that a playwright is interested in anything but popular success—there may be some point in comparing the two estates.

The sort of life that I had had previous to this popular

success was one that required endurance, a life of clawing and scratching along a sheer surface and holding on tight with raw fingers to every inch of rock higher than the one caught hold of before, but it was a good life because it was the sort of life for which the human organism is created.

I was not aware of how much vital energy had gone into this struggle until the struggle was removed. I was out on a level plateau with my arms still thrashing and my lungs still grabbing at air that no longer resisted. This was security at last.

I sat down and looked about me and was suddenly very depressed. I thought to myself, this is just a period of adjustment. Tomorrow morning I will wake up in this first-class hotel suite above the discreet hum of an East Side boulevard and I will appreciate its elegance and luxuriate in its comforts and know that I have arrived at our American plan of Olympus. Tomorrow morning when I look at the green satin sofa I will fall in love with it. It is only temporarily that the green satin looks like slime on stagnant water.

But in the morning the inoffensive little sofa looked more revolting than the night before and I was already getting too fat for the $125 suit which a fashionable acquaintance had selected for me. In the suite things began to break accidentally. An arm came off the sofa. Cigarette burns appeared on the polished surface of the furniture. Windows were left open and a rain storm flooded the suite. But the maid always put it straight and the patience of the management was inexhaustible. Late parties could not offend them seriously. Nothing short of a demolition bomb seemed to bother my neighbors.

I lived on room service. But in this, too, there was a disenchantment. Some time between the moment when I ordered dinner over the phone and when it was rolled into my living room like a corpse on a rubber-wheeled table, I lost all interest in it. Once I ordered a sirloin steak and a chocolate sundae, but everything was so cunningly disguised on the table that

I mistook the chocolate sauce for gravy and poured it over the sirloin steak.

Of course all this was the more trivial aspect of a spiritual dislocation that began to manifest itself in far more disturbing ways. I soon found myself becoming indifferent to people. A well of cynicism rose in me. Conversations all sounded as if they had been recorded years ago and were being played back on a turntable. Sincerity and kindliness seemed to have gone out of my friends' voices. I suspected them of hypocrisy. I stopped calling them, stopped seeing them. I was impatient of what I took to be inane flattery.

I got so sick of hearing people say, "I loved your play!" that I could not say thank you any more. I choked on the words and turned rudely away from the usually sincere person. I no longer felt any pride in the play itself but began to dislike it, probably because I felt too lifeless inside ever to create another. I was walking around dead in my shoes and I knew it but there were no friends I knew or trusted sufficiently, at that time, to take them aside and tell them what was the matter.

This curious condition persisted about three months, till late spring, when I decided to have another eye operation mainly because of the excuse it gave me to withdraw from the world behind a gauze mask. It was my fourth eye operation, and perhaps I should explain that I had been afflicted for about five years with a cataract on my left eye which required a series of needling operations and finally an operation on the muscle of the eye. (The eye is still in my head. So much for that.)

Well, the gauze mask served a purpose. While I was resting in the hospital the friends whom I had neglected or affronted in one way or another began to call on me and now that I was in pain and darkness, their voices seemed to have changed, or rather that unpleasant mutation which I had suspected earlier in the season had now disappeared and they sounded now as they had used to sound in the lamented days of my obscurity. Once more they were sincere and kindly voices with the ring of truth in them and that quality of understanding for which I had originally sought them out.

As far as my physical vision was concerned, this last operation was only relatively successful (although it left me with an apparently clear black pupil in the right position, or nearly so) but in another, figurative way, it had served a much deeper purpose.

When the gauze mask was removed I found myself in a readjusted world. I checked out of the handsome suite at the first-class hotel, packed my papers and a few incidental belongings and left for Mexico, an elemental country where you can quickly forget the false dignities and conceits imposed by success, a country where vagrants innocent as children curl up to sleep on the pavements and human voices, especially when their language is not familiar to the ear, are soft as birds'. My public self, that artifice of mirrors, did not exist here and so my natural being was resumed.

Then, as a final act of restoration, I settled for a while at Chapala to work on a play called "The Poker Night," which later became "A Streetcar Named Desire." It is only in his work that an artist can find reality and satisfaction, for the actual world is less intense than the world of his invention and consequently his life, without recourse to violent disorder, does not seem very substantial. The right condition for him is that in which his work is not only convenient but unavoidable.

For me a convenient place to work is a remote place among strangers where there is good swimming. But life should require a certain minimal effort. You should not have too many people waiting on you, you should have to do most things for yourself. Hotel service is embarrassing. Maids, waiters, bellhops, porters and so forth are the most embarrassing people in the world for they continually remind you of inequities which we accept as the proper thing. The sight of an ancient woman, gasping and wheezing as she drags a heavy pail of water down a hotel corridor to mop up the mess of some drunken overprivileged guest, is one that sickens and weighs upon the heart and withers it with shame for this world in which it is not only tolerated but regarded as proof positive that the wheels of Democracy are functioning as they should without interference from above or below. Nobody should have to clean up anybody else's mess in this world. It is terribly bad for both parties, but probably worse for the one receiving the service.

I have been corrupted as much as anyone else by the vast number of menial services which our society has grown to expect and depend on. We should do for ourselves or let the machines do for us, the glorious technology that is supposed to be the new light of the world. We are like a man who has bought a great amount of equipment for a camping trip, who has the canoe and the tent and the fishing lines and the axe and the guns, the mackinaw and the blankets, but who now, when all the preparations and the provisions are piled expertly together, is suddenly too timid to set out on the journey but remains where he was yesterday and the day before and the day before that, looking suspiciously through white lace curtains at the clear sky he distrusts. Our great technology is a God-given chance for adventure and for progress which we are afraid to attempt. Our ideas and our ideals remain exactly what they were and where they were three centuries ago. No. I beg your pardon. It is no longer safe for a man even to declare them!

This is a long excursion from a small theme into a large one which I did not intend to make, so let me go back to what I was saying before.

This is an oversimplification. One does not escape that

easily from the seduction of an effete way of life. You cannot arbitrarily say to yourself, I will now continue my life as it was before this thing, Success, happened to me. But once you fully apprehend the vacuity of a life without struggle you are equipped with the basic means of salvation. Once you know this is true, that the heart of man, his body and his brain, are forged in a white-hot furnace for the purpose of conflict (the struggle of creation) and that with the conflict removed, the man is a sword cutting daisies, that not privation but luxury is the wolf at the door and that the fangs of this wolf are all the little vanities and conceits and laxities that Success is heir to—why, then with this knowledge you are at least in a position of knowing where danger lies.

You know, then, that the public Somebody you are when you "have a name" is a fiction created with mirrors and that the only somebody worth being is the solitary and unseen you that existed from your first breath and which is the sum of your actions and so is constantly in a state of becoming under your own violation—and knowing these things, you can even survive the catastrophe of Success!

It is never altogether too late, unless you embrace the Bitch Goddess, as William James called her, with both arms and find in her smothering caresses exactly what the homesick little boy in you always wanted, absolute protection and utter effortlessness. Security is a kind of death, I think, and it can come to you in a storm of royalty checks beside a kidney-shaped pool in Beverly Hills or anywhere at all that is removed from the conditions that made you an artist, if that's what you are or were or intended to be. Ask anyone who has experienced the kind of success I am talking about— What good is it? Perhaps to get an honest answer you will have to give him a shot of truth serum but the word he will finally groan is unprintable in genteel publications.

Then what is good? The obsessive interest in human affairs,

plus a certain amount of compassion and moral conviction, that first made the experience of living something that must be translated into pigment or music or bodily movement or poetry or prose or anything that's dynamic and expressive—that's what's good for you if you're at all serious in your aims. William Saroyan wrote a great play on this theme, that purity of heart is the one success worth having. "In the time of your life—live!" That time is short and it doesn't return again. It is slipping away while I write this and while you read it, and the monosyllable of the clock is Loss, loss, loss, unless you devote your heart to its opposition.

SCENE ONE

The Wingfield apartment is in the rear of the building, one of those vast hive-like conglomerations of cellular living-units that flower as warty growths in overcrowded urban centers of lower middle-class population and are symptomatic of the impulse of this largest and fundamentally enslaved section of American society to avoid fluidity and differentiation and to exist and function as one interfused mass of automatism.

The apartment faces an alley and is entered by a fire escape, a structure whose name is a touch of accidental poetic truth, for all of these huge buildings are always burning with the slow and implacable fires of human desperation. The fire escape is part of what we see—that is, the landing of it and steps descending from it.

The scene is memory and is therefore nonrealistic. Memory takes a lot of poetic license. It omits some details; others are exaggerated, according to the emotional value of the articles it touches, for memory is seated predominantly in the heart. The interior is therefore rather dim and poetic.

At the rise of the curtain, the audience is faced with the dark, grim rear wall of the Wingfield tenement. This building is flanked on both sides by dark, narrow alleys which run into murky canyons of tangled clotheslines, garbage cans, and the sinister latticework of neighboring fire escapes. It is up and down these side alleys that exterior entrances and exits are made during the play. At the end of Tom's opening commentary, the dark tenement wall slowly becomes transparent and reveals the interior of the ground-floor Wingfield apartment.

Nearest the audience is the living room, which also serves as a sleeping room for Laura, the sofa unfolding to make her bed. Just beyond, separated from the living room by a wide arch or second proscenium with transparent faded portieres (or second curtain), is the dining room. In an old-fashioned whatnot in the living room are seen scores of transparent glass animals. A blown-up photograph of the father hangs on the wall of the living room, to the left of the archway. It is the face of a very handsome young man in a doughboy's First World War cap. He is gallantly smiling, ineluctably smiling, as if to say "I will be smiling forever."

Also hanging on the wall, near the photograph, are a typewriter keyboard chart and a Gregg shorthand diagram. An upright typewriter on a small table stands beneath the charts.

The audience hears and sees the opening scene in the dining room through both the transparent fourth wall of the building and the transparent gauze portieres of the dining-room arch. It is during this revealing scene that the fourth wall slowly ascends, out of sight. This transparent exterior wall is not brought down again until the very end of the play, during Tom's final speech.

The narrator is an undisguised convention of the play. He takes whatever license with dramatic convention is convenient to his purposes.

Tom enters, dressed as a merchant sailor, and strolls across to the fire escape. There he stops and lights a cigarette. He addresses the audience.

TOM: Yes, I have tricks in my pocket, I have things up my sleeve. But I am the opposite of a stage magician. He gives you illusion that has the appearance of truth. I give you truth in the pleasant disguise of illusion.

To begin with, I turn back time. I reverse it to that quaint period, the thirties, when the huge middle class of America was matriculating in a school for the blind. Their eyes had failed them, or they had failed their eyes, and so they were having their fingers pressed forcibly down on the fiery Braille alphabet of a dissolving economy.
In Spain there was revolution. Here there was only shouting and confusion. In Spain there was Guernica. Here there were disturbances of labor, sometimes pretty violent, in otherwise peaceful cities such as Chicago, Cleveland, Saint Louis . . .
This is the social background of the play.

[*Music begins to play.*]

The play is memory. Being a memory play, it is dimly lighted, it is sentimental, it is not realistic. In memory everything seems to happen to music. That explains the fiddle in the wings.
I am the narrator of the play, and also a character in it. The other characters are my mother, Amanda, my sister, Laura, and a gentleman caller who appears in the final scenes. He is the most realistic character in the play, being an emissary from a world of reality that we were somehow set apart from. But since I have a poet's weakness for symbols, I am using this character also as a symbol; he is the long-delayed but always expected something that we live for.
There is a fifth character in the play who doesn't appear except in this larger-than-life-size photograph over the mantel. This is our father who left us a long time ago. He was a telephone man who fell in love with long distances; he gave up his job with the telephone company and skipped the light fantastic out of town . . .
The last we heard of him was a picture postcard from Mazatlan, on the Pacific coast of Mexico, containing a message of two words: "Hello—Goodbye!" and no address.
I think the rest of the play will explain itself. . . .

[*Amanda's voice becomes audible through the portieres.*]

[*Legend on screen:* "Ou sont les neiges."]

[*Tom divides the portieres and enters the dining room. Amanda and Laura are seated at a drop-leaf table. Eating is indicated by gestures without food or utensils. Amanda faces the audience. Tom and Laura are seated in profile. The interior has lit up softly and through the scrim we see Amanda and Laura seated at the table.*]

AMANDA [*calling*]: Tom?

TOM: Yes, Mother.

AMANDA: We can't say grace until you come to the table!

TOM: Coming, Mother. [*He bows slightly and withdraws, reappearing a few moments later in his place at the table.*]

AMANDA [*to her son*]: Honey, don't *push* with your *fingers.* If you have to push with something, the thing to push with is a crust of bread. And chew—chew! Animals have secretions in their stomachs which enable them to digest food without mastication, but human beings are supposed to chew their food before they swallow it down. Eat food leisurely, son, and really enjoy it. A well-cooked meal has lots of delicate flavors that have to be held in the mouth for appreciation. So chew your food and give your salivary glands a chance to function!

[*Tom deliberately lays his imaginary fork down and pushes his chair back from the table.*]

TOM: I haven't enjoyed one bite of this dinner because of your constant directions on how to eat it. It's you that make me rush through meals with your hawklike attention to every bite I take. Sickening—spoils my appetite—all this discussion of—animals' secretion—salivary glands—mastication!

AMANDA [*lightly*]: Temperament like a Metropolitan star!

[*Tom rises and walks toward the living room.*]

You're not excused from the table.

TOM: I'm getting a cigarette.

AMANDA: You smoke too much.

[*Laura rises.*]

LAURA: I'll bring in the blanc mange.

[*Tom remains standing with his cigarette by the portieres.*]

AMANDA [*rising*]: No, sister, no, sister—you be the lady this time and I'll be the darky.

LAURA: I'm already up.

AMANDA: Resume your seat, little sister—I want you to stay fresh and pretty—for gentlemen callers!

LAURA [*sitting down*]: I'm not expecting any gentlemen callers.

AMANDA [*crossing out to the kitchenette, airily*]: Sometimes they come when they are least expected! Why, I remember one Sunday afternoon in Blue Mountain—

[*She enters the kitchenette.*]

TOM: I know what's coming!

LAURA: Yes. But let her tell it.

TOM: Again?

LAURA: She loves to tell it.

[*Amanda returns with a bowl of dessert*].

AMANDA: One Sunday afternoon in Blue Mountain—your mother received—*seventeen!*—gentlemen callers! Why, sometimes there weren't chairs enough to accommodate them all. We had to send the nigger over to bring in folding chairs from the parish house.

TOM [*remaining at the portieres*]: How did you entertain those gentlemen callers?

AMANDA: I understood the art of conversation!

TOM: I bet you could talk.

AMANDA: Girls in those days *knew* how to talk, I can tell you.

TOM: Yes?

[*Image on screen*: Amanda as a girl on a porch, greeting callers.]

AMANDA: They knew how to entertain their gentlemen callers. It wasn't enough for a girl to be possessed of a pretty face and a graceful figure—although I wasn't slighted in either respect. She also needed to have a nimble wit and a tongue to meet all occasions.

TOM: What did you talk about?

AMANDA: Things of importance going on in the world! Never anything coarse or common or vulgar.

[*She addresses Tom as though he were seated in the vacant chair at the table though he remains by the portieres. He plays this scene as though reading from a script.*]

My callers were gentlemen—all! Among my callers were some of the most prominent young planters of the Mississippi Delta—planters and sons of planters!

[*Tom motions for music and a spot of light on Amanda. Her eyes lift, her face glows, her voice becomes rich and elegiac.*]

[*Screen legend*: "Ou sont les neiges d'antan?"]

There was young Champ Laughlin who later became vice-president of the Delta Planters Bank. Hadley Stevenson who was drowned in Moon Lake and left his widow one hundred and fifty thousand in Government bonds. There were the Cutrere brothers, Wesley and Bates. Bates was one of my bright particular beaux! He got in a quarrel with that wild Wainwright boy. They shot it out on the floor of Moon Lake Casino. Bates was shot through the stomach. Died in the ambulance on his way to Memphis. His widow was also well provided-for, came into eight or ten thousand acres, that's all. She married him on the rebound—never loved her—carried my picture on him the night he died! And there was that boy that every girl in the Delta had set her cap for! That beautiful, brilliant young Fitzhugh boy from Greene County!

TOM: What did he leave his widow?

AMANDA: He never married! Gracious, you talk as though all of my old admirers had turned up their toes to the daisies!

TOM: Isn't this the first you've mentioned that still survives?

AMANDA: That Fitzhugh boy went North and made a fortune—came to be known as the Wolf of Wall Street! He had the Midas touch, whatever he touched turned to gold! And I could have been Mrs. Duncan J. Fitzhugh, mind you! But—I picked your *father!*

LAURA [*rising*]: Mother, let me clear the table.

AMANDA: No, dear, you go in front and study your typewriter chart. Or practice your shorthand a little. Stay fresh and pretty!—It's almost time for our gentlemen callers to start arriving. [*She flounces girlishly toward the kitchenette*] How many do you suppose we're going to entertain this afternoon?

[*Tom throws down the paper and jumps up with a groan.*]

LAURA [*alone in the dining room*]: I don't believe we're going to receive any, Mother.

AMANDA [*reappearing, airily*]: What? No one—not one? You must be joking!

[*Laura nervously echoes her laugh. She slips in a fugitive manner through the half-open portieres and draws them gently behind her. A shaft of very clear light is thrown on her face against the faded tapestry of the curtains. Faintly the music of "The Glass Menagerie" is heard as she continues, lightly*:]

Not one gentleman caller? It can't be true! There must be a flood, there must have been a tornado!

LAURA: It isn't a flood, it's not a tornado, Mother. I'm just not popular like you were in Blue Mountain. . . .

[*Tom utters another groan. Laura glances at him with a faint, apologetic smile. Her voice catches a little*:]

Mother's afraid I'm going to be an old maid.

[*The scene dims out with the "Glass Menagerie" music.*]

SCENE TWO

On the dark stage the screen is lighted with the image of blue roses. Gradually Laura's figure becomes apparent and the screen goes out. The music subsides.

Laura is seated in the delicate ivory chair at the small claw-foot table. She wears a dress of soft violet material for a kimono—her hair is tied back from her forehead with a ribbon. She is washing and polishing her collection of glass. Amanda appears on the fire escape steps. At the sound of her ascent, Laura catches her breath, thrusts the bowl of ornaments away, and seats herself stiffly before the diagram of the typewriter keyboard as though it held her spellbound. Something has happened to Amanda. It is written in her face as she climbs to the landing: a look that is grim and hopeless and a little absurd. She has on one of those cheap or imitation velvety-looking cloth coats with imitation fur collar. Her hat is five or six years old, one of those dreadful cloche hats that were worn in the late Twenties, and she is clutching an enormous black patent-leather pocketbook with nickel clasps and initials. This is her full-dress outfit, the one she usually wears to the D.A.R. Before entering she looks through the door. She purses her lips, opens her eyes very wide, rolls them upward and shakes her head. Then she slowly lets herself in the door. Seeing her mother's expression Laura touches her lips with a nervous gesture.

LAURA: Hello, Mother, I was— [*She makes a nervous gesture toward the chart on the wall. Amanda leans against the shut door and stares at Laura with a martyred look.*]

AMANDA: Deception? Deception? [*She slowly removes her hat and gloves, continuing the sweet suffering stare. She lets the hat and gloves fall on the floor—a bit of acting.*]

LAURA [*shakily*]: How was the D.A.R. meeting?

[*Amanda slowly opens her purse and removes a dainty white handkerchief which she shakes out delicately and delicately touches to her lips and nostrils.*]

Didn't you go to the D.A.R. meeting, Mother?

AMANDA [*faintly, almost inaudibly*]: —No.—No. [*then more forcibly*:] I did not have the strength—to go to the D.A.R. In fact, I did not have the courage! I wanted to find a hole in the ground and hide myself in it forever! [*She crosses slowly to the wall and removes the diagram of the typewriter keyboard. She holds it in front of her for a second, staring at it sweetly and sorrowfully—then bites her lips and tears it in two pieces.*]

LAURA [*faintly*]: Why did you do that, Mother?

[*Amanda repeats the same procedure with the chart of the Gregg Alphabet.*]

Why are you—

AMANDA: Why? Why? How old are you, Laura?

LAURA: Mother, you know my age.

AMANDA: I thought that you were an adult; it seems that I was mistaken. [*She crosses slowly to the sofa and sinks down and stares at Laura.*]

LAURA: Please don't stare at me, Mother.

[*Amanda closes her eyes and lowers her head. There is a ten-second pause.*]

AMANDA: What are we going to do, what is going to become of us, what is the future?

[*There is another pause.*]

LAURA: Has something happened, Mother?

[*Amanda draws a long breath, takes out the handkerchief again, goes through the dabbing process.*]

Mother, has—something happened?

AMANDA: I'll be all right in a minute, I'm just bewildered —[*She hesitates.*]—by life. . . .

LAURA: Mother, I wish that you would tell me what's happened!

AMANDA: As you know, I was supposed to be inducted into my office at the D.A.R. this afternoon.

[*Screen image*: A swarm of typewriters.]

But I stopped off at Rubicam's Business College to speak to your teachers about your having a cold and ask them what progress they thought you were making down there.

LAURA: Oh. . . .

AMANDA: I went to the typing instructor and introduced myself as your mother. She didn't know who you were. "Wingfield," she said, "We don't have any such student enrolled at the school!"
I assured her she did, that you had been going to classes since early in January.
"I wonder," she said, "If you could be talking about that terribly shy little girl who dropped out of school after only a few days' attendance?"
"No," I said, "Laura, my daughter, has been going to school every day for the past six weeks!"
"Excuse me," she said. She took the attendance book out and there was your name, unmistakably printed, and all the dates you were absent until they decided that you had dropped out of school.

I still said, "No, there must have been some mistake! There must have been some mix-up in the records!"
And she said, "No—I remember her perfectly now. Her hands shook so that she couldn't hit the right keys! The first time we gave a speed test, she broke down completely—was sick at the stomach and almost had to be carried into the wash room! After that morning she never showed up any more. We phoned the house but never got any answer"—While I was working at Famous–Barr, I suppose, demonstrating those—

[*She indicates a brassiere with her hands.*]

Oh! I felt so weak I could barely keep on my feet! I had to sit down while they got me a glass of water! Fifty dollars' tuition, all of our plans—my hopes and ambitions for you—just gone up the spout, just gone up the spout like that.

[*Laura draws a long breath and gets awkwardly to her feet. She crosses to the Victrola and winds it up.*]

What are you doing?

LAURA: Oh! [*She releases the handle and returns to her seat.*]

AMANDA: Laura, where have you been going when you've gone out pretending that you were going to business college?

LAURA: I've just been going out walking.

AMANDA: That's not true.

LAURA: It is. I just went walking.

AMANDA: Walking? Walking? In winter? Deliberately courting pneumonia in that light coat? Where did you walk to, Laura?

LAURA: All sorts of places—mostly in the park.

AMANDA: Even after you'd started catching that cold?

LAURA: It was the lesser of two evils, Mother.

[*Screen image*: Winter scene in a park.]

I couldn't go back there. I—threw up—on the floor!

AMANDA: From half past seven till after five every day you mean to tell me you walked around in the park, because you wanted to make me think that you were still going to Rubicam's Business College?

LAURA: It wasn't as bad as it sounds. I went inside places to get warmed up.

AMANDA: Inside where?

LAURA: I went in the art museum and the bird houses at the Zoo. I visited the penguins every day! Sometimes I did without lunch and went to the movies. Lately I've been spending most of my afternoons in the Jewel Box, that big glass house where they raise the tropical flowers.

AMANDA: You did all this to deceive me, just for deception?

[*Laura looks down.*] Why?

LAURA: Mother, when you're disappointed, you get that awful suffering look on your face, like the picture of Jesus' mother in the museum!

AMANDA: Hush!

LAURA: I couldn't face it.

[*There is a pause. A whisper of strings is heard. Legend on screen*: "The Crust of Humility."]

AMANDA [*hopelessly fingering the huge pocketbook*]: So what are we going to do the rest of our lives? Stay home and

watch the parades go by? Amuse ourselves with the glass menagerie, darling? Eternally play those worn-out phonograph records your father left as a painful reminder of him? We won't have a business career—we've given that up because it gave us nervous indigestion! [*She laughs wearily.*] What is there left but dependency all our lives? I know so well what becomes of unmarried women who aren't prepared to occupy a position. I've seen such pitiful cases in the South—barely tolerated spinsters living upon the grudging patronage of sister's husband or brother's wife!—stuck away in some little mousetrap of a room—encouraged by one in-law to visit another—little birdlike women without any nest—eating the crust of humility all their life!
Is that the future that we've mapped out for ourselves? I swear it's the only alternative I can think of! [*She pauses.*] It isn't a very pleasant alternative, is it? [*She pauses again.*] Of course—some girls *do marry.*

[*Laura twists her hands nervously.*]

Haven't you ever liked some boy?

LAURA: Yes. I liked one once. [*She rises.*] I came across his picture a while ago.

AMANDA [*with some interest*]: He gave you his picture?

LAURA: No, it's in the yearbook.

AMANDA [*disappointed*]: Oh—a high school boy.

[*Screen image*: Jim as the high school hero bearing a silver cup.]

LAURA: Yes. His name was Jim. [*She lifts the heavy annual from the claw-foot table.*] Here he is in *The Pirates of Penzance.*

AMANDA [*absently*]: The what?

LAURA: The operetta the senior class put on. He had a wonderful voice and we sat across the aisle from each other Mondays, Wednesdays and Fridays in the Aud. Here he is with the silver cup for debating! See his grin?

AMANDA [*absently*]: He must have had a jolly disposition.

LAURA: He used to call me—Blue Roses.

[*Screen image*: Blue roses.]

AMANDA: Why did he call you such a name as that?

LAURA: When I had that attack of pleurosis—he asked me what was the matter when I came back. I said pleurosis—he thought that I said Blue Roses! So that's what he always called me after that. Whenever he saw me, he'd holler, "Hello, Blue Roses!" I didn't care for the girl that he went out with. Emily Meisenbach. Emily was the best-dressed girl at Soldan. She never struck me, though, as being sincere . . . It says in the Personal Section—they're engaged. That's—six years ago! They must be married by now.

AMANDA: Girls that aren't cut out for business careers usually wind up married to some nice man. [*She gets up with a spark of revival.*] Sister, that's what you'll do!

[*Laura utters a startled, doubtful laugh. She reaches quickly for a piece of glass.*]

LAURA: But, Mother—

AMANDA: Yes? [*She goes over to the photograph.*]

LAURA [*in a tone of frightened apology*]: I'm—crippled!

AMANDA: Nonsense! Laura, I've told you never, never to use that word. Why, you're not crippled, you just have a little defect—hardly noticeable, even! When people have some slight disadvantage like that, they cultivate other things to make up for it—develop charm—and vivacity—and—*charm!* That's all you have to do! [*She turns again to the photograph.*] One thing your father had *plenty of*—was *charm!*

[*The scene fades out with music.*]

SCENE THREE

Legend on screen: "After the fiasco—"

Tom speaks from the fire escape landing.

TOM: After the fiasco at Rubicam's Business College, the idea of getting a gentleman caller for Laura began to play a more and more important part in Mother's calculations. It became an obsession. Like some archetype of the universal unconscious, the image of the gentleman caller haunted our small apartment. . . .

[*Screen image*: A young man at the door of a house with flowers.]

An evening at home rarely passed without some allusion to this image, this specter, this hope. . . . Even when he wasn't mentioned, his presence hung in Mother's preoccupied look and in my sister's frightened, apologetic manner—hung like a sentence passed upon the Wingfields!
Mother was a woman of action as well as words. She began to take logical steps in the planned direction. Late that winter and in the early spring—realizing that extra money would be needed to properly feather the nest and plume the bird—she conducted a vigorous campaign on the telephone, roping in subscribers to one of those magazines for matrons called *The Homemaker's Companion,* the type of journal that features the serialized sublimations of ladies of letters who think in terms of delicate cuplike breasts, slim, tapering waists, rich, creamy thighs, eyes like wood smoke in autumn, fingers that soothe and caress like strains of music, bodies as powerful as Etruscan sculpture.

[*Screen image*: The cover of a glamor magazine.]

[*Amanda enters with the telephone on a long extension cord. She is spotlighted in the dim stage.*]

AMANDA: Ida Scott? This is Amanda Wingfield! We *missed* you at the D.A.R. last Monday! I said to myself: She's probably suffering with that sinus condition! How is that sinus condition?
Horrors! Heaven have mercy!—You're a Christian martyr, yes, that's what your are, a Christian martyr!
Well, I just now happened to notice that your subscription to the *Companion*'s about to expire! Yes, it expires with the next issue, honey!—just when that wonderful new serial by Bessie Mae Hopper is getting off to such an exciting start. Oh, honey, it's something that you can't miss! You remember how *Gone with the Wind* took everybody by storm? You simply couldn't go out if you hadn't read it. All everybody *talked* was Scarlett O'Hara. Well, this is a book that critics already compare to *Gone with the Wind*. It's the *Gone with the Wind* of the post-World-War generation!—What?—Burning?—Oh, honey, don't let them burn, go take a look in the oven and I'll hold the wire! Heavens—I think she's hung up!

[*The scene dims out.*]

[*Legend on screen*: "You think I'm in love with Continental Shoemakers?"]

[*Before the lights come up again, the violent voices of Tom and Amanda are heard. They are quarreling behind the portieres. In front of them stands Laura with clenched hands and panicky expression. A clear pool of light is on her figure throughout this scene.*]

TOM: What in Christ's name am I—

AMANDA [*shrilly*]: Don't you use that—

TOM: —supposed to do!

AMANDA: —expression! Not in my—

TOM: Ohhh!

AMANDA: —presence! Have you gone out of your senses?

TOM: I have, that's true, *driven* out!

AMANDA: What is the matter with you, you—big—big—IDIOT!

TOM: Look!—I've got *no thing,* no single thing—

AMANDA: Lower your voice!

TOM: —in my life here that I can call my OWN! Everything is—

AMANDA: Stop that shouting!

TOM: Yesterday you confiscated my books! You had the nerve to—

AMANDA: I took that horrible novel back to the library—yes! That hideous book by that insane Mr. Lawrence.

[*Tom laughs wildly.*]

I cannot control the output of diseased minds or people who cater to them—

[*Tom laughs still more wildly.*]

BUT I WON'T ALLOW SUCH FILTH BROUGHT INTO MY HOUSE! No, no, no, no, no!

TOM: House, house! Who pays rent on it, who makes a slave of himself to—

AMANDA [*fairly screeching*]: Don't you DARE to—

TOM: No, no, *I* mustn't say things! *I've* got to just—

AMANDA: Let me tell you—

TOM: I don't want to hear any more!

[*He tears the portieres open. The dining-room area is lit with a turgid smoky red glow. Now we see Amanda; her hair is in metal curlers and she is wearing a very old bathrobe, much too large for her slight figure, a relic of the faithless Mr. Wingfield. The upright typewriter now stands on the drop-leaf table, along with a wild disarray of manuscripts. The quarrel was probably precipitated by Amanda's interruption of Tom's creative labor. A chair lies overthrown on the floor. Their gesticulating shadows are cast on the ceiling by the fiery glow.*]

AMANDA: You *will* hear more, you—

TOM: No, I won't hear more, I'm going out!

AMANDA: You come right back in—

TOM: Out, out, out! Because I'm—

AMANDA: Come back here, Tom Wingfield! I'm not through talking to you!

TOM: Oh, go—

LAURA [*desperately*]: —Tom!

AMANDA: You're going to listen, and no more insolence from you! I'm at the end of my patience!

[*He comes back toward her.*]

TOM: What do you think I'm at? Aren't I supposed to have any patience to reach the end of, Mother? I know, I know. It seems unimportant to you, what I'm *doing*—what I *want* to do—having a little *difference* between them! You don't think that—

AMANDA: I think you've been doing things that you're ashamed of. That's why you act like this. I don't believe that you go every night to the movies. Nobody goes to the movies night after night. Nobody in their right minds goes to the movies as often as you pretend to. People don't go to the movies at nearly midnight, and movies don't let out at two A.M. Come in stumbling. Muttering to yourself like a maniac! You get three hours' sleep and then go to work. Oh, I can picture the way you're doing down there. Moping, doping, because you're in no condition.

TOM [*wildly*]: No, I'm in no condition!

AMANDA: What right have you got to jeopardize your job? Jeopardize the security of us all? How do you think we'd manage if you were—

TOM: Listen! You think I'm crazy about the *warehouse?* [*He bends fiercely toward her slight figure.*] You think I'm in love with the Continental Shoemakers? You think I want to spend fifty-five *years* down there in that—*celotex interior!* with—*fluorescent—tubes!* Look! I'd rather somebody picked up a crowbar and battered out my brains—than go back mornings! I *go!* Every time you come in yelling that God-damn *"Rise and Shine!" "Rise and Shine!"* I say to myself, "How *lucky dead* people are!" But I get up. I *go!* For sixty-five dollars a month I give up all that I dream of doing and being *ever!* And you say self—*self's* all I ever think of. Why, listen, if self is what I thought of, Mother, I'd be where he is—GONE! [*He points to his father's picture.*] As far as the system of transportation reaches! [*He starts past her. She grabs his arm.*] Don't grab at me, Mother!

AMANDA: Where are you going?

TOM: I'm going to the *movies!*

AMANDA: I don't believe that lie!

[*Tom crouches toward her, overtowering her tiny figure. She backs away, gasping.*]

TOM: I'm going to opium dens! Yes, opium dens, dens of vice and criminals' hangouts, Mother. I've joined the Hogan Gang, I'm a hired assassin, I carry a tommy gun in a violin case! I run a string of cat houses in the Valley! They call me Killer, Killer Wingfield, I'm leading a double-life, a simple, honest warehouse worker by day, by night a dynamic *czar* of the *underworld, Mother.* I go to gambling casinos, I spin away fortunes on the roulette table! I wear a patch over one eye and a false mustache, sometimes I put on green whiskers. On those occasions they call me—*El Diablo!* Oh, I could tell you many things to make you sleepless! My enemies plan to dynamite this place. They're going to blow us all sky-high some night! I'll be glad, very happy, and so will you! You'll go up, up on a broomstick, over Blue Mountain with seventeen gentlemen callers! You ugly—babbling old—*witch*. . . . [*He goes through a series of violent, clumsy movements, seizing his overcoat, lunging to the door, pulling it fiercely open. The women watch him, aghast. His arm catches in the sleeve of the coat as he struggles to pull it on. For a moment he is pinioned by the bulky garment. With an outraged groan he tears the coat off again, splitting the shoulder of it, and hurls it across the room. It strikes against the shelf of Laura's glass collection, and there is a tinkle of shattering glass. Laura cries out as if wounded.*]

[*Music.*]

[*Screen legend*: "The Glass Menagerie."]

LAURA [*shrilly*]: *My glass!*—menagerie. . . . [*She covers her face and turns away.*]

[*But Amanda is still stunned and stupefied by the "ugly witch" so that she barely notices this occurrence. Now she recovers her speech.*]

AMANDA [*in an awful voice*]: I won't speak to you—until you apologize!

[*She crosses through the portieres and draws them together behind her. Tom is left with Laura. Laura clings weakly to the mantel with her face averted. Tom stares at her stupidly for a moment. Then he crosses to the shelf. He drops awkwardly on his knees to collect the fallen glass, glancing at Laura as if he would speak but couldn't.*]

["*The Glass Menagerie" music steals in as the scene dims out.*]

SCENE FOUR

The interior of the apartment is dark. There is a faint light in the alley. A deep-voiced bell in a church is tolling the hour of five.

Tom appears at the top of the alley. After each solemn boom of the bell in the tower, he shakes a little noisemaker or rattle as if to express the tiny spasm of man in contrast to the sustained power and dignity of the Almighty. This and the unsteadiness of his advance make it evident that he has been drinking. As he climbs the few steps to the fire escape landing light steals up inside. Laura appears in the front room in a nightdress. She notices that Tom's bed is empty. Tom fishes in his pockets for his door key, removing a motley assortment of articles in the search, including a shower of movie ticket stubs and an empty bottle. At last he finds the key, but just as he is about to insert it, it slips from his fingers. He strikes a match and crouches below the door.

TOM [*bitterly*]: One crack—and it falls through!

[*Laura opens the door.*]

LAURA: Tom! Tom, what are you doing?

TOM: Looking for a door key.

LAURA: Where have you been all this time?

TOM: I have been to the movies.

LAURA: All this time at the movies?

TOM: There was a very long program. There was a Garbo picture and a Mickey Mouse and a travelogue and a newsreel and a preview of coming attractions. And there was an organ solo and a collection for the Milk Fund—simultaneously—

which ended up in a terrible fight between a fat lady and an usher!

LAURA [*innocently*]: Did you have to stay through everything?

TOM: Of course! And, oh, I forgot! There was a big stage show! The headliner on this stage show was Malvolio the Magician. He performed wonderful tricks, many of them, such as pouring water back and forth between pitchers. First it turned to wine and then it turned to beer and then it turned to whisky. I know it was whisky it finally turned into because he needed somebody to come up out of the audience to help him, and I came up—both shows! It was Kentucky Straight Bourbon. A very generous fellow, he gave souvenirs. [*He pulls from his back pocket a shimmering rainbow-colored scarf.*] He gave me this. This is his magic scarf. You can have it, Laura. You wave it over a canary cage and you get a bowl of goldfish. You wave it over the goldfish bowl and they fly away canaries. . . . But the wonderfullest trick of all was the coffin trick. We nailed him into a coffin and he got out of the coffin without removing one nail. [*He has come inside.*] There is a trick that would come in handy for me—get me out of this two-by-four situation! [*He flops onto the bed and starts removing his shoes.*]

LAURA: Tom—shhh!

TOM: What're you shushing me for?

LAURA: You'll wake up Mother.

TOM: Goody, goody! Pay 'er back for all those "Rise an' Shines." [*He lies down, groaning.*] You know it don't take much intelligence to get yourself into a nailed-up coffin, Laura. But who in hell ever got himself out of one without removing one nail?

[As if in answer, the father's grinning photograph lights up. The scene dims out.]

[Immediately following, the church bell is heard striking six. At the sixth stroke the alarm clock goes off in Amanda's room, and after a few moments we hear her calling: "Rise and Shine! Rise and Shine! Laura, go tell your brother to rise and shine!"]

TOM *[sitting up slowly]*: I'll rise—but I won't shine.

[The light increases.]

AMANDA: Laura, tell your brother his coffee is ready.

[Laura slips into the front room.]

LAURA: Tom!—It's nearly seven. Don't make Mother nervous.

[He stares at her stupidly.]

[beseechingly:] Tom, speak to Mother this morning. Make up with her, apologize, speak to her!

TOM: She won't to me. It's her that started not speaking.

LAURA: If you just say you're sorry she'll start speaking.

TOM: Her not speaking—is that such a tragedy?

LAURA: Please—please!

AMANDA *[calling from the kitchenette]*: Laura, are you going to do what I asked you to do, or do I have to get dressed and go out myself?

LAURA: Going, going—soon as I get on my coat!

[She pulls on a shapeless felt hat with a nervous, jerky movement, pleadingly glancing at Tom. She rushes awk-

wardly for her coat. The coat is one of Amanda's, inaccurately made-over, the sleeves too short for Laura.]

Butter and what else?

AMANDA [*entering from the kitchenette*]: Just butter. Tell them to charge it.

LAURA: Mother, they make such faces when I do that.

AMANDA: Sticks and stones can break our bones, but the expression on Mr. Garfinkel's face won't harm us! Tell your brother his coffee is getting cold.

LAURA [*at the door*]: Do what I asked you, will you, will you, Tom?

[*He looks sullenly away.*]

AMANDA: Laura, go now or just don't go at all!

LAURA [*rushing out*]: Going—going!

[*A second later she cries out. Tom springs up and crosses to the door. Tom opens the door.*]

TOM: Laura?

LAURA: I'm all right. I slipped, but I'm all right.

AMANDA [*peering anxiously after her*]: If anyone breaks a leg on those fire-escape steps, the landlord ought to be sued for every cent he possesses! [*She shuts the door. Now she remembers she isn't speaking to Tom and returns to the other room.*]

[*As Tom comes listlessly for his coffee, she turns her back to him and stands rigidly facing the window on the gloomy gray vault of the areaway. Its light on her face with its aged but childish features is cruelly sharp, satirical as a Daumier print.*]

[*The music of "Ave Maria," is heard softly.*]

[*Tom glances sheepishly but sullenly at her averted figure and slumps at the table. The coffee is scalding hot; he sips it and gasps and spits it back in the cup. At his gasp, Amanda catches her breath and half turns. Then she catches herself and turns back to the window. Tom blows on his coffee, glancing sidewise at his mother. She clears her throat. Tom clears his. He starts to rise, sinks back down again, scratches his head, clears his throat again. Amanda coughs. Tom raises his cup in both hands to blow on it, his eyes staring over the rim of it at his mother for several moments. Then he slowly sets the cup down and awkwardly and hesitantly rises from the chair.*]

TOM [*hoarsely*]: Mother. I—I apologize, Mother.

[*Amanda draws a quick, shuddering breath. Her face works grotesquely. She breaks into childlike tears.*]

I'm sorry for what I said, for everything that I said, I didn't mean it.

AMANDA [*sobbingly*]: My devotion has made me a witch and so I make myself hateful to my children!

TOM: *No,* you *don't.*

AMANDA: I worry so much, don't sleep, it makes me nervous!

TOM [*gently*]: I understand that.

AMANDA: I've had to put up a solitary battle all these years. But you're my right-hand bower! Don't fall down, don't fail!

TOM [*gently*]: I try, Mother.

AMANDA [*with great enthusiasm*]: Try and you will *succeed!* [*The notion makes her breathless.*] Why, you—you're just *full* of natural endowments! Both of my children—they're *unusual* children! Don't you think I know it? I'm so—*proud!* Happy and—feel I've—so much to be thankful for but— promise me one thing, son!

TOM: What, Mother?

AMANDA: Promise, son, you'll—never be a drunkard!

TOM [*turns to her grinning*]: I will never be a drunkard, Mother.

AMANDA: That's what frightened me so, that you'd be drinking! Eat a bowl of Purina!

TOM: Just coffee, Mother.

AMANDA: Shredded wheat biscuit?

TOM: No. No, Mother, just coffee.

AMANDA: You can't put in a day's work on an empty stomach. You've got ten minutes—don't gulp! Drinking too-hot liquids makes cancer of the stomach. . . . Put cream in.

TOM: No, thank you.

AMANDA: To cool it.

TOM: No! No, thank you, I want it black.

AMANDA: I know, but it's not good for you. We have to do all that we can to build ourselves up. In these trying times we live in, all that we have to cling to is—each other. . . . That's why it's so important to— Tom, I— I sent out your sister so I could discuss something with you. If you hadn't spoken I would have spoken to you. [*She sits down.*]

TOM [*gently*]: What is it, Mother, that you want to discuss?

AMANDA: *Laura!*

[*Tom puts his cup down slowly.*]

[*Legend on screen*: "Laura." *Music*: "*The Glass Menagerie.*"]

TOM: —Oh.—Laura . . .

AMANDA [*touching his sleeve*]: You know how Laura is. So quiet but—still water runs deep! She notices things and I think she—broods about them.

[*Tom looks up.*]

A few days ago I came in and she was crying.

TOM: What about?

AMANDA: You.

TOM: Me?

AMANDA: She has an idea that you're not happy here.

TOM: What gave her that idea?

AMANDA: What gives her any idea? However, you do act strangely. I—I'm not criticizing, understand *that!* I know your ambitions do not lie in the warehouse, that like everybody in the whole wide world—you've had to—make sacrifices, but—Tom—Tom—life's not easy, it calls for—Spartan endurance! There's so many things in my heart that I cannot describe to you! I've never told you but I—*loved* your father. . . .

TOM [*gently*]: I know that, Mother.

AMANDA: And you—when I see you taking after his ways! Staying out late—and—well, you *had* been drinking the night you were in that—terrifying condition! Laura says that you hate the apartment and that you go out nights to get away from it! Is that true, Tom?

TOM: No. You say there's so much in your heart that you can't describe to me. That's true of me, too. There's so much in my heart that I can't describe to *you!* So let's respect each other's—

AMANDA: But, why—*why,* Tom—are you always so *restless?* Where do you *go* to, nights?

TOM: I—go to the movies.

AMANDA: Why do you go to the movies so much, Tom?

TOM: I go to the movies because—I like adventure. Adventure is something I don't have much of at work, so I go to the movies.

AMANDA: But, Tom, you go to the movies *entirely* too *much!*

TOM: I like a lot of adventure.

[*Amanda looks baffled, then hurt. As the familiar inquisition resumes, Tom becomes hard and impatient again. Amanda slips back into her querulous attitude toward him.*]

[*Image on screen*: A sailing vessel with Jolly Roger.]

AMANDA: Most young men find adventure in their careers.

TOM: Then most young men are not employed in a warehouse.

AMANDA: The world is full of young men employed in warehouses and offices and factories.

TOM: Do all of them find adventure in their careers?

AMANDA: They do or they do without it! Not everybody has a craze for adventure.

TOM: Man is by instinct a lover, a hunter, a fighter, and none of those instincts are given much play at the warehouse!

AMANDA: Man is by instinct! Don't quote instinct to me! Instinct is something that people have got away from! It belongs to animals! Christian adults don't want it!

TOM: What do Christian adults want, then, Mother?

AMANDA: Superior things! Things of the mind and the spirit! Only animals have to satisfy instincts! Surely your aims are somewhat higher than theirs! Than monkeys—pigs—

TOM: I reckon they're not.

AMANDA: You're joking. However, that isn't what I wanted to discuss.

TOM [*rising*]: I haven't much time.

AMANDA [*pushing his shoulders*]: Sit down.

TOM: You want me to punch in red at the warehouse, Mother?

AMANDA: You have five minutes. I want to talk about Laura.

[*Screen legend*: "Plans and Provisions."]

TOM: All right! What about Laura?

AMANDA: We have to be making some plans and provisions for her. She's older than you, two years, and nothing has happened. She just drifts along doing nothing. It frightens me terribly how she just drifts along.

TOM: I guess she's the type that people call home girls.

AMANDA: There's no such type, and if there is, it's a pity! That is unless the home is hers, with a husband!

TOM: What?

AMANDA: Oh, I can see the handwriting on the wall as plain as I see the nose in front of my face! It's terrifying! More and more you remind me of your father! He was out all hours without explanation!—Then *left! Goodbye!* And me with the bag to hold. I saw that letter you got from the Merchant Marine. I know what you're dreaming of. I'm not standing here blindfolded. [*She pauses.*] Very well, then. Then *do* it! But not till there's somebody to take your place.

TOM: What do you mean?

AMANDA: I mean that as soon as Laura has got somebody to take care of her, married, a home of her own, independent —why, then you'll be free to go wherever you please, on land, on sea, whichever way the wind blows you! But until that time you've got to look out for your sister. I don't say me because I'm old and don't matter! I say for your sister because she's young and dependent.

I put her in business college—a dismal failure! Frightened her so it made her sick at the stomach. I took her over to the Young People's League at the church. Another fiasco. She spoke to nobody, nobody spoke to her. Now all she does is fool with those pieces of glass and play those worn-out records. What kind of a life is that for a girl to lead?

TOM: What can I do about it?

AMANDA: Overcome selfishness! Self, self, self is all that you ever think of!

[*Tom springs up and crosses to get his coat. It is ugly and bulky. He pulls on a cap with earmuffs.*]

Where is your muffler? Put your wool muffler on!

[*He snatches it angrily from the closet, tosses it around his neck and pulls both ends tight.*]

Tom! I haven't said what I had in mind to ask you.

TOM: I'm too late to—

AMANDA [*catching his arm—very importunately; then shyly*]: Down at the warehouse, aren't there some—nice young men?

TOM: No!

AMANDA: There *must* be—*some* . . .

TOM: Mother—[*He gestures.*]

AMANDA: Find out one that's clean-living—doesn't drink and ask him out for sister!

TOM: What?

AMANDA: For *sister!* To *meet!* Get *acquainted!*

TOM [*stamping to the door*]: Oh, my *go-osh!*

AMANDA: Will you?

[*He opens the door. She says, imploringly:*]

Will you?

[*He starts down the fire escape.*]

Will you? *Will* you, dear?

TOM [*calling back*]: *Yes!*

[*Amanda closes the door hesitantly and with a troubled but faintly hopeful expression.*]

[*Screen image*: The cover of a glamor magazine.]

[*The spotlight picks up Amanda at the phone.*]

AMANDA: Ella Cartwright? This is Amanda Wingfield!
How are you, honey?
How is that kidney condition?

[*There is a five-second pause.*]

Horrors!

[*There is another pause.*]

You're a Christian martyr, yes, honey, that's what you are, a Christian martyr! Well, I just now happened to notice in my little red book that your subscription to the *Companion* has just run out! I knew that you wouldn't want to miss out on the wonderful serial starting in this new issue. It's by Bessie Mae Hopper, the first thing she's written since *Honeymoon for Three.* Wasn't that a strange and interesting story? Well, this one is even lovelier, I believe. It has a sophisticated, society background. It's all about the horsey set on Long Island!

[*The light fades out.*]

SCENE FIVE

Legend on the screen: "Annunciation."

Music is heard as the light slowly comes on.

It is early dusk of a spring evening. Supper has just been finished in the Wingfield apartment. Amanda and Laura, in light-colored dresses, are removing dishes from the table in the dining room, which is shadowy, their movements formalized almost as a dance or ritual, their moving forms as pale and silent as moths. Tom, in white shirt and trousers, rises from the table and crosses toward the fire escape.

AMANDA [*as he passes her*]: Son, will you do me a favor?

TOM: What?

AMANDA: Comb your hair! You look so pretty when your hair is combed!

[*Tom slouches on the sofa with the evening paper. Its enormous headline reads: "Franco Triumphs."*]

There is only one respect in which I would like you to emulate your father.

TOM: What respect is that?

AMANDA: The care he always took of his appearance. He never allowed himself to look untidy.

[*He throws down the paper and crosses to the fire escape.*]

Where are you going?

TOM: I'm going out to smoke.

AMANDA: You smoke too much. A pack a day at fifteen cents a pack. How much would that amount to in a month?

Thirty times fifteen is how much, Tom? Figure it out and you will be astounded at what you could save. Enough to give you a night-school course in accounting at Washington U.! Just think what a wonderful thing that would be for you, son!

[*Tom is unmoved by the thought.*]

TOM: I'd rather smoke. [*He steps out on the landing, letting the screen door slam.*]

AMANDA [*sharply*]: I know! That's the tragedy of it. . . . [*Alone, she turns to look at her husband's picture.*]

[*Dance music: "The World Is Waiting for the Sunrise!"*]

TOM [*to the audience*]: Across the alley from us was the Paradise Dance Hall. On evenings in spring the windows and doors were open and the music came outdoors. Sometimes the lights were turned out except for a large glass sphere that hung from the ceiling. It would turn slowly about and filter the dusk with delicate rainbow colors. Then the orchestra played a waltz or a tango, something that had a slow and sensuous rhythm. Couples would come outside, to the relative privacy of the alley. You could see them kissing behind ash pits and telephone poles. This was the compensation for lives that passed like mine, without any change or adventure. Adventure and change were imminent in this year. They were waiting around the corner for all these kids. Suspended in the mist over Berchtesgaden, caught in the folds of Chamberlain's umbrella. In Spain there was Guernica! But here there was only hot swing music and liquor, dance halls, bars, and movies, and sex that hung in the gloom like a chandelier and flooded the world with brief, deceptive rainbows. . . . All the world was waiting for bombardments!

[*Amanda turns from the picture and comes outside.*]

AMANDA [*sighing*]: A fire escape landing's a poor excuse for a porch. [*She spreads a newspaper on a step and sits down, gracefully and demurely as if she were settling into a swing on a Mississippi veranda.*] What are you looking at?

TOM: The moon.

AMANDA: Is there a moon this evening?

TOM: It's rising over Garfinkel's Delicatessen.

AMANDA: So it is! A little silver slipper of a moon. Have you made a wish on it yet?

TOM: Um-hum.

AMANDA: What did you wish for?

TOM: That's a secret.

AMANDA: A secret, huh? Well, I won't tell mine either. I will be just as mysterious as you.

TOM: I bet I can guess what yours is.

AMANDA: Is my head so transparent?

TOM: You're not a sphinx.

AMANDA: No, I don't have secrets. I'll tell you what I wished for on the moon. Success and happiness for my precious children! I wish for that whenever there's a moon, and when there isn't a moon, I wish for it, too.

TOM: I thought perhaps you wished for a gentleman caller.

AMANDA: Why do you say that?

TOM: Don't you remember asking me to fetch one?

AMANDA: I remember suggesting that it would be nice for your sister if you brought home some nice young man from the warehouse. I think that I've made that suggestion more than once.

TOM: Yes, you have made it repeatedly.

AMANDA: Well?

TOM: We are going to have one.

AMANDA: *What?*

TOM: A gentleman caller!

[*The annunciation is celebrated with music.*]

[*Amanda rises.*]

[*Image on screen*: A caller with a bouquet.]

AMANDA: You mean you have asked some nice young man to come over?

TOM: Yep. I've asked him to dinner.

AMANDA: You really did?

TOM: I did!

AMANDA: You did, and did he—*accept?*

TOM: He did!

AMANDA: Well, well—well, well! That's—lovely!

TOM: I thought that you would be pleased.

AMANDA: It's definite then?

TOM: Very definite.

AMANDA: Soon?

TOM: Very soon.

AMANDA: For heaven's sake, stop putting on and tell me some things, will you?

TOM: What things do you want me to tell you?

AMANDA: *Naturally* I would like to know when he's *coming!*

TOM: He's coming tomorrow.

AMANDA: *Tomorrow?*

TOM: Yep. Tomorrow.

AMANDA: But, Tom!

TOM: Yes, Mother?

AMANDA: Tomorrow gives me no time!

TOM: Time for what?

AMANDA: Preparations! Why didn't you phone me at once, as soon as you asked him, the minute that he accepted? Then, don't you see, I could have been getting ready!

TOM: You don't have to make any fuss.

AMANDA: Oh, Tom, Tom, Tom, of course I have to make a fuss! I want things nice, not sloppy! Not thrown together. I'll certainly have to do some fast thinking, won't I?

TOM: I don't see why you have to think at all.

AMANDA: You just don't know. We can't have a gentleman caller in a pigsty! All my wedding silver has to be polished, the monogrammed table linen ought to be laundered! The windows have to be washed and fresh curtains put up. And how about clothes? We have to *wear* something, don't we?

TOM: Mother, this boy is no one to make a fuss over!

AMANDA: Do you realize he's the first young man we've introduced to your sister? It's terrible, dreadful, disgraceful that poor little sister has never received a single gentleman caller! Tom, come inside! [*She opens the screen door.*]

TOM: What for?

AMANDA: I want to ask you some things.

TOM: If you're going to make such a fuss, I'll call it off, I'll tell him not to come!

AMANDA: You certainly won't do anything of the kind. Nothing offends people worse than broken engagements. It simply means I'll have to work like a Turk! We won't be brilliant, but we will pass inspection. Come on inside.

[*Tom follows her inside, groaning.*]

Sit down.

TOM: Any particular place you would like me to sit?

AMANDA: Thank heavens I've got that new sofa! I'm also making payments on a floor lamp I'll have sent out! And put the chintz covers on, they'll brighten things up! Of course I'd hoped to have these walls re-papered. . . . What is the young man's name?

TOM: His name is O'Connor.

AMANDA: That, of course, means fish—tomorrow is Friday! I'll have that salmon loaf—with Durkee's dressing! What does he do? He works at the warehouse?

TOM: Of course! How else would I—

AMANDA: Tom, he—doesn't drink?

TOM: Why do you ask me that?

AMANDA: Your father *did!*

TOM: Don't get started on that!

AMANDA: He *does* drink, then?

TOM: Not that I know of!

AMANDA: Make sure, be certain! The last thing I want for my daughter's a boy who drinks!

TOM: Aren't you being a little bit premature? Mr. O'Connor has not yet appeared on the scene!

AMANDA: But will tomorrow. To meet your sister, and what do I know about his character? Nothing! Old maids are better off than wives of drunkards!

TOM: Oh, my God!

AMANDA: Be still!

TOM [*leaning forward to whisper*]: Lots of fellows meet girls whom they don't marry!

AMANDA: Oh, talk sensibly, Tom—and don't be sarcastic! [*She has gotten a hairbrush.*]

TOM: What are you doing?

AMANDA: I'm brushing that cowlick down! [*She attacks his hair with the brush.*] What is this young man's position at the warehouse?

TOM [*submitting grimly to the brush and the interrogation*]: This young man's position is that of a shipping clerk, Mother.

AMANDA: Sounds to me like a fairly responsible job, the sort of a job *you* would be in if you just had more *get-up*. What is his salary? Have you any idea?

TOM: I would judge it to be approximately eighty-five dollars a month.

AMANDA: Well—not princely, but—

TOM: Twenty more than I make.

AMANDA: Yes, how well I know! But for a family man, eighty-five dollars a month is not much more than you can just get by on. . . .

TOM: Yes, but Mr. O'Connor is not a family man.

AMANDA: He might be, mightn't he? Some time in the future?

TOM: I see. Plans and provisions.

AMANDA: You are the only young man that I know of who ignores the fact that the future becomes the present, the present the past, and the past turns into everlasting regret if you don't plan for it!

TOM: I will think that over and see what I can make of it.

AMANDA: Don't be supercilious with your mother! Tell me some more about this—what do you call him?

TOM: James D. O'Connor. The D. is for Delaney.

AMANDA: Irish on *both* sides! *Gracious!* And doesn't drink?

TOM: Shall I call him up and ask him right this minute?

AMANDA: The only way to find out about those things is to make discreet inquiries at the proper moment. When I was a girl in Blue Mountain and it was suspected that a young man drank, the girl whose attentions he had been receiving, if any girl *was,* would sometimes speak to the minister of his church, or rather her father would if her father was living, and sort of feel him out on the young man's character. That is the way such things are discreetly handled to keep a young woman from making a tragic mistake!

TOM: Then how did you happen to make a tragic mistake?

AMANDA: That innocent look of your father's had everyone fooled! He *smiled*—the world was *enchanted!* No girl can do worse than put herself at the mercy of a handsome appearance! I hope that Mr. O'Connor is not too good-looking.

TOM: No, he's not too good-looking. He's covered with freckles and hasn't too much of a nose.

AMANDA: He's not right-down homely, though?

TOM: Not right-down homely. Just medium homely, I'd say.

AMANDA: Character's what to look for in a man.

TOM: That's what I've always said, Mother.

AMANDA: You've never said anything of the kind and I suspect you would never give it a thought.

TOM: Don't be so suspicious of me.

AMANDA: At least I hope he's the type that's up and coming.

TOM: I think he really goes in for self-improvement.

AMANDA: What reason have you to think so?

TOM: He goes to night school.

AMANDA [*beaming*]: Splendid! What does he do, I mean study?

TOM: Radio engineering and public speaking!

AMANDA: Then he has visions of being advanced in the world! Any young man who studies public speaking is aiming to have an executive job some day! And radio engineering? A thing for the future! Both of these facts are very illuminating. Those are the sort of things that a mother should know concerning any young man who comes to call on her daughter. Seriously or—not.

TOM: One little warning. He doesn't know about Laura. I didn't let on that we had dark ulterior motives. I just said, why don't you come and have dinner with us? He said okay and that was the whole conversation.

AMANDA: I bet it was! You're eloquent as an oyster. However, he'll know about Laura when he gets here. When he sees how lovely and sweet and pretty she is, he'll thank his lucky stars he was asked to dinner.

TOM: Mother, you mustn't expect too much of Laura.

AMANDA: What do you mean?

TOM: Laura seems all those things to you and me because she's ours and we love her. We don't even notice she's crippled any more.

AMANDA: Don't say crippled! You know that I never allow that word to be used!

TOM: But face facts, Mother. She is and—that's not all—

AMANDA: What do you mean "not all"?

TOM: Laura is very different from other girls.

AMANDA: I think the difference is all to her advantage.

TOM: Not quite all—in the eyes of others—strangers—she's terribly shy and lives in a world of her own and those things make her seem a little peculiar to people outside the house.

AMANDA: Don't say peculiar.

TOM: Face the facts. She is.

[*The dance hall music changes to a tango that has a minor and somewhat ominous tone.*]

AMANDA: In what way is she peculiar—may I ask?

TOM [*gently*]: She lives in a world of her own—a world of little glass ornaments, Mother. . . .

[*He gets up. Amanda remains holding the brush, looking at him, troubled.*]

She plays old phonograph records and—that's about all—[*He glances at himself in the mirror and crosses to the door.*]

AMANDA [*sharply*]: Where are you going?

TOM: I'm going to the movies. [*He goes out the screen door.*]

AMANDA: Not to the movies, every night to the movies! [*She follows quickly to the screen door.*] I don't believe you always go to the movies!

[*He is gone. Amanda looks worriedly after him for a moment. Then vitality and optimism return and she turns from the door, crossing to the portieres.*]

Laura! Laura!

[*Laura answers from the kitchenette.*]

LAURA: Yes, Mother.

AMANDA: Let those dishes go and come in front!

[*Laura appears with a dish towel. Amanda speaks to her gaily.*]

Laura, come here and make a wish on the moon!

[*Screen image*: The Moon.]

LAURA [*entering*]: Moon—moon?

AMANDA: A little silver slipper of a moon. Look over your left shoulder, Laura, and make a wish!

[*Laura looks faintly puzzled as if called out of sleep. Amanda seizes her shoulders and turns her at an angle by the door.*]

Now! Now, darling, *wish!*

LAURA: What shall I wish for, Mother?

AMANDA [*her voice trembling and her eyes suddenly filling with tears*]: Happiness! Good fortune!

[*The sound of the violin rises and the stage dims out.*]

SCENE SIX

The light comes up on the fire escape landing. Tom is leaning against the grill, smoking.

[*Screen image*: The high school hero.]

TOM: And so the following evening I brought Jim home to dinner. I had known Jim slightly in high school. In high school Jim was a hero. He had tremendous Irish good nature and vitality with the scrubbed and polished look of white chinaware. He seemed to move in a continual spotlight. He was a star in basketball, captain of the debating club, president of the senior class and the glee club and he sang the male lead in the annual light operas. He was always running or bounding, never just walking. He seemed always at the point of defeating the law of gravity. He was shooting with such velocity through his adolescence that you would logically expect him to arrive at nothing short of the White House by the time he was thirty. But Jim apparently ran into more interference after his graduation from Soldan. His speed had definitely slowed. Six years after he left high school he was holding a job that wasn't much better than mine.

[*Screen image*: The Clerk.]

He was the only one at the warehouse with whom I was on friendly terms. I was valuable to him as someone who could remember his former glory, who had seen him win basketball games and the silver cup in debating. He knew of my secret practice of retiring to a cabinet of the washroom to work on poems when business was slack in the warehouse. He called me Shakespeare. And while the other boys in the warehouse regarded me with suspicious hostility, Jim took a humorous attitude toward me. Gradually his attitude affected the others, their hostility wore off and they also began to smile at me as people smile at an oddly fashioned dog who trots across their path at some distance.

I knew that Jim and Laura had known each other at Soldan, and I had heard Laura speak admiringly of his voice. I didn't know if Jim remembered her or not. In high school Laura had been as unobtrusive as Jim had been astonishing. If he did remember Laura, it was not as my sister, for when I asked him to dinner, he grinned and said, "You know, Shakespeare, I never thought of you as having folks!"

He was about to discover that I did. . . .

[*Legend on screen*: "The accent of a coming foot."]

[*The light dims out on Tom and comes up in the Wingfield living room—a delicate lemony light. It is about five on a Friday evening of late spring which comes "scattering poems in the sky."*]

[*Amanda has worked like a Turk in preparation for the gentleman caller. The results are astonishing. The new floor lamp with its rose silk shade is in place, a colored paper lantern conceals the broken light fixture in the ceiling, new billowing white curtains are at the windows, chintz covers are on the chairs and sofa, a pair of new sofa pillows make their initial appearance. Open boxes and tissue paper are scattered on the floor.*]

[*Laura stands in the middle of the room with lifted arms while Amanda crouches before her, adjusting the hem of a new dress, devout and ritualistic. The dress is colored and designed by memory. The arrangement of Laura's hair is changed; it is softer and more becoming. A fragile, unearthly prettiness has come out in Laura: she is like a piece of translucent glass touched by light, given a momentary radiance, not actual, not lasting.*]

AMANDA [*impatiently*]: Why are you trembling?

LAURA: Mother, you've made me so nervous!

AMANDA: How have I made you nervous?

LAURA: By all this fuss! You make it seem so important!

AMANDA: I don't understand you, Laura. You couldn't be satisfied with just sitting home, and yet whenever I try to arrange something for you, you seem to resist it. [*She gets up.*] Now take a look at yourself. No, wait! Wait just a moment—I have an idea!

LAURA: What is it now?

[*Amanda produces two powder puffs which she wraps in handkerchiefs and stuffs in Laura's bosom.*]

LAURA: Mother, what are you doing?

AMANDA: They call them "Gay Deceivers"!

LAURA: I won't wear them!

AMANDA: You will!

LAURA: Why should I?

AMANDA: Because, to be painfully honest, your chest is flat.

LAURA: You make it seem like we were setting a trap.

AMANDA: All pretty girls are a trap, a pretty trap, and men expect them to be.

[*Legend on screen*: "A pretty trap."]

Now look at yourself, young lady. This is the prettiest you will ever be! [*She stands back to admire Laura.*] I've got to fix myself now! You're going to be surprised by your mother's appearance!

[*Amanda crosses through the portieres, humming gaily. Laura moves slowly to the long mirror and stares solemnly at herself. A wind blows the white curtains inward in a slow, graceful motion and with a faint, sorrowful sighing.*]

AMANDA [*from somewhere behind the portieres*]: It isn't dark enough yet.

[*Laura turns slowly before the mirror with a troubled look.*]

[*Legend on screen*: "This is my sister: Celebrate her with strings!" *Music plays.*]

AMANDA [*laughing, still not visible*]: I'm going to show you something. I'm going to make a spectacular appearance!

LAURA: What is it, Mother?

AMANDA: Possess your soul in patience—you will see! Something I've resurrected from that old trunk! Styles haven't changed so terribly much after all. . . . [*She parts the portieres.*] Now just look at your mother! [*She wears a girlish frock of yellowed voile with a blue silk sash. She carries a bunch of jonquils—the legend of her youth is nearly revived. Now she speaks feverishly*:] This is the dress in which I led the cotillion. Won the cakewalk twice at Sunset Hill, wore one Spring to the Governor's Ball in Jackson! See how I sashayed around the ballroom, Laura? [*She raises her skirt and does a mincing step around the room.*] I wore it on Sundays for my gentlemen callers! I had it on the day I met your father. . . . I had malaria fever all that Spring. The change of climate from East Tennessee to the Delta—weakened resistance. I had a little temperature all the time—not enough to be serious—just enough to make me restless and giddy! Invitations poured in—parties all over the Delta! "Stay in bed," said Mother, "you have a fever!"—but I just wouldn't. I took quinine but kept on going, going! Evenings, dances!

Afternoons, long, long rides! Picnics—lovely! So lovely, that country in May—all lacy with dogwood, literally flooded with jonquils! That was the spring I had the craze for jonquils. Jonquils became an absolute obsession. Mother said, "Honey, there's no more room for jonquils." And still I kept on bringing in more jonquils. Whenever, wherever I saw them, I'd say, "Stop! Stop! I see jonquils!" I made the young men help me gather the jonquils! It was a joke, Amanda and her jonquils. Finally there were no more vases to hold them, every available space was filled with jonquils. No vases to hold them? All right, I'll hold them myself! And then I—[*She stops in front of the picture. Music plays.*] met your father! Malaria fever and jonquils and then—this—boy. . . . [*She switches on the rose-colored lamp.*] I hope they get here before it starts to rain. [*She crosses the room and places the jonquils in a bowl on the table.*] I gave your brother a little extra change so he and Mr. O'Connor could take the service car home.

LAURA [*with an altered look*]: What did you say his name was?

AMANDA: O'Connor.

LAURA: What is his first name?

AMANDA: I don't remember. Oh, yes, I do. It was—Jim!

[*Laura sways slightly and catches hold of a chair.*]

[*Legend on screen*: "Not Jim!"]

LAURA [*faintly*]: Not—Jim!

AMANDA: Yes, that was it, it was Jim! I've never known a Jim that wasn't nice!

[*The music becomes ominous.*]

LAURA: Are you sure his name is Jim O'Connor?

AMANDA: Yes. Why?

LAURA: Is he the one that Tom used to know in high school?

AMANDA: He didn't say so. I think he just got to know him at the warehouse.

LAURA: There was a Jim O'Connor we both knew in high school—[*then, with effort*] If that is the one that Tom is bringing to dinner—you'll have to excuse me, I won't come to the table.

AMANDA: What sort of nonsense is this?

LAURA: You asked me once if I'd ever liked a boy. Don't you remember I showed you this boy's picture?

AMANDA: You mean the boy you showed me in the yearbook?

LAURA: Yes, that boy.

AMANDA: Laura, Laura, were you in love with that boy?

LAURA: I don't know, Mother. All I know is I couldn't sit at the table if it was him!

AMANDA: It won't be him! It isn't the least bit likely. But whether it is or not, you will come to the table. You will not be excused.

LAURA: I'll have to be, Mother.

AMANDA: I don't intend to humor your silliness, Laura. I've had too much from you and your brother, both! So just sit down and compose yourself till they come. Tom has forgotten his key so you'll have to let them in, when they arrive.

LAURA [*panicky*]: Oh, Mother—*you* answer the door!

AMANDA [*lightly*]: I'll be in the kitchen—busy!

LAURA: Oh, Mother, please answer the door, don't make me do it!

AMANDA [*crossing into the kitchenette*]: I've got to fix the dressing for the salmon. Fuss, fuss—silliness!—over a gentleman caller!

[*The door swings shut. Laura is left alone.*]

[*Legend on screen*: "Terror!"]

[*She utters a low moan and turns off the lamp—sits stiffly on the edge of the sofa, knotting her fingers together.*]

[*Legend on screen*: "The Opening of a Door!"]

[*Tom and Jim appear on the fire escape steps and climb to the landing. Hearing their approach, Laura rises with a panicky gesture. She retreats to the portieres. The doorbell rings. Laura catches her breath and touches her throat. Low drums sound.*]

AMANDA [*calling*]: Laura, sweetheart! The door!

[*Laura stares at it without moving.*]

JIM: I think we just beat the rain.

TOM: Uh-huh. [*He rings again, nervously. Jim whistles and fishes for a cigarette.*]

AMANDA [*very, very gaily*]: Laura, that is your brother and Mr. O'Connor! Will you let them in, darling?

[*Laura crosses toward the kitchenette door.*]

LAURA [*breathlessly*]: Mother—you go to the door!

Amanda steps out of the kitchenette and stares furiously at Laura. She points imperiously at the door.]

LAURA: Please, please!

AMANDA [*in a fierce whisper*]: What is the matter with you, you silly thing?

LAURA [*desperately*]: Please, you answer it, *please!*

AMANDA: I told you I wasn't going to humor you, Laura. Why have you chosen this moment to lose your mind?

LAURA: Please, please, please, you go!

AMANDA: You'll have to go to the door because I can't!

LAURA [*despairingly*]: I can't either!

AMANDA: *Why?*

LAURA: I'm *sick!*

AMANDA: I'm sick, too—of your nonsense! Why can't you and your brother be normal people? Fantastic whims and behavior!

[*Tom gives a long ring.*]

Preposterous goings on! Can you give me one reason—[*She calls out lyrically.*] *Coming! Just one second!*—why you should be afraid to open a door? Now you answer it, Laura!

LAURA: Oh, oh, oh . . . [*She returns through the portieres, darts to the Victrola, winds it frantically and turns it on.*]

AMANDA: Laura Wingfield, you march right to that door!

LAURA: *Yes—yes, Mother!*

[*A faraway, scratchy rendition of "Dardanella" softens the air and gives her strength to move through it. She slips to the door and draws it cautiously open. Tom enters with the caller, Jim O'Connor.*]

TOM: Laura, this is Jim. Jim, this is my sister, Laura.

JIM [*stepping inside*]: I didn't know that Shakespeare had a sister!

LAURA [*retreating, stiff and trembling, from the door*]: How—how do you do?

JIM [*heartily, extending his hand*]: Okay!

[*Laura touches it hesitantly with hers.*]

JIM: Your hand's *cold,* Laura!

LAURA: Yes, well—I've been playing the Victrola. . . .

JIM: Must have been playing classical music on it! You ought to play a little hot swing music to warm you up!

LAURA: Excuse me—I haven't finished playing the Victrola. . . . [*She turns awkwardly and hurries into the front room. She pauses a second by the Victrola. Then she catches her breath and darts through the portieres like a frightened deer.*]

JIM [*grinning*]: What was the matter?

TOM: Oh—with Laura? Laura is—terribly shy.

JIM: Shy, huh? It's unusual to meet a shy girl nowadays. I don't believe you ever mentioned you had a sister.

TOM: Well, now you know. I have one. Here is the *Post Dispatch.* You want a piece of it?

JIM: Uh-huh.

TOM: What piece? The comics?

JIM: Sports! [*He glances at it.*] Ole Dizzy Dean is on his bad behavior.

TOM [*uninterested*]: Yeah? [*He lights a cigarette and goes over to the fire-escape door.*]

JIM: Where are *you* going?

TOM: I'm going out on the terrace.

JIM [*going after him*]: You know, Shakespeare—I'm going to sell you a bill of goods!

TOM: What goods?

JIM: A course I'm taking.

TOM: Huh?

JIM: In public speaking! You and me, we're not the warehouse type.

TOM: Thanks—that's good news. But what has public speaking got to do with it?

JIM: It fits you for—executive positions!

TOM: Awww.

JIM: I tell you it's done a helluva lot for me.

[*Image on screen*: Executive at his desk.]

TOM: In what respect?

JIM: In every! Ask yourself what is the difference between you an' me and men in the office down front? Brains?—No! —Ability?—No! Then what? Just one little thing—

TOM: What is that one little thing?

JIM: Primarily it amounts to—social poise! Being able to square up to people and hold your own on any social level!

AMANDA [*from the kitchenette*]: Tom?

TOM: Yes, Mother?

AMANDA: Is that you and Mr. O'Connor?

TOM: Yes, Mother.

AMANDA: Well, you just make yourselves comfortable in there.

TOM: Yes, Mother.

AMANDA: Ask Mr. O'Connor if he would like to wash his hands.

JIM: Aw, no—no—thank you—I took care of that at the warehouse. Tom—

TOM: Yes?

JIM: Mr. Mendoza was speaking to me about you.

TOM: Favorably?

JIM: What do you think?

TOM: Well—

JIM: You're going to be out of a job if you don't wake up.

TOM: I am waking up—

JIM: You show no signs.

TOM: The signs are interior.

[*Image on screen*: The sailing vessel with the Jolly Roger again.]

TOM: I'm planning to change. [*He leans over the fire-escape rail, speaking with quiet exhilaration. The incandescent marquees and signs of the first-run movie houses light his face from across the alley. He looks like a voyager.*] I'm right at the point of committing myself to a future that doesn't include the warehou : and Mr. Mendoza or even a night-school course in public speaking.

JIM: What are you gassing about?

TOM: I'm tired of the movies.

JIM: Movies!

TOM: Yes, movies! Look at them— [*a wave toward the marvels of Grand Avenue*] All of those glamorous people—having adventures—hogging it all, gobbling the whole thing up! You know what happens? People go to the *movies* instead of *moving!* Hollywood characters are supposed to have all the adventures for everybody in America, while everybody in America sits in a dark room and watches them have them! Yes, until there's a war. That's when adventure becomes available to the masses! *Everyone's* dish, not only Gable's! Then the people in the dark room come out of the dark room to have some adventures themselves—goody, goody! It's our turn now, to go to the South Sea Island—to make a safari—to be exotic, far-off! But I'm not patient. I don't want to wait till then. I'm tired of the *movies* and I am *about* to *move!*

JIM [*incredulously*]: Move?

TOM: Yes.

JIM: When?

TOM: Soon!

JIM: Where? Where?

[*The music seems to answer the question, while Tom thinks it over. He searches in his pockets.*]

TOM: I'm starting to boil inside. I know I seem dreamy, but inside—well, I'm boiling! Whenever I pick up a shoe, I shudder a little thinking how short life is and what I am doing! Whatever that means, I know it doesn't mean shoes—except as something to wear on a traveler's feet! [*He finds what he has been searching for in his pockets and holds out a paper to Jim.*] Look—

JIM: What?

TOM: I'm a member.

JIM [*reading*]: The Union of Merchant Seamen.

TOM: I paid my dues this month, instead of the light bill.

JIM: You will regret it when they turn the lights off.

TOM: I won't be here.

JIM: How about your mother?

TOM: I'm like my father. The bastard son of a bastard! Did you notice how he's grinning in his picture in there? And he's been absent going on sixteen years!

JIM: You're just talking, you drip. How does your mother feel about it?

TOM: Shhh! Here comes Mother! Mother is not acquainted with my plans!

AMANDA [*coming through the portieres*]: Where are you all?

TOM: On the terrace, Mother.

[*They start inside. She advances to them. Tom is distinctly shocked at her appearance. Even Jim blinks a little. He is making his first contact with girlish Southern vivacity and in spite of the night-school course in public speaking is somewhat thrown off the beam by the unexpected outlay of social charm. Certain responses are attempted by Jim but are swept aside by Amanda's gay laughter and chatter. Tom is embarrassed but after the first shock Jim reacts very warmly. He grins and chuckles, is altogether won over.*]

[*Image on screen*: Amanda as a girl.]

AMANDA [*coyly smiling, shaking her girlish ringlets*]: Well, well, well, so this is Mr. O'Connor. Introductions entirely unnecessary. I've heard so much about you from my boy. I finally said to him, Tom—good gracious!—why don't you bring this paragon to supper? I'd like to meet this nice young man at the warehouse!—instead of just hearing him sing your praises so much! I don't know why my son is so stand-offish—that's not Southern behavior!

Let's sit down and—I think we could stand a little more air in here! Tom, leave the door open. I felt a nice fresh breeze a moment ago. Where has it gone to? Mmm, so warm already! And not quite summer, even. We're going to burn up when summer really gets started. However, we're having—we're having a very light supper. I think light things are better fo' this time of year. The same as light clothes are. Light clothes an' light food are what warm weather calls fo'. You know our blood gets so thick during th' winter—it takes a while fo' us to *adjust* ou'selves!—when the season changes . . . It's come so quick this year. I wasn't prepared. All of a sudden—heavens! Already summer! I ran to the trunk an' pulled out this light dress—terribly old! Historical almost! But feels so good—so good an' co-ol, y' know. . . .

TOM: Mother—

AMANDA: Yes, honey?

TOM: How about—supper?

AMANDA: Honey, you go ask Sister if supper is ready! You know that Sister is in full charge of supper! Tell her you hungry boys are waiting for it. [*to Jim*] Have you met Laura?

JIM: She—

AMANDA: Let you in? Oh, good, you've met already! It's rare for a girl as sweet an' pretty as Laura to be domestic! But Laura is, thank heavens, not only pretty but also very domestic. I'm not at all. I never was a bit. I never could make a thing but angel-food cake. Well, in the South we had so many servants. Gone, gone, gone. All vestige of gracious living! Gone completely! I wasn't prepared for what the future brought me. All of my gentlemen callers were sons of planters and so of course I assumed that I would be married to one and raise my family on a large piece of land with plenty of servants. But man proposes—and woman accepts the proposal! To vary that old, old saying a little bit—I married no planter! I married a man who worked for the telephone company! That gallantly smiling gentleman over there! [*She points to the picture.*] A telephone man who—fell in love with long-distance! Now he travels and I don't even know where! But what am I going on for about my—tribulations? Tell me yours—I hope you don't have any! Tom?

TOM [*returning*]: Yes, Mother?

AMANDA: Is supper nearly ready?

TOM: It looks to me like supper is on the table.

AMANDA: Let me look— [*She rises prettily and looks through the portieres.*] Oh, lovely! But where is Sister?

TOM: Laura is not feeling well and she says that she thinks she'd better not come to the table.

AMANDA: What? Nonsense! Laura? Oh, Laura!

LAURA [*from the kitchenette, faintly*]: Yes, Mother.

AMANDA: You really must come to the table. We won't be seated until you come to the table! Come in, Mr. O'Connor. You sit over there, and I'll. . . . Laura? Laura Wingfield! You're keeping us waiting, honey! We can't say grace until you come to the table!

[*The kitchenette door is pushed weakly open and Laura comes in. She is obviously quite faint, her lips trembling, her eyes wide and staring. She moves unsteadily toward the table.*]

[*Screen legend*: "Terror!"]

[*Outside a summer storm is coming on abruptly. The white curtains billow inward at the windows and there is a sorrowful murmur from the deep blue dusk.*]

[*Laura suddenly stumbles; she catches at a chair with a faint moan.*]

TOM: Laura!

AMANDA: Laura!

[*There is a clap of thunder.*]

[*Screen legend*: "Ah!"]

[*despairingly*] Why, Laura, you *are* ill, darling! Tom, help your sister into the living room, dear! Sit in the living room, Laura—rest on the sofa. Well! [*to Jim as Tom helps his sister to the sofa in the living room*] Standing over the hot stove made her ill! I told her that it was just too warm this evening, but—

[*Tom comes back to the table.*]

Is Laura all right now?

TOM: Yes.

AMANDA: What *is* that? Rain? A nice cool rain has come up! [*She gives Jim a frightened look.*] I think we may—have grace—now . . .

[*Tom looks at her stupidly.*] Tom, honey—you say grace!

TOM: Oh . . . "For these and all thy mercies—"

[*They bow their heads, Amanda stealing a nervous glance at Jim. In the living room Laura, stretched on the sofa, clenches her hand to her lips, to hold back a shuddering sob.*]

God's Holy Name be praised—

[*The scene dims out.*]

SCENE SEVEN

It is half an hour later. Dinner is just being finished in the dining room, Laura is still huddled upon the sofa, her feet drawn under her, her head resting on a pale blue pillow, her eyes wide and mysteriously watchful. The new floor lamp with its shade of rose-colored silk gives a soft, becoming light to her face, bringing out the fragile, unearthly prettiness which usually escapes attention. From outside there is a steady murmur of rain, but it is slackening and soon stops; the air outside becomes pale and luminous as the moon breaks through the clouds. A moment after the curtain rises, the lights in both rooms flicker and go out.

JIM: Hey, there, Mr. Light Bulb!

[*Amanda laughs nervously.*]

[*Legend on screen*: "Suspension of a public service."]

AMANDA: Where was Moses when the lights went out? Ha-ha. Do you know the answer to that one, Mr. O'Connor?

JIM: No, Ma'am, what's the answer?

AMANDA: In the dark!

[*Jim laughs appreciatively.*]

Everybody sit still. I'll light the candles. Isn't it lucky we have them on the table? Where's a match? Which of you gentlemen can provide a match?

JIM: Here.

AMANDA: Thank you, Sir.

JIM: Not at all, Ma'am!

AMANDA [*as she lights the candles*]: I guess the fuse has burnt out. Mr. O'Connor, can you tell a burnt-out fuse? I know I can't and Tom is a total loss when it comes to mechanics.

[*They rise from the table and go into the kitchenette, from where their voices are heard.*]

Oh, be careful you don't bump into something. We don't want our gentleman caller to break his neck. Now wouldn't that be a fine howdy-do?

JIM: Ha-ha! Where is the fuse-box?

AMANDA: Right here next to the stove. Can you see anything?

JIM: Just a minute.

AMANDA: Isn't electricity a mysterious thing? Wasn't it Benjamin Franklin who tied a key to a kite? We live in such a mysterious universe, don't we? Some people say that science clears up all the mysteries for us. In my opinion it only creates more! Have you found it yet?

JIM: No, Ma'am. All these fuses look okay to me.

AMANDA: Tom!

TOM: Yes, Mother?

AMANDA: That light bill I gave you several days ago. The one I told you we got the notices about?

[*Legend on screen*: "Ha!"]

TOM: Oh—yeah.

AMANDA: You didn't neglect to pay it by any chance?

TOM: Why, I—

AMANDA: Didn't! I might have known it!

JIM: Shakespeare probably wrote a poem on that light bill, Mrs. Wingfield.

AMANDA: I might have known better than to trust him with it! There's such a high price for negligence in this world!

JIM: Maybe the poem will win a ten-dollar prize.

AMANDA: We'll just have to spend the remainder of the evening in the nineteenth century, before Mr. Edison made the Mazda lamp!

JIM: Candlelight is my favorite kind of light.

AMANDA: That shows you're romantic! But that's no excuse for Tom. Well, we got through dinner. Very considerate of them to let us get through dinner before they plunged us into everlasting darkness, wasn't it, Mr. O'Connor?

JIM: Ha-ha!

AMANDA: Tom, as a penalty for your carelessness you can help me with the dishes.

JIM: Let me give you a hand.

AMANDA: Indeed you will not!

JIM: I ought to be good for something.

AMANDA: Good for something? [*Her tone is rhapsodic.*] *You?* Why, Mr. O'Connor, nobody, *nobody's* given me this much entertainment in years—as you have!

JIM: Aw, now, Mrs. Wingfield!

AMANDA: I'm not exaggerating, not one bit! But Sister is all by her lonesome. You go keep her company in the parlor! I'll give you this lovely old candelabrum that used to be on the altar at the Church of the Heavenly Rest. It was melted a little out of shape when the church burnt down. Lightning struck it one spring. Gypsy Jones was holding a revival at the time and he intimated that the church was destroyed because the Episcopalians gave card parties.

JIM: Ha-ha.

AMANDA: And how about you coaxing Sister to drink a little wine? I think it would be good for her! Can you carry both at once?

JIM: Sure. I'm Superman!

AMANDA: Now, Thomas, get into this apron!

[*Jim comes into the dining room, carrying the candelabrum, its candles lighted, in one hand and a glass of wine in the other. The door of the kitchenette swings closed on Amanda's gay laughter; the flickering light approaches the portieres. Laura sits up nervously as Jim enters. She can hardly speak from the almost intolerable strain of being alone with a stranger.*]

[*Screen legend*: "I don't suppose you remember me at all!"]

[*At first, before Jim's warmth overcomes her paralyzing shyness, Laura's voice is thin and breathless, as though she had just run up a steep flight of stairs. Jim's attitude is gently humorous. While the incident is apparently unimportant, it is to Laura the climax of her secret life.*]

JIM: Hello there, Laura.

LAURA [*faintly*]: Hello.

[*She clears her throat.*]

JIM: How are you feeling now? Better?

LAURA: Yes. Yes, thank you.

JIM: This is for you. A little dandelion wine. [*He extends the glass toward her with extravagant gallantry.*]

LAURA: Thank you.

JIM: Drink it—but don't get drunk!

[*He laughs heartily. Laura takes the glass uncertainly; she laughs shyly.*]

Where shall I set the candles?

LAURA: Oh—oh, anywhere . . .

JIM: How about here on the floor? Any objections?

LAURA: No.

JIM: I'll spread a newspaper under to catch the drippings. I like to sit on the floor. Mind if I do?

LAURA: Oh, no.

JIM: Give me a pillow?

LAURA: What?

JIM: A pillow!

LAURA: Oh . . . [*She hands him one quickly.*]

JIM: How about you? Don't you like to sit on the floor?

LAURA: Oh—yes.

JIM: Why don't you, then?

LAURA: I—will.

JIM: Take a pillow!

[*Laura does. She sits on the floor on the other side of the candelabrum. Jim crosses his legs and smiles engagingly at her.*] I can't hardly see you sitting way over there.

LAURA: I can—see you.

JIM: I know, but that's not fair, I'm in the limelight.

[*Laura moves her pillow closer.*]

Good! Now I can see you! Comfortable?

LAURA: Yes.

JIM: So am I. Comfortable as a cow! Will you have some gum?

LAURA: No, thank you.

JIM: I think that I will indulge, with your permission. [*He musingly unwraps a stick of gum and holds it up.*] Think of the fortune made by the guy that invented the first piece of chewing gum. Amazing, huh? The Wrigley Building is one of the sights of Chicago—I saw it when I went up to the Century of Progress. Did you take in the Century of Progress?

LAURA: No, I didn't.

JIM: Well, it was quite a wonderful exposition. What impressed me most was the Hall of Science. Gives you an idea of what the future will be in America, even more wonderful than the present time is! [*There is a pause. Jim smiles at her.*] Your brother tells me you're shy. Is that right, Laura?

LAURA: I—don't know.

JIM: I judge you to be an old-fashioned type of girl. Well, I think that's a pretty good type to be. Hope you don't think I'm being too personal—do you?

LAURA [*hastily, out of embarrassment*]: I believe I *will* take a piece of gum, if you—don't mind. [*clearing her throat*] Mr. O'Connor, have you—kept up with your singing?

JIM: Singing? Me?

LAURA: Yes. I remember what a beautiful voice you had.

JIM: When did you hear me sing?

[*Laura does not answer, and in the long pause which follows a man's voice is heard singing offstage.*]

VOICE:

O blow, ye winds, heigh-ho,
A-roving I will go!
  I'm off to my love
  With a boxing glove—
Ten thousand miles away!

JIM: You say you've heard me sing?

LAURA: Oh, yes! Yes, very often . . . I—don't suppose—you remember me—at all?

JIM [*smiling doubtfully*]: You know I have an idea I've seen you before. I had that idea soon as you opened the door. It seemed almost like I was about to remember your name. But the name that I started to call you—wasn't a name! And so I stopped myself before I said it.

LAURA: Wasn't it—Blue Roses?

JIM [*springing up, grinning*]: Blue Roses! My gosh, yes—Blue Roses! That's what I had on my tongue when you opened the door! Isn't it funny what tricks your memory plays? I didn't connect you with high school somehow or other. But that's where it was; it was high school. I didn't even know you were Shakespeare's sister! Gosh, I'm sorry.

LAURA: I didn't expect you to. You—barely knew me!

JIM: But we did have a speaking acquaintance, huh?

LAURA: Yes, we—spoke to each other.

JIM: When did you recognize me?

LAURA: Oh, right away!

JIM: Soon as I came in the door?

LAURA: When I heard your name I thought it was probably you. I knew that Tom used to know you a little in high school. So when you came in the door—well, then I was—sure.

JIM: Why didn't you *say* something, then?

LAURA [*breathlessly*]: I didn't know what to say, I was —too surprised!

JIM: For goodness' sakes! You know, this sure is funny!

LAURA: Yes! Yes, isn't it, though . . .

JIM: Didn't we have a class in something together?

LAURA: Yes, we did.

JIM: What class was that?

LAURA: It was—singing—chorus!

JIM: Aw!

LAURA: I sat across the aisle from you in the Aud.

JIM: Aw.

LAURA: Mondays, Wednesdays, and Fridays.

JIM: Now I remember—you always came in late.

LAURA: Yes, it was so hard for me, getting upstairs. I had that brace on my leg—it clumped so loud!

JIM: I never heard any clumping.

LAURA [*wincing at the recollection*]: To me it sounded like—thunder!

JIM: Well, well, well, I never even noticed.

LAURA: And everybody was seated before I came in. I had to walk in front of all those people. My seat was in the back row. I had to go clumping all the way up the aisle with everyone watching!

JIM: You shouldn't have been self-conscious.

LAURA: I know, but I was. It was always such a relief when the singing started.

JIM: Aw, yes, I've placed you now! I used to call you Blue Roses. How was it that I got started calling you that?

LAURA: I was out of school a little while with pleurosis. When I came back you asked me what was the matter. I said I had pleurosis—you thought I said *Blue Roses*. That's what you always called me after that!

JIM: I hope you didn't mind.

LAURA: Oh, no—I liked it. You see, I wasn't acquainted with many—people. . . .

JIM: As I remember you sort of stuck by yourself.

LAURA: I—I—never have had much luck at—making friends.

JIM: I don't see why you wouldn't.

LAURA: Well, I—started out badly.

JIM: You mean being—

LAURA: Yes, it sort of—stood between me—

JIM: You shouldn't have let it!

LAURA: I know, but it did, and—

JIM: You were shy with people!

LAURA: I tried not to be but never could—

JIM: Overcome it?

LAURA: No, I—I never could!

JIM: I guess being shy is something you have to work out of kind of gradually.

LAURA [*sorrowfully*]: Yes—I guess it—

JIM: Takes time!

LAURA: Yes—

JIM: People are not so dreadful when you know them. That's what you have to remember! And everybody has problems, not just you, but practically everybody has got some problems. You think of yourself as having the only problems, as being the only one who is disappointed. But just look around you and you will see lots of people as disappointed as you are. For instance, I hoped when I was going to high school that I would be further along at this time, six years later, than I am now. You remember that wonderful write-up I had in *The Torch?*

LAURA: Yes! [*She rises and crosses to the table.*]

JIM: It said I was bound to succeed in anything I went into!

[*Laura returns with the high school yearbook.*]

Holy Jeez! *The Torch!*

[*He accepts it reverently. They smile across the book with mutual wonder. Laura crouches beside him and they begin to turn the pages. Laura's shyness is dissolving in his warmth.*]

LAURA: Here you are in *The Pirates of Penzance!*

JIM [*wistfully*]: I sang the baritone lead in that operetta.

LAURA [*raptly*]: So—*beautifully!*

JIM [*protesting*]: Aw—

LAURA: Yes, yes—beautifully—beautifully!

JIM: You heard me?

LAURA: All three times!

JIM: No!

LAURA: Yes!

JIM: All three performances?

LAURA [*looking down*]: Yes.

JIM: Why?

LAURA: I—wanted to ask you to—autograph my program. [*She takes the program from the back of the yearbook and shows it to him.*]

JIM: Why didn't you ask me to?

LAURA: You were always surrounded by your own friends so much that I never had a chance to.

JIM: You should have just—

LAURA: Well, I—thought you might think I was—

JIM: Thought I might think you was—what?

LAURA: Oh—

JIM [*with reflective relish*]: I was beleaguered by females in those days.

LAURA: You were terribly popular!

JIM: Yeah—

LAURA: You had such a—friendly way—

JIM: I was spoiled in high school.

LAURA: Everybody—liked you!

JIM: Including you?

LAURA: I—yes, I—did, too— [*She gently closes the book in her lap.*]

JIM: Well, well, well! Give me that program, Laura.

[*She hands it to him. He signs it with a flourish.*]

There you are—better late than never!

LAURA: Oh, I—what a—surprise!

JIM: My signature isn't worth very much right now. But some day—maybe—it will increase in value! Being disappointed is one thing and being discouraged is something else. I am disappointed but I am not discouraged. I'm twenty-three years old. How old are you?

LAURA: I'll be twenty-four in June.

JIM: That's not old age!

LAURA: No, but—

JIM: You finished high school?

LAURA [*with difficulty*]: I didn't go back.

JIM: You mean you dropped out?

LAURA: I made bad grades in my final examinations. [*She rises and replaces the book and the program on the table. Her voice is strained.*] How is—Emily Meisenbach getting along?

JIM: Oh, that kraut-head!

LAURA: Why do you call her that?

JIM: That's what she was.

LAURA: You're not still—going with her?

JIM: I never see her.

LAURA: It said in the "Personal" section that you were—engaged!

JIM: I know, but I wasn't impressed by that—propaganda!

LAURA: It wasn't—the truth?

JIM: Only in Emily's optimistic opinion!

LAURA: Oh—

[*Legend*: "What have you done since high school?"]

[*Jim lights a cigarette and leans indolently back on his elbows smiling at Laura with a warmth and charm which lights her inwardly with altar candles. She remains by the table, picks up a piece from the glass menagerie collection, and turns it in her hands to cover her tumult.*]

JIM [*after several reflective puffs on his cigarette*]: What have you done since high school?

[*She seems not to hear him.*]

Huh?

[*Laura looks up.*]

I said what have you done since high school, Laura?

LAURA: Nothing much.

JIM: You must have been doing something these six long years.

LAURA: Yes.

JIM: Well, then, such as what?

LAURA: I took a business course at business college—

JIM: How did that work out?

LAURA: Well, not very—well—I had to drop out, it gave me—indigestion—

[*Jim laughs gently.*]

JIM: What are you doing now?

LAURA: I don't do anything—much. Oh, please don't think I sit around doing nothing! My glass collection takes up a good deal of time. Glass is something you have to take good care of.

JIM: What did you say—about glass?

LAURA: Collection I said—I have one— [*She clears her throat and turns away again, acutely shy.*]

JIM [*abruptly*]: You know what I judge to be the trouble with you? Inferiority complex! Know what that is? That's what they call it when someone low-rates himself! I understand it because I had it, too. Although my case was not so aggravated as yours seems to be. I had it until I took up public speaking, developed my voice, and learned that I had an aptitude for science. Before that time I never thought of myself as being outstanding in any way whatsoever! Now I've never made a regular study of it, but I have a friend who says I can analyze people better than doctors that make a profession of it. I don't claim that to be necessarily true, but I can sure guess a person's psychology, Laura! [*He takes out his gum.*] Excuse me, Laura. I always take it out when the flavor is gone. I'll use this scrap of paper to wrap it in. I know how it is to get it stuck on a shoe. [*He wraps the gum in paper and puts it in his pocket.*] Yep—that's what I judge to be your principal trouble. A lack of confidence in yourself as a person. You don't have the proper amount of faith in yourself. I'm basing that fact on a number of your remarks and also on certain observations I've made. For instance that clumping you thought was so awful in high school. You say that you even dreaded to walk into class. You see what you did? You dropped out of school, you gave up an education because of a clump, which as far as I know was practically non-existent! A little physical defect is what you have. Hardly noticeable even! Magnified thousands of times by imagination! You know what my strong advice to you is? Think of yourself as *superior* in some way!

LAURA: In what way would I think?

JIM: Why, man alive, Laura! Just look about you a little. What do you see? A world full of common people! All of 'em born and all of 'em going to die! Which of them has one-tenth of your good points! Or mine! Or anyone else's, as far as that goes—gosh! Everybody excels in some one thing. Some in many! [*He unconsciously glances at himself in the mirror.*] All you've got to do is discover in *what!* Take me, for instance. [*He adjusts his tie at the mirror.*] My interest happens to lie in electro-dynamics. I'm taking a course in radio engineering at night school, Laura, on top of a fairly responsible job at the warehouse. I'm taking that course and studying public speaking.

LAURA: Ohhhh.

JIM: Because I believe in the future of television! [*turning his back to her.*] I wish to be ready to go up right along with it. Therefore I'm planning to get in on the ground floor. In fact I've already made the right connections and all that remains is for the industry itself to get under way! Full steam —[*His eyes are starry.*] *Knowledge*—Zzzzzp! *Money*—Zzzzzzp!—*Power!* That's the cycle democracy is built on!

[*His attitude is convincingly dynamic. Laura stares at him, even her shyness eclipsed in her absolute wonder. He suddenly grins.*]

I guess you think I think a lot of myself!

LAURA: No—o-o-o, I—

JIM: Now how about you? Isn't there something you take more interest in than anything else?

LAURA: Well, I do—as I said—have my—glass collection—

[*A peal of girlish laughter rings from the kitchenette.*]

JIM: I'm not right sure I know what you're talking about. What kind of glass is it?

LAURA: Little articles of it, they're ornaments mostly! Most of them are little animals made out of glass, the tiniest little animals in the world. Mother calls them a glass menagerie! Here's an example of one, if you'd like to see it! This one is one of the oldest. It's nearly thirteen.

[*Music*: "The Glass Menagerie."]

[*He stretches out his hand.*]

Oh, be careful—if you breathe, it breaks!

JIM: I'd better not take it. I'm pretty clumsy with things.

LAURA: Go on, I trust you with him! [*She places the piece in his palm.*] There now—you're holding him gently! Hold him over the light, he loves the light! You see how the light shines through him?

JIM: It sure does shine!

LAURA: I shouldn't be partial, but he is my favorite one.

JIM: What kind of a thing is this one supposed to be?

LAURA: Haven't you noticed the single horn on his forehead?

JIM: A unicorn, huh?

LAURA: Mmmm-hmmm!

JIM: Unicorns—aren't they extinct in the modern world?

LAURA: I know!

JIM: Poor little fellow, he must feel sort of lonesome.

LAURA [*smiling*]: Well, if he does, he doesn't complain about it. He stays on a shelf with some horses that don't have horns and all of them seem to get along nicely together.

JIM: How do you know?

LAURA [*lightly*]: I haven't heard any arguments among them!

JIM [*grinning*]: No arguments, huh? Well, that's a pretty good sign! Where shall I set him?

LAURA: Put him on the table. They all like a change of scenery once in a while!

JIM: Well, well, well, well—[*He places the glass piece on the table, then raises his arms and stretches.*] Look how big my shadow is when I stretch!

LAURA: Oh, oh, yes—it stretches across the ceiling!

JIM [*crossing to the door*]: I think it's stopped raining. [*He opens the fire-escape door and the background music changes to a dance tune.*] Where does the music come from?

LAURA: From the Paradise Dance Hall across the alley.

JIM: How about cutting the rug a little, Miss Wingfield?

LAURA: Oh, I—

JIM: Or is your program filled up? Let me have a look at it. [*He grasps an imaginary card.*] Why, every dance is taken! I'll just have to scratch some out.

[*Waltz music*: "La Golondrina."]

Ahhh, a waltz! [*He executes some sweeping turns by himself, then holds his arms toward Laura.*]

LAURA [*breathlessly*]: I—can't dance!

JIM: There you go, that inferiority stuff!

LAURA: I've never danced in my life!

JIM: Come on, try!

LAURA: Oh, but I'd step on you!

JIM: I'm not made out of glass.

LAURA: How—how—how do we start?

JIM: Just leave it to me. You hold your arms out a little.

LAURA: Like this?

JIM [*taking her in his arms*]: A little bit higher. Right. Now don't tighten up, that's the main thing about it—relax.

LAURA [*laughing breathlessly*]: It's hard not to.

JIM: Okay.

LAURA: I'm afraid you can't budge me.

JIM: What do you bet I can't? [*He swings her into motion.*]

LAURA: Goodness, yes, you can!

JIM: Let yourself go, now, Laura, just let yourself go.

LAURA: I'm—

JIM: Come on!

LAURA:—trying!

JIM: Not so stiff—easy does it!

LAURA: I know but I'm—

JIM: Loosen th' backbone! There now, that's a lot better.

LAURA: Am I?

JIM: Lots, lots better! [*He moves her about the room in a clumsy waltz.*]

LAURA: Oh, my!

JIM: Ha-ha!

LAURA: Oh, my goodness!

JIM: Ha-ha-ha!

[*They suddenly bump into the table, and the glass piece on it falls to the floor. Jim stops the dance.*]

What did we hit on?

LAURA: Table.

JIM: Did something fall off it? I think—

LAURA: Yes.

JIM: I hope that it wasn't the little glass horse with the horn!

LAURA: Yes. [*She stoops to pick it up.*]

JIM: Aw, aw, aw. Is it broken?

LAURA: Now it is just like all the other horses.

JIM: It's lost its—

LAURA: Horn! It doesn't matter. Maybe it's a blessing in disguise.

JIM: You'll never forgive me. I bet that that was your favorite piece of glass.

LAURA: I don't have favorites much. It's no tragedy, Freckles. Glass breaks so easily. No matter how careful you are. The traffic jars the shelves and things fall off them.

JIM: Still I'm awfully sorry that I was the cause.

LAURA [*smiling*]: I'll just imagine he had an operation. The horn was removed to make him feel less—freakish!

[*They both laugh.*]

Now he will feel more at home with the other horses, the ones that don't have horns. . . .

JIM: Ha-ha, that's very funny! [*Suddenly he is serious.*] I'm glad to see that you have a sense of humor. You know

—you're—well—very different! Surprisingly different from anyone else I know! [*His voice becomes soft and hesitant with a genuine feeling.*] Do you mind me telling you that?

[*Laura is abashed beyond speech.*]

I mean it in a nice way—

[*Laura nods shyly, looking away.*]

You make me feel sort of—I don't know how to put it! I'm usually pretty good at expressing things, but—this is something that I don't know how to say!

[*Laura touches her throat and clears it—turns the broken unicorn in her hands. His voice becomes softer.*]

Has anyone ever told you that you were pretty?

[*There is a pause, and the music rises slightly. Laura looks up slowly, with wonder, and shakes her head.*]

Well, you are! In a very different way from anyone else. And all the nicer because of the difference, too.

[*His voice becomes low and husky. Laura turns away, nearly faint with the novelty of her emotions.*]

I wish that you were my sister. I'd teach you to have some confidence in yourself. The different people are not like other people, but being different is nothing to be ashamed of. Because other people are not such wonderful people. They're one hundred times one thousand. You're one times one! They walk all over the earth. You just stay here. They're common as—weeds, but—you—well, you're—*Blue Roses!*

[*Image on screen*: Blue Roses.]

[*The music changes.*]

LAURA: But blue is wrong for—roses. . . .

JIM: It's right for you! You're—pretty!

LAURA: In what respect am I pretty?

JIM: In all respects—believe me! Your eyes—your hair—are pretty! Your hands are pretty! [*He catches hold of her hand.*] You think I'm making this up because I'm invited to dinner and have to be nice. Oh, I could do that! I could put on an act for you, Laura, and say lots of things without being very sincere. But this time I am. I'm talking to you sincerely. I happened to notice you had this inferiority complex that keeps you from feeling comfortable with people. Somebody needs to build your confidence up and make you proud instead of shy and turning away and—blushing. Somebody—ought to—*kiss* you, Laura!

[*His hand slips slowly up her arm to her shoulder as the music swells tumultuously. He suddenly turns her about and kisses her on the lips. When he releases her, Laura sinks on the sofa with a bright, dazed look. Jim backs away and fishes in his pocket for a cigarette.*]

[*Legend on screen*: "A souvenir."]

Stumblejohn!

[*He lights the cigarette, avoiding her look. There is a peal of girlish laughter from Amanda in the kitchenette. Laura slowly raises and opens her hand. It still contains the little broken glass animal. She looks at it with a tender, bewildered expression.*]

Stumblejohn! I shouldn't have done that—that was way off the beam. You don't smoke, do you?

[*She looks up, smiling, not hearing the question. He sits beside her rather gingerly. She looks at him speechlessly—*

waiting. He coughs decorously and moves a little farther aside as he considers the situation and senses her feelings, dimly, with perturbation. He speaks gently.]

Would you—care for a—mint?

[*She doesn't seem to hear him but her look grows brighter even.*]

Peppermint? Life Saver? My pocket's a regular drugstore—wherever I go . . . . [*He pops a mint in his mouth. Then he gulps and decides to make a clean breast of it. He speaks slowly and gingerly.*] Laura, you know, if I had a sister like you, I'd do the same thing as Tom. I'd bring out fellows and—introduce her to them. The right type of boys—of a type to—appreciate her. Only—well—he made a mistake about me. Maybe I've got no call to be saying this. That may not have been the idea in having me over. But what if it was? There's nothing wrong about that. The only trouble is that in my case—I'm not in a situation to—do the right thing. I can't take down your number and say I'll phone. I can't call up next week and—ask for a date. I thought I had better explain the situation in case you—misunderstood it and—I hurt your feelings. . . .

[*There is a pause. Slowly, very slowly, Laura's look changes, her eyes returning slowly from his to the glass figure in her palm. Amanda utters another gay laugh in the kitchenette.*]

LAURA [*faintly*]: You—won't—call again?

JIM: No, Laura, I can't. [*He rises from the sofa.*] As I was just explaining, I've—got strings on me. Laura, I've—been going steady! I go out all the time with a girl named Betty. She's a home-girl like you, and Catholic, and Irish, and in a great many ways we—get along fine. I met her last summer on a moonlight boat trip up the river to Alton, on the *Majestic.* Well—right away from the start it was—love!

[*Legend*: Love!]

[*Laura sways slightly forward and grips the arm of the sofa. He fails to notice, now enrapt in his own comfortable being.*]

Being in love has made a new man of me!

[*Leaning stiffly forward, clutching the arm of the sofa, Laura struggles visibly with her storm. But Jim is oblivious; she is a long way off.*]

The power of love is really pretty tremendous! Love is something that—changes the whole world, Laura!

[*The storm abates a little and Laura leans back. He notices her again.*]

It happened that Betty's aunt took sick, she got a wire and had to go to Centralia. So Tom—when he asked me to dinner—I naturally just accepted the invitation, not knowing that you—that he—that I— [*He stops awkwardly.*] Huh—I'm a stumblejohn!

[*He flops back on the sofa. The holy candles on the altar of Laura's face have been snuffed out. There is a look of almost infinite desolation. Jim glances at her uneasily.*]

I wish that you would—say something.

[*She bites her lip which was trembling and then bravely smiles. She opens her hand again on the broken glass figure. Then she gently takes his hand and raises it level with her own. She carefully places the unicorn in the palm of his hand, then pushes his fingers closed upon it.*]

What are you—doing that for? You want me to have him? Laura?

[*She nods.*]

What for?

LAURA: A—souvenir . . . .

[*She rises unsteadily and crouches beside the Victrola to wind it up.*]

[*Legend on screen*: "Things have a way of turning out so badly!" *Or image*: "Gentleman caller waving goodbye—gaily."]

[*At this moment Amanda rushes brightly back into the living room. She bears a pitcher of fruit punch in an old-fashioned cut-glass pitcher, and a plate of macaroons. The plate has a gold border and poppies painted on it.*]

AMANDA: Well, well, well! Isn't the air delightful after the shower? I've made you children a little liquid refreshment.

[*She turns gaily to Jim.*] Jim, do you know that song about lemonade?

"Lemonade, lemonade
Made in the shade and stirred with a spade—
Good enough for any old maid!"

JIM [*uneasily*]: Ha-ha! No—I never heard it.

AMANDA: Why, Laura! You look so serious!

JIM: We were having a serious conversation.

AMANDA: Good! Now you're better acquainted!

JIM [*uncertainly*]: Ha-ha! Yes.

AMANDA: You modern young people are much more serious-minded than my generation. I was so gay as a girl!

JIM: You haven't changed, Mrs. Wingfield.

AMANDA: Tonight I'm rejuvenated! The gaiety of the occasion, Mr. O'Connor! [*She tosses her head with a peal of laughter, spilling some lemonade.*] Oooo! I'm baptizing myself!

JIM: Here—let me—

AMANDA [*setting the pitcher down*]: There now. I discovered we had some maraschino cherries. I dumped them in, juice and all!

JIM: You shouldn't have gone to that trouble, Mrs. Wingfield.

AMANDA: Trouble, trouble? Why, it was loads of fun! Didn't you hear me cutting up in the kitchen? I bet your ears were burning! I told Tom how outdone with him I was for keeping you to himself so long a time! He should have brought you over much, much sooner! Well, now that you've found your way, I want you to be a very frequent caller! Not just occasional but all the time. Oh, we're going to have a lot of gay times together! I see them coming! Mmm, just breathe that air! So fresh, and the moon's so pretty! I'll skip back out—I know where my place is when young folks are having a—serious conversation!

JIM: Oh, don't go out, Mrs. Wingfield. The fact of the matter is I've got to be going.

AMANDA: Going, now? You're joking! Why, it's only the shank of the evening, Mr. O'Connor!

JIM: Well, you know how it is.

AMANDA: You mean you're a young workingman and have to keep workingmen's hours. We'll let you off early tonight. But only on the condition that next time you stay later. What's the best night for you? Isn't Saturday night the best night for you workingmen?

JIM: I have a couple of time-clocks to punch, Mrs. Wingfield. One at morning, another one at night!

AMANDA: My, but you *are* ambitious! You work at night, too?

JIM: No, Ma'am, not work but—Betty!

[*He crosses deliberately to pick up his hat. The band at the Paradise Dance Hall goes into a tender waltz.*]

AMANDA: Betty? Betty? Who's—Betty!

[*There is an ominous cracking sound in the sky.*]

JIM: Oh, just a girl. The girl I go steady with!

[*He smiles charmingly. The sky falls.*]

[*Legend*: "The Sky Falls."]

AMANDA [*a long-drawn exhalation*]: Ohhhh . . . Is it a serious romance, Mr. O'Connor?

JIM: We're going to be married the second Sunday in June.

AMANDA: Ohhhh—how nice! Tom didn't mention that you were engaged to be married.

JIM: The cat's not out of the bag at the warehouse yet. You know how they are. They call you Romeo and stuff like that. [*He stops at the oval mirror to put on his hat. He carefully shapes the brim and the crown to give a discreetly dashing effect.*] It's been a wonderful evening, Mrs. Wingfield. I guess this is what they mean by Southern hospitality.

AMANDA: It really wasn't anything at all.

JIM: I hope it don't seem like I'm rushing off. But I promised Betty I'd pick her up at the Wabash depot, an' by the time I get my jalopy down there her train'll be in. Some women are pretty upset if you keep 'em waiting.

AMANDA: Yes, I know—the tyranny of women! [*She extends her hand.*] Goodbye, Mr. O'Connor. I wish you luck—and happiness—and success! All three of them, and so does Laura! Don't you, Laura?

LAURA: Yes!

JIM [*taking Laura's hand*]: Goodbye, Laura. I'm certainly going to treasure that souvenir. And don't you forget the good advice I gave you. [*He raises his voice to a cheery shout.*] So long, Shakespeare! Thanks again, ladies. Good night!

[*He grins and ducks jauntily out. Still bravely grimacing, Amanda closes the door on the gentleman caller. Then she turns back to the room with a puzzled expression. She and Laura don't dare to face each other. Laura crouches beside the Victrola to wind it.*]

AMANDA [*faintly*]: Things have a way of turning out so badly. I don't believe that I would play the Victrola. Well, well—well! Our gentleman caller was engaged to be married! [*She raises her voice.*] Tom!

TOM [*from the kitchenette*]: Yes, Mother?

AMANDA: Come in here a minute. I want to tell you something awfully funny.

TOM [*entering with a macaroon and a glass of the lemonade*]: Has the gentleman caller gotten away already?

AMANDA: The gentleman caller has made an early departure. What a wonderful joke you played on us!

TOM: How do you mean?

AMANDA: You didn't mention that he was engaged to be married.

TOM: Jim? Engaged?

AMANDA: That's what he just informed us.

TOM: I'll be jiggered! I didn't know about that.

AMANDA: That seems very peculiar.

TOM: What's peculiar about it?

AMANDA: Didn't you call him your best friend down at the warehouse?

TOM: He is, but how did I know?

AMANDA: It seems extremely peculiar that you wouldn't know your best friend was going to be married!

TOM: The warehouse is where I work, not where I know things about people!

AMANDA: You don't know things anywhere! You live in a dream; you manufacture illusions!

[*He crosses to the door.*]

Where are you going?

TOM: I'm going to the movies.

AMANDA: That's right, now that you've had us make such fools of ourselves. The effort, the preparations, all the expense! The new floor lamp, the rug, the clothes for Laura! All for what? To entertain some other girl's fiancé! Go to the movies, go! Don't think about us, a mother deserted, an unmarried sister who's crippled and has no job! Don't let anything interfere with your selfish pleasure! Just go, go, go—to the movies!

TOM: All right, I will! The more you shout about my selfishness to me the quicker I'll go, and I won't go to the movies!

AMANDA: Go, then! Go to the moon—you selfish dreamer!

[*Tom smashes his glass on the floor. He plunges out on the fire escape, slamming the door. Laura screams in fright. The dance-hall music becomes louder. Tom stands on the fire escape, gripping the rail. The moon breaks through the storm clouds, illuminating his face.*]

[*Legend on screen*: "And so goodbye . . ."]

[*Tom's closing speech is timed with what is happening inside the house. We see, as though through soundproof glass, that Amanda appears to be making a comforting speech to Laura, who is huddled upon the sofa. Now that we cannot hear the mother's speech, her silliness is gone and she has dignity and tragic beauty. Laura's hair hides her face until, at the end of the speech, she lifts her head to smile at her mother. Amanda's gestures are slow and graceful, almost dancelike, as she comforts her daughter. At the end of her speech she glances a moment at the father's picture—then withdraws through the portieres. At the close of Tom's speech, Laura blows out the candles, ending the play.*]

TOM: I didn't go to the moon, I went much further—for time is the longest distance between two places. Not long after that I was fired for writing a poem on the lid of a shoe-box. I left Saint Louis. I descended the steps of this fire escape for a last time and followed, from then on, in my father's footsteps, attempting to find in motion what was lost in space. I traveled around a great deal. The cities swept about me like dead leaves, leaves that were brightly colored but torn away from the branches. I would have stopped, but I was pursued by something. It always came upon me unawares, taking me altogether by surprise. Perhaps it was a familiar bit of music. Perhaps it was only a piece of transparent glass. Perhaps I am walking along a street at night, in some strange city, before I have found companions. I pass the lighted window of a shop where perfume is sold. The window is filled with pieces of colored glass, tiny transparent bottles in delicate colors, like bits of a shattered rainbow. Then all at once my sister touches my shoulder. I turn around and look into her eyes. Oh, Laura, Laura, I tried to leave you behind me, but I am more faithful than I intended to be! I reach for a cigarette, I cross the street, I run into the movies or a bar, I buy a drink, I speak to the nearest stranger—anything that can blow your candles out!

[*Laura bends over the candles.*]

For nowadays the world is lit by lightning! Blow out your candles, Laura—and so goodbye. . . .

[*She blows the candles out.*]

A STREETCAR NAMED DESIRE

And so it was I entered the broken world
To trace the visionary company of love, its voice
An instant in the wind (I know not whither hurled)
But not for long to hold each desperate choice.

"*The Broken Tower*" *by* HART CRANE

A Streetcar Named Desire was presented at the Barrymore Theatre in New York on December 3, 1947, by Irene Selznick. It was directed by Elia Kazan,with the following cast:

Negro Woman	Gee Gee James
Eunice Hubbell	Peg Hillias
Stanley Kowalski	Marlon Brando
Stella Kowalski	Kim Hunter
Steve Hubbell	Rudy Bond
Harold Mitchell (Mitch)	Karl Malden
Mexican Woman	Edna Thomas
Blanche DuBois	Jessica Tandy
Pablo Gonzales	Nick Dennis
A Young Collector	Vito Christi
Nurse	Ann Dere
Doctor	Richard Garrick

Scenery and lighting by Jo Meilziner, costumes by Lucinda Ballard. The action of the play takes place in the spring, summer, and early fall in New Orleans. It was performed with intermissions after Scene Four and Scene Six.

Assistant to the producer	Irving Schneider
Musical Advisor	Lehman Engel

THE CHARACTERS

BLANCHE

STELLA

STANLEY

MITCH

EUNICE

STEVE

PABLO

A NEGRO WOMAN

A DOCTOR

A NURSE

A YOUNG COLLECTOR

A MEXICAN WOMAN

SCENE ONE

The exterior of a two-story corner building on a street in New Orleans which is named Elysian Fields and runs between the L&N tracks and the river. The section is poor but, unlike corresponding sections in other American cities, it has a raffish charm. The houses are mostly white frame, weathered grey, with rickety outside stairs and galleries and quaintly ornamented gables. This building contains two flats, upstairs and down. Faded white stairs ascend to the entrances of both.

It is first dark of an evening early in May. The sky that shows around the dim white building is a peculiarly tender blue, almost a turquoise, which invests the scene with a kind of lyricism and gracefully attenuates the atmosphere of decay. You can almost feel the warm breath of the brown river beyond the river warehouses with their faint redolences of bananas and coffee. A corresponding air is evoked by the music of Negro entertainers at a barroom around the corner. In this part of New Orleans you are practically always just around the corner, or a few doors down the street, from a tinny piano being played with the infatuated fluency of brown fingers. This "blue piano" expresses the spirit of the life which goes on here.

Two women, one white and one colored, are taking the air on the steps of the building. The white woman is Eunice, who occupies the upstairs flat; the colored woman a neighbor, for New Orleans is a cosmopolitan city where there is a relatively warm and easy intermingling of races in the old part of town.

Above the music of the "blue piano" the voices of people on the street can be heard overlapping.

[Two men come around the corner, Stanley Kowalski and Mitch. They are about twenty-eight or thirty years old, roughly dressed in blue denim work clothes. Stanley carries his bowling jacket and a red-stained package from a butcher's. They stop at the foot of the steps.]

STANLEY *[bellowing]*:
Hey, there! Stella, baby!

[Stella comes out on the first floor landing, a gentle young woman, about twenty-five, and of a background obviously quite different from her husband's.]

STELLA *[mildly]*:
Don't holler at me like that. Hi, Mitch.

STANLEY:
Catch!

STELLA:
What?

STANLEY:
Meat!

[He heaves the package at her. She cries out in protest but manages to catch it: then she laughs breathlessly. Her husband and his companion have already started back around the corner.]

STELLA *[calling after him]*:
Stanley! Where are you going?

STANLEY:
Bowling!

STELLA:
Can I come watch?

STANLEY:

Come on. [*He goes out.*]

STELLA:

Be over soon. [*to the white woman*] Hello, Eunice. How are you?

EUNICE:

I'm all right. Tell Steve to get him a poor boy's sandwich 'cause nothing's left here.

[*They all laugh; the colored woman does not stop. Stella goes out.*]

COLORED WOMAN:

What was that package he th'ew at 'er? [*She rises from steps, laughing louder.*]

EUNICE:

You hush, now!

NEGRO WOMAN:

Catch *what!*

[*She continues to laugh. Blanche comes around the corner, carrying a valise. She looks at a slip of paper, then at the building, then again at the slip and again at the building. Her expression is one of shocked disbelief. Her appearace is incongruous to this setting. She is daintily dressed in a white suit with a fluffy bodice, necklace and earrings of pearl, white gloves and hat, looking as if she were arriving at a summer tea or cocktail party in the garden district. She is about five years older than Stella. Her delicate beauty must avoid a strong light. There is something about her uncertain manner, as well as her white clothes, that suggests a moth.*]

EUNICE [*finally*]:

What's the matter, honey? Are you lost?

BLANCHE [*with faintly hysterical humor*]:

They told me to take a street-car named Desire, and then transfer to one called Cemeteries and ride six blocks and get off at—Elysian Fields!

EUNICE:

That's where you are now.

BLANCHE:

At Elysian Fields?

EUNICE:

This here is Elysian Fields.

BLANCHE:

They mustn't have—understood—what number I wanted . . .

EUNICE:

What number you lookin' for?

[*Blanche wearily refers to the slip of paper.*]

BLANCHE:

Six thirty-two.

EUNICE:

You don't have to look no further.

BLANCHE [*uncomprehendingly*]:

I'm looking for my sister, Stella DuBois. I mean—Mrs. Stanley Kowalski.

EUNICE:

That's the party.—You just did miss her, though.

BLANCHE:

This—can this be—her home?

EUNICE:
She's got the downstairs here and I got the up.

BLANCHE:
Oh. She's—out?

EUNICE:
You noticed that bowling alley around the corner?

BLANCHE:
I'm—not sure I did.

EUNICE:
Well, that's where she's at, watchin' her husband bowl. [*There is a pause*] You want to leave your suitcase here an' go find her?

BLANCHE:
No.

NEGRO WOMAN:
I'll go tell her you come.

BLANCHE:
Thanks.

NEGRO WOMAN:
You welcome. [*She goes out.*]

EUNICE:
She wasn't expecting you?

BLANCHE:
No. No, not tonight.

EUNICE:
Well, why don't you just go in and make yourself at home till they get back.

BLANCHE:
How could I—do that?

EUNICE:
We own this place so I can let you in.

[*She gets up and opens the downstairs door. A light goes on behind the blind, turning it light blue. Blanche slowly follows her into the downstairs flat. The surrounding areas dim out as the interior is lighted.*]

[*Two rooms can be seen, not too clearly defined. The one first entered is primarily a kitchen but contains a folding bed to be used by Blanche. The room beyond this is a bedroom. Off this room is a narrow door to a bathroom.*]

EUNICE [*defensively, noticing Blanche's look*]:
It's sort of messed up right now but when it's clean it's real sweet.

BLANCHE:
Is it?

EUNICE:
Uh-huh, I think so. So you're Stella's sister?

BLANCHE:
Yes. [*wanting to get rid of her*] Thanks for letting me in.

EUNICE:
Por nada, as the Mexicans say, *por nada!* Stella spoke of you.

BLANCHE:
Yes?

EUNICE:

I think she said you taught school.

BLANCHE:

Yes.

EUNICE:

And you're from Mississippi, huh?

BLANCHE:

Yes.

EUNICE:

She showed me a picture of your home-place, the plantation.

BLANCHE:

Belle Reve?

EUNICE:

A great big place with white columns.

BLANCHE:

Yes...

EUNICE:

A place like that must be awful hard to keep up.

BLANCHE:

If you will excuse me, I'm just about to drop.

EUNICE:

Sure, honey. Why don't you set down?

BLANCHE:

What I meant was I'd like to be left alone.

EUNICE [*offended*]:

Aw. I'll make myself scarce, in that case.

BLANCHE:

I didn't mean to be rude, but—

EUNICE:

I'll drop by the bowling alley an' hustle her up. [*She goes out the door.*]

[*Blanche sits in a chair very stiffly with her shoulders slightly hunched and her legs pressed close together and her hands tightly clutching her purse as if she were quite cold. After a while the blind look goes out of her eyes and she begins to look slowly around. A cat screeches. She catches her breath with a startled gesture. Suddenly she notices something in a half opened closet. She springs up and crosses to it, and removes a whiskey bottle. She pours a half tumbler of whiskey and tosses it down. She carefully replaces the bottle and washes out the tumbler at the sink. Then she resumes her seat in front of the table.*]

BLANCHE [*faintly to herself*]:

I've got to keep hold of myself!

[*Stella comes quickly around the corner of the building and runs to the door of the downstairs flat.*]

STELLA [*calling out joyfully*]:

Blanche!

[*For a moment they stare at each other. Then Blanche springs up and runs to her with a wild cry.*]

BLANCHE:

Stella, oh, Stella, Stella! Stella for Star!

[*She begins to speak with feverish vivacity as if she feared for either of them to stop and think. They catch each other in a spasmodic embrace.*]

BLANCHE:

Now, then, let me look at you. But don't you look at me, Stella, no, no, no, not till later, not till I've bathed and rested! And turn that over-light off! Turn that off! I won't be looked at in this merciless glare! [*Stella laughs and complies*] Come back here now! Oh, my baby! Stella! Stella for Star! [*She embraces her again*] I thought you would never come back to this horrible place! What am I saying? I didn't mean to say that. I meant to be nice about it and say—Oh, what a convenient location and such—Ha-a-ha! Precious lamb! You haven't said a *word* to me.

STELLA:

You haven't given me a chance to, honey! [*She laughs, but her glance at Blanche is a little anxious.*]

BLANCHE:

Well, now you talk. Open your pretty mouth and talk while I look around for some liquor! I know you must have some liquor on the place! Where could it be, I wonder? Oh, I spy, I spy!

[*She rushes to the closet and removes the bottle; she is shaking all over and panting for breath as she tries to laugh. The bottle nearly slips from her grasp.*]

STELLA [*noticing*]:

Blanche, you sit down and let me pour the drinks. I don't know what we've got to mix with. Maybe a coke's in the icebox. Look'n see, honey, while I'm—

BLANCHE:

No coke, honey, not with my nerves tonight! Where—where—where is—?

STELLA:

Stanley? Bowling! He loves it. They're having a—found some soda!—tournament...

BLANCHE:

Just water, baby, to chase it! Now don't get worried, your sister hasn't turned into a drunkard, she's just all shaken up and hot and tired and dirty! You sit down, now, and explain this place to me! What are you doing in a place like this?

STELLA:

Now, Blanche—

BLANCHE:

Oh, I'm not going to be hypocritical, I'm going to be honestly critical about it! Never, never, never in my worst dreams could I picture— Only Poe! Only Mr. Edgar Allan Poe!—could do it justice! Out there I suppose is the ghoul-haunted woodland of Weir! [*She laughs.*]

STELLA:

No, honey, those are the L & N tracks.

BLANCHE:

No, now seriously, putting joking aside. Why didn't you tell me, why didn't you write me, honey, why didn't you let me know?

STELLA [*carefully, pouring herself a drink*]:

Tell you what, Blanche?

BLANCHE:

Why, that you had to live in these conditions!

STELLA:

Aren't you being a little intense about it? It's not that bad at all! New Orleans isn't like other cities.

BLANCHE:

This has got nothing to do with New Orleans. You might as well say—forgive me, blessed baby! [*She suddenly stops short*] The subject is closed!

STELLA [*a little drily*]:

Thanks.

[*During the pause, Blanche stares at her. She smiles at Blanche.*]

BLANCHE [*looking down at her glass, which shakes in her hand*]:

You're all I've got in the world, and you're not glad to see me!

STELLA [*sincerely*]:

Why, Blanche, you know that's not true.

BLANCHE:

No?—I'd forgotten how quiet you were.

STELLA:

You never did give me a chance to say much, Blanche. So I just got in the habit of being quiet around you.

BLANCHE [*vaguely*]:

A good habit to get into... [*then, abruptly*] You haven't asked me how I happened to get away from the school before the spring term ended.

STELLA:

Well, I thought you'd volunteer that information—if you wanted to tell me.

BLANCHE:

You thought I'd been fired?

STELLA:

No, I—thought you might have—resigned...

BLANCHE:

I was so exhausted by all I'd been through my—nerves broke. [*nervously tamping cigarette*] I was on the verge of—lunacy, almost! So Mr. Graves—Mr. Graves is the high school superintendent—he suggested I take a leave of absence. I couldn't put all of those details into the wire... [*She drinks quickly*] Oh, this buzzes right through me and feels so *good!*

STELLA:

Won't you have another?

BLANCHE:

No, one's my limit.

STELLA:

Sure?

BLANCHE:

You haven't said a word about my appearance.

STELLA:

You look just fine.

BLANCHE:

God love you for a liar! Daylight never exposed so total a ruin! But you—you've put on some weight, yes, you're just as plump as a little partridge! And it's so becoming to you!

STELLA:

Now, Blanche—

BLANCHE:

Yes, it is, it is or I wouldn't say it! You just have to watch around the hips a little. Stand up.

STELLA:

Not now.

BLANCHE:

You hear me? I said stand up! [*Stella complies reluctantly*] You messy child, you, you've spilt something on that pretty white lace collar! About your hair—you ought to have it cut in a feather bob with your dainty features. Stella, you have a maid, don't you?

STELLA:

No. With only two rooms it's—

BLANCHE:

What? *Two* rooms, did you say?

STELLA:

This one and—[*She is embarrassed.*]

BLANCHE:

The other one? [*She laughs sharply. There is an embarrassed silence.*]

BLANCHE:

The other one? [*She laughs sharply. There is an embarrassed silence.*] I am going to take just one little tiny nip more, sort of to put the stopper on, so to speak.... Then put the bottle away so I won't be tempted. [*She rises*] I want you to look at *my* figure! [*She turns around*] You know I haven't put on one ounce in ten years, Stella? I weigh what I weighed the summer you left Belle Reve. The summer Dad died and you left us . . .

STELLA [*a little wearily*]:

It's just incredible, Blanche, how well you're looking.

BLANCHE [*They both laugh uncomfortably.*]:
But, Stella, there's only two rooms, I don't see where you're going to put me!

STELLA:
We're going to put you in here.

BLANCHE:
What kind of bed's this—one of those collapsible things? [*She sits on it.*]

STELLA:
Does it feel all right?

BLANCHE [*dubiously*]:
Wonderful, honey. I don't like a bed that gives much. But there's no door between the two rooms, and Stanley —will it be decent?

STELLA:
Stanley is Polish, you know.

BLANCHE:
Oh, yes. They're something like Irish, aren't they?

STELLA:
Well—

BLANCHE:
Only not so—highbrow? [*They both laugh again in the same way*] I brought some nice clothes to meet all your lovely friends in.

STELLA:
I'm afraid you won't think they are lovely.

BLANCHE:
What are they like?

STELLA:

They're Stanley's friends.

BLANCHE:

Polacks?

STELLA:

They're a mixed lot, Blanche.

BLANCHE:

Heterogeneous—types?

STELLA:

Oh, yes. Yes, types is right!

BLANCHE:

Well—anyhow—I brought nice clothes and I'll wear them. I guess you're hoping I'll say I'll put up at a hotel, but I'm not going to put up at a hotel. I want to be *near* you, got to be *with* somebody, I *can't* be *alone!* Because—as you must have noticed—I'm—*not* very *well* . . . [*Her voice drops and her look is frightened.*]

STELLA:

You seem a little bit nervous or overwrought or something.

BLANCHE:

Will Stanley like me, or will I be just a visiting in-law, Stella? I couldn't stand that.

STELLA:

You'll get along fine together, if you'll just try not to—well—compare him with men that we went out with at home.

BLANCHE:

Is he so—different?

STELLA:

Yes. A different species.

BLANCHE:

In what way; what's he like?

STELLA:

Oh, you can't describe someone you're in love with! Here's a picture of him! [*She hands a photograph to Blanche.*]

BLANCHE:

An officer?

STELLA:

A Master Sergeant in the Engineers' Corps. Those are decorations!

BLANCHE:

He had those on when you met him?

STELLA:

I assure you I wasn't just blinded by all the brass.

BLANCHE:

That's not what I—

STELLA:

But of course there were things to adjust myself to later on.

BLANCHE:

Such as his civilian background! [*Stella laughs uncertainly*] How did he take it when you said I was coming?

STELLA:

Oh, Stanley doesn't know yet.

BLANCHE [*frightened*]:
You—haven't told him?

STELLA:
He's on the road a good deal.

BLANCHE:
Oh. Travels?

STELLA:
Yes.

BLANCHE:
Good. I mean—isn't it?

STELLA [*half to herself*]:
I can hardly stand it when he is away for a night...

BLANCHE:
Why, Stella!

STELLA:
When he's away for a week I nearly go wild!

BLANCHE:
Gracious!

STELLA:
And when he comes back I cry on his lap like a baby... [*She smiles to herself.*]

BLANCHE:
I guess that is what is meant by being in love... [*Stella looks up with a radiant smile.*] Stella—

STELLA:
What?

BLANCHE [*in an uneasy rush*]:
I haven't asked you the things you probably thought I

was going to ask. And so I'll expect you to be understanding about what *I* have to tell *you.*

STELLA:

What, Blanche? [*Her face turns anxious.*]

BLANCHE:

Well, Stella—you're going to reproach me, I know that you're bound to reproach me—but before you do—take into consideration—you left! I stayed and struggled! You came to New Orleans and looked out for yourself! *I* stayed at *Belle Reve* and tried to hold it together! I'm not meaning this in any reproachful way, but *all* the burden descended on *my* shoulders.

STELLA:

The best I could do was make my own living, Blanche.

[*Blanche begins to shake again with intensity.*]

BLANCHE:

I know, I know. But you are the one that abandoned Belle Reve, not I! I stayed and fought for it, bled for it, almost died for it!

STELLA:

Stop this hysterical outburst and tell me what's happened? What do you mean fought and bled? What kind of—

BLANCHE:

I knew you would, Stella. I knew you would take this attitude about it!

STELLA:

About—what?—please!

BLANCHE [*slowly*]:

The loss—the loss . . .

STELLA:

Belle Reve? Lost, is it? No!

BLANCHE:

Yes, Stella.

[*They stare at each other across the yellow-checked linoleum of the table. Blanche slowly nods her head and Stella looks slowly down at her hands folded on the table. The music of the "blue piano" grows louder. Blanche touches her handkerchief to her forehead.*]

STELLA:

But how did it go? What happened?

BLANCHE [*springing up*]:

You're a fine one to ask me how it went!

STELLA:

Blanche!

BLANCHE:

You're a fine one to sit there *accusing me* of it!

STELLA:

Blanche!

BLANCHE:

I, I, *I* took the blows in my face and my body! All of those deaths! The long parade to the graveyard! Father, mother! Margaret, that dreadful way! So big with it, it couldn't be put in a coffin! But had to be burned like rubbish! You just came home in time for the funerals, Stella. And funerals are pretty compared to deaths. Funerals are quiet, but deaths—not always. Sometimes their breathing is hoarse, and sometimes it rattles, and sometimes they even cry out to you, "Don't let me go!"

Even the old, sometimes, say, "Don't let me go." As if you were able to stop them! But funerals are quiet, with pretty flowers. And, oh, what gorgeous boxes they pack them away in! Unless you were there at the bed when they cried out, "Hold me!" you'd never suspect there was the struggle for breath and bleeding. You didn't dream, but I saw! *Saw! Saw!* And now you sit there telling me with your eyes that I let the place go! How in hell do you think all that sickness and dying was paid for? Death is expensive, Miss Stella! And old Cousin Jessie's right after Margaret's, hers! Why, the Grim Reaper had put up his tent on our doorstep! . . . Stella. Belle Reve was his headquarters! Honey—that's how it slipped through my fingers! Which of them left us a fortune? Which of them left a cent of insurance even? Only poor Jessie—one hundred to pay for her coffin. That was all, Stella! And I with my pitiful salary at the school. Yes, accuse me! Sit there and stare at me, thinking I let the place go! *I* let the place go? Where were *you!* In bed with your—Polack!

STELLA [*springing*]:
Blanche! You be still! That's enough! [*She starts out.*]

BLANCHE:
Where are you going?

STELLA:
I'm going into the bathroom to wash my face.

BLANCHE:
Oh, Stella, Stella, you're crying!

STELLA:
Does that surprise you?

BLANCHE:

Forgive me—I didn't mean to—

[*The sound of men's voices is heard. Stella goes into the bathroom, closing the door behind her. When the men appear, and Blanche realizes it must be Stanley returning, she moves uncertainly from the bathroom door to the dressing table, looking apprehensively toward the front door. Stanley enters, followed by Steve and Mitch. Stanley pauses near his door, Steve by the foot of the spiral stair, and Mitch is slightly above and to the right of them, about to go out. As the men enter, we hear some of the following dialogue.*]

STANLEY:

Is that how he got it?

STEVE:

Sure that's how he got it. He hit the old weather-bird for 300 bucks on a six-number-ticket.

MITCH:

Don't tell him those things; he'll believe it.

[*Mitch starts out.*]

STANLEY [*restraining Mitch*]:

Hey, Mitch—come back here.

[*Blanche, at the sound of voices, retires in the bedroom. She picks up Stanley's photo from dressing table, looks at it, puts it down. When Stanley enters the apartment, she darts and hides behind the screen at the head of bed.*]

STEVE [*to Stanley and Mitch*]:

Hey, are we playin' poker tomorrow?

STANLEY:

Sure—at Mitch's.

MITCH [*hearing this, returns quickly to the stair rail*]:

No—not at my place. My mother's still sick!

STANLEY:

Okay, at my place . . . [*Mitch starts out again*] But you bring the beer!

[*Mitch pretends not to hear—calls out "Goodnight, all," and goes out, singing.*]

EUNICE [*heard from above*]:

Break it up down there! I made the spaghetti dish and ate it myself.

STEVE [*going upstairs*]:

I told you and phoned you we was playing. [*to the men*] Jax beer!

EUNICE:

You never phoned me once.

STEVE:

I told you at breakfast—and phoned you at lunch . . .

EUNICE:

Well, never mind about that. You just get yourself home here once in a while.

STEVE:

You want it in the papers?

[*More laughter and shouts of parting come from the men. Stanley throws the screen door of the kitchen open and comes in. He is of medium height, about five feet eight or nine, and strongly, compactly built. Animal joy in his being is implicit in all his movements and attitudes. Since earliest manhood the center of his life has been pleasure with women, the giving and taking of it, not with weak indulgence, dependently, but with the power and pride of a richly feathered male bird among hens. Branching out from this complete and satisfying center are all the auxiliary channels of his life, such as his heartiness with men, his appreciation of rough humor, his love of good drink and food and games, his car, his radio, everything that is his, that bears his emblem of the gaudy seed-bearer. He sizes women up at a glance, with sexual classifications, crude images flashing into his mind and determining the way he smiles at them.*]

BLANCHE [*drawing involuntarily back from his stare*]:
You must be Stanley. I'm Blanche.

STANLEY:
Stella's sister?

BLANCHE:
Yes.

STANLEY:
H'lo. Where's the little woman?

BLANCHE:
In the bathroom.

STANLEY:
Oh. Didn't know you were coming in town

BLANCHE:
I—uh—

STANLEY:
Where you from, Blanche?

BLANCHE:
Why, I—live in Laurel.

[*He has crossed to the closet and removed the whiskey bottle.*]

STANLEY:

In Laurel, huh? Oh, yeah. Yeah, in Laurel, that's right. Not in my territory. Liquor goes fast in hot weather.

[*He holds the bottle to the light to observe its depletion.*]

Have a shot?

BLANCHE:

No, I—rarely touch it.

STANLEY:

Some people rarely touch it, but it touches them often.

BLANCHE [*faintly*]:

Ha-ha.

STANLEY:

My clothes're stickin' to me. Do you mind if I make myself comfortable? [*He starts to remove his shirt.*]

BLANCHE:

Please, please do.

STANLEY:

Be comfortable is my motto.

BLANCHE:

It's mine, too. It's hard to stay looking fresh. I haven't washed or even powdered my face and—here you are!

STANLEY:

You know you can catch cold sitting around in damp things, especially when you been exercising hard like bowling is. You're a teacher, aren't you?

BLANCHE:

Yes.

STANLEY:

What do you teach, Blanche?

BLANCHE:

English.

STANLEY:

I never was a very good English student. How long you here for, Blanche?

BLANCHE:

I—don't know yet.

STANLEY:

You going to shack up here?

BLANCHE:

I thought I would if it's not inconvenient for you all.

STANLEY:

Good.

BLANCHE:

Traveling wears me out.

STANLEY:

Well, take it easy.

[*A cat screeches near the window. Blanche springs up.*]

BLANCHE:

What's that?

STANLEY:

Cats . . . Hey, Stella!

STELLA [*faintly, from the bathroom*]:

Yes, Stanley.

STANLEY:

Haven't fallen in, have you? [*He grins at Blanche. She tries unsuccessfully to smile back. There is a silence*] I'm afraid I'll strike you as being the unrefined type. Stella's spoke of you a good deal. You were married once, weren't you?

[*The music of the polka rises up, faint in the distance.*]

BLANCHE:

Yes. When I was quite young.

STANLEY:

What happened?

BLANCHE:

The boy—the boy died. [*She sinks back down*] I'm afraid I'm—going to be sick!

[*Her head falls on her arms.*]

SCENE TWO

It is six o'clock the following evening. Blanche is bathing. Stella is completing her toilette. Blanche's dress, a flowered print, is laid out on Stella's bed.

Stanley enters the kitchen from outside, leaving the door open on the perpetual "blue piano" around the corner.

STANLEY:

What's all this monkey doings?

STELLA:

Oh, Stan! [*She jumps up and kisses him, which he accepts with lordly composure*] I'm taking Blanche to Galatoire's for supper and then to a show, because it's your poker night.

STANLEY:

How about my supper, huh? I'm not going to no Galatoire's for supper!

STELLA:

I put you a cold plate on ice.

STANLEY:

Well, isn't that just dandy!

STELLA:

I'm going to try to keep Blanche out till the party breaks up because I don't know how she would take it. So we'll go to one of the little places in the Quarter afterward and you'd better give me some money.

STANLEY:

Where is she?

STELLA:

She's soaking in a hot tub to quiet her nerves. She's terribly upset.

STANLEY:

Over what?

STELLA:

She's been through such an ordeal.

STANLEY:

Yeah?

STELLA:

Stan, we've—lost Belle Reve!

STANLEY:

The place in the country?

STELLA:

Yes.

STANLEY:

How?

STELLA [*vaguely*]:

Oh, it had to be—sacrificed or something. [*There is a pause while Stanley considers. Stella is changing into her dress*] When she comes in be sure to say something nice about her appearance. And, oh! Don't mention the baby. I haven't said anything yet, I'm waiting until she gets in a quieter condition.

STANLEY [*ominously*]:

So?

STELLA:

And try to understand her and be nice to her, Stan.

BLANCHE [*singing in the bathroom*]:

"From the land of the sky blue water,
They brought a captive maid!"

STELLA:

She wasn't expecting to find us in such a small place. You see I'd tried to gloss things over a little in my letters.

STANLEY:

So?

STELLA:

And admire her dress and tell her she's looking wonderful. That's important with Blanche. Her little weakness!

STANLEY:

Yeah. I get the idea. Now let's skip back a little to where you said the country place was disposed of.

STELLA:

Oh!—yes...

STANLEY:

How about that? Let's have a few more details on that subjeck.

STELLA:

It's best not to talk much about it until she's calmed down.

STANLEY:

So that's the deal, huh? Sister Blanche cannot be annoyed with business details right now!

STELLA:

You saw how she was last night.

STANLEY:

Uh-hum, I saw how she was. Now let's have a gander at the bill of sale.

STELLA:

I haven't seen any.

STANLEY:

She didn't show you no papers, no deed of sale or nothing like that, huh?

STELLA:

It seems like it wasn't sold.

STANLEY:

Well, what in hell was it then, give away? To charity?

STELLA:

Shhh! She'll hear you.

STANLEY:

I don't care if she hears me. Let's see the papers!

STELLA:

There weren't any papers, she didn't show any papers, I don't care about papers.

STANLEY:

Have you ever heard of the Napoleonic code?

STELLA:

No, Stanley, I haven't heard of the Napoleonic code and if I have, I don't see what it—

STANLEY:

Let me enlighten you on a point or two, baby.

STELLA:

Yes?

STANLEY:

In the state of Louisiana we have the Napoleonic code according to which what belongs to the wife belongs to the husband and vice versa. For instance if I had a piece of property, or you had a piece of property—

STELLA:

My head is swimming!

STANLEY:

All right. I'll wait till she gets through soaking in a hot tub and then I'll inquire if *she* is acquainted with the Napoleonic code. It looks to me like you have been swindled, baby, and when you're swindled under the Napoleonic code I'm swindled *too*. And I don't like to be *swindled.*

STELLA:

There's plenty of time to ask her questions later but if you do now she'll go to pieces again. I don't understand what happened to Belle Reve but you don't know how ridiculous you are being when you suggest that my sister or I or anyone of our family could have perpetrated a swindle on anyone else.

STANLEY:

Then where's the money if the place was sold?

STELLA:

Not sold—*lost, lost!*

[*He stalks into bedroom, and she follows him.*]

Stanley!

[*He pulls open the wardrobe trunk standing in middle of room and jerks out an armful of dresses.*]

STANLEY:

Open your eyes to this stuff! You think she got them out of a teacher's pay?

STELLA:

Hush!

STANLEY:

Look at these feathers and furs that she come here to preen herself in! What's this here? A solid-gold dress, I believe! And this one! What is these here? Fox-pieces! [*He blows on them*] Genuine fox fur-pieces, a half a mile long! Where are your fox-pieces, Stella? Bushy snow-white ones, no less! Where are your white fox-pieces?

STELLA:

Those are inexpensive summer furs that Blanche has had a long time.

STANLEY:

I got an acquaintance who deals in this sort of merchandise. I'll have him in here to appraise it. I'm willing to bet you there's thousands of dollars invested in this stuff here!

STELLA:

Don't be such an idiot, Stanley!

[*He hurls the furs to the day bed. Then he jerks open small drawer in the trunk and pulls up a fistful of costume jewelry.*]

STANLEY:

And what have we here? The treasure chest of a pirate!

STELLA:

Oh, Stanley!

STANLEY:

Pearls! Ropes of them! What is this sister of yours, a deep-sea diver? Bracelets of solid gold, too! Where are your pearls and gold bracelets?

STELLA:

Shhh! Be still, Stanley!

STANLEY:

And diamonds! A crown for an empress!

STELLA:

A rhinestone tiara she wore to a costume ball.

STANLEY:

What's rhinestone?

STELLA:

Next door to glass.

STANLEY:

Are you kidding? I have an acquaintance that works in a jewelry store. I'll have him in here to make an appraisal of this. Here's your plantation, or what was left of it, here!

STELLA:

You have no idea how stupid and horrid you're being! Now close that trunk before she comes out of the bathroom!

[*He kicks the trunk partly closed and sits on the kitchen table.*]

STANLEY:

The Kowalskis and the DuBoises have different notions.

STELLA [*angrily*]:

Indeed they have, thank heavens!—*I'm* going outside.

[*She snatches up her white hat and gloves and crosses to the outside door*] You come out with me while Blanche is getting dressed.

STANLEY:

Since when do you give me orders?

STELLA:

Are you going to stay here and insult her?

STANLEY:

You're damn tootin' I'm going to stay here.

[*Stella goes out to the porch. Blanche comes out of the bathroom in a red satin robe.*]

BLANCHE [*airily*]:

Hello, Stanley! Here I am, all freshly bathed and scented, and feeling like a brand new human being!

[*He lights a cigarette.*]

STANLEY:

That's good.

BLANCHE [*drawing the curtains at the windows*]:

Excuse me while I slip on my pretty new dress!

STANLEY:

Go right ahead, Blanche.

[*She closes the drapes between the rooms.*]

BLANCHE:

I understand there's to be a little card party to which we ladies are cordially *not* invited!

STANLEY [*ominously*]:

Yeah?

[*Blanche throws off her robe and slips into a flowered print dress.*]

BLANCHE:

Where's Stella?

STANLEY:

Out on the porch.

BLANCHE:

I'm going to ask a favor of you in a moment.

STANLEY:

What could that be, I wonder?

BLANCHE:

Some buttons in back! You may enter!

[*He crosses through drapes with a smoldering look.*]

How do I look?

STANLEY:

You look all right.

BLANCHE:

Many thanks! Now the buttons!

STANLEY:

I can't do nothing with them.

BLANCHE:

You men with your big clumsy fingers. May I have a drag on your cig?

STANLEY:

Have one for yourself.

BLANCHE:

Why, thanks! . . . It looks like my trunk has exploded.

STANLEY:

Me an' Stella were helping you unpack.

BLANCHE:

Well, you certainly did a fast and thorough job of it!

STANLEY:

It looks like you raided some stylish shops in Paris.

BLANCHE:

Ha-ha! Yes—clothes are my passion!

STANLEY:

What does it cost for a string of fur-pieces like that?

BLANCHE:

Why, those were a tribute from an admirer of mine!

STANLEY:

He must have had a lot of—admiration!

BLANCHE:

Oh, in my youth I excited some admiration. But look at me now! [*She smiles at him radiantly*] Would you think it possible that I was once considered to be—attractive?

STANLEY:

Your looks are okay.

BLANCHE:

I was fishing for a compliment, Stanley.

STANLEY:

I don't go in for that stuff.

BLANCHE:

What—stuff?

STANLEY:

Compliments to women about their looks. I never met a woman that didn't know if she was good-looking or not without being told, and some of them give themselves credit for more than they've got. I once went out with a doll who said to me, "I am the glamorous type, I am the glamorous type!" I said, "So what?"

BLANCHE:
And what did she say then?

STANLEY:
She didn't say nothing. That shut her up like a clam.

BLANCHE:
Did it end the romance?

STANLEY:
It ended the conversation—that was all. Some men are took in by this Hollywood glamor stuff and some men are not.

BLANCHE:
I'm sure you belong in the second category.

STANLEY:
That's right.

BLANCHE:
I cannot imagine any witch of a woman casting a spell over you.

STANLEY:
That's—right.

BLANCHE:
You're simple, straightforward and honest, a little bit on the primitive side I should think. To interest you a woman would have to— [*She pauses with an indefinite gesture.*]

STANLEY [*slowly*]:
Lay . . . her cards on the table.

BLANCHE [*smiling*]:
Well, I never cared for wishy-washy people. That was

why, when you walked in here last night, I said to myself—"My sister has married a man!"—Of course that was all that I could tell about you.

STANLEY [*booming*]:
Now let's cut the re-bop!

BLANCHE [*pressing hands to her ears*]:
Ouuuuu!

STELLA [*calling from the steps*]:
Stanley! You come out here and let Blanche finish dressing!

BLANCHE:
I'm through dressing, honey.

STELLA:
Well, you come out, then.

STANLEY:
Your sister and I are having a little talk.

BLANCHE [*lightly*]:
Honey, do me a favor. Run to the drugstore and get me a lemon Coke with plenty of chipped ice in it!—Will you do that for me, sweetie?

STELLA [*uncertainly*]:
Yes. [*She goes around the corner of the building.*]

BLANCHE:
The poor little thing was out there listening to us, and I have an idea she doesn't understand you as well as I do. . . . All right; now, Mr. Kowalski, let us proceed without any more double-talk. I'm ready to answer all questions. I've nothing to hide. What is it?

STANLEY:
There is such a thing in this state of Louisiana as the

Napoleonic code, according to which whatever belongs to my wife is also mine—and vice versa.

BLANCHE:

My, but you have an impressive judicial air!

[*She sprays herself with her atomizer; then playfully sprays him with it. He seizes the atomizer and slams it down on the dresser. She throws back her head and laughs.*]

STANLEY:

If I didn't know that you was my wife's sister I'd get ideas about you!

BLANCHE:

Such as what!

STANLEY:

Don't play so dumb. You know what!

BLANCHE [*she puts the atomizer on the table*]:

All right. Cards on the table. That suits me. [*She turns to Stanley.*] I know I fib a good deal. After all, a woman's charm is fifty per cent illusion, but when a thing is important I tell the truth, and this is the truth: I haven't cheated my sister or you or anyone else as long as I have lived.

STANLEY:

Where's the papers? In the trunk?

BLANCHE:

Everything that I own is in that trunk.

[*Stanley crosses to the trunk, shoves it roughly open and begins to open compartments.*]

BLANCHE:

What in the name of heaven are you thinking of! What's

in the back of that little boy's mind of yours? That I am absconding with something, attempting some kind of treachery on my sister?—Let me do that! It will be faster and simpler . . . [*She crosses to the trunk and takes out a box*] I keep my papers mostly in this tin box. [*She opens it.*]

STANLEY:

What's them underneath? [*He indicates another sheaf of paper.*]

BLANCHE

These are love-letters, yellowing with antiquity, all from one boy. [*He snatches them up. She speaks fiercely*] Give those back to me!

STANLEY:

I'll have a look at them first!

BLANCHE:

The touch of your hands insults them!

STANLEY:

Don't pull that stuff!

[*He rips off the ribbon and starts to examine them. Blanche snatches them from him, and they cascade to the floor.*]

BLANCHE:

Now that you've touched them I'll burn them!

STANLEY [*staring, baffled*]:

What in hell are they?

BLANCHE [*on the floor gathering them up*]:

Poems a dead boy wrote. I hurt him the way that you would like to hurt me, but you can't! I'm not young and vulnerable any more. But my young husband was and I —never mind about that! Just give them back to me!

STANLEY:

What do you mean by saying you'll have to burn them?

BLANCHE:

I'm sorry, I must have lost my head for a moment. Everyone has something he won't let others touch because of their—intimate nature . . .

[*She now seems faint with exhaustion and she sits down with the strong box and puts on a pair of glasses and goes methodically through a large stack of papers.*]

Ambler & Ambler. Hmmmmm. . . . Crabtree. . . . More Ambler & Ambler.

STANLEY:

What is Ambler & Ambler?

BLANCHE:

A firm that made loans on the place.

STANLEY:

Then it *was* lost on a mortgage?

BLANCHE [*touching her forehead*]:

That must've been what happened.

STANLEY:

I don't want no ifs, ands or buts! What's all the rest of them papers?

[*She hands him the entire box. He carries it to the table and starts to examine the papers.*]

BLANCHE [*picking up a large envelope containing more papers*]:

There are thousands of papers, stretching back over hundreds of years, affecting Belle Reve as, piece by piece, our improvident grandfathers and father and uncles and brothers exchanged the land for their epic fornications—to put it plainly! [*She removes her glasses with an exhausted laugh*] The four-letter word deprived us of our plantation, till finally all that was left—and Stella can verify that!—was the house itself and about twenty acres of ground, including a graveyard, to which now all but Stella and I have retreated. [*She pours the contents of the envelope on the table*] Here all of them are, all papers! I hereby endow you with them! Take them, peruse them—commit them to memory, even! I think it's wonderfully fitting that Belle Reve should finally be this bunch of old papers in your big, capable hands! . . . I wonder if Stella's come back with my lemon Coke . . . [*She leans back and closes her eyes.*]

STANLEY:

I have a lawyer acquaintance who will study these out.

BLANCHE:

Present them to him with a box of aspirin tablets.

STANLEY [*becoming somewhat sheepish*]:

You see, under the Napoleonic code—a man has to take an interest in his wife's affairs—especially now that she's going to have a baby.

[*Blanche opens her eyes. The "blue piano" sounds louder.*]

BLANCHE:

Stella? Stella going to have a baby? [*dreamily*] I didn't know she was going to have a baby!

[*She gets up and crosses to the outside door. Stella*

appears around the corner with a carton from the drugstore.

[*Stanley goes into the bedroom with the envelope and the box.*

[*The inner rooms fade to darkness and the outside wall of the house is visible. Blanche meets Stella at the foot of the steps to the sidewalk.*]

BLANCHE:

Stella, Stella for star! How lovely to have a baby! It's all right. Everything's all right.

STELLA:

I'm sorry he did that to you.

BLANCHE:

Oh, I guess he's just not the type that goes for jasmine perfume, but maybe he's what we need to mix with our blood now that we've lost Belle Reve. We thrashed it out. I feel a bit shaky, but I think I handled it nicely, I laughed and treated it all as a joke. [*Steve and Pablo appear, carrying a case of beer.*] I called him a little boy and laughed and flirted. Yes, I was flirting with your husband! [*as the men approach*] The guests are gathering for the poker party. [*The two men pass between them, and enter the house.*] Which way do we go now, Stella—this way?

STELLA:

No, this way. [*She leads Blanche away.*]

BLANCHE [*laughing*]:

The blind are leading the blind!

[*A tamale Vendor is heard calling.*]

VENDOR'S VOICE:

Red-hot!

SCENE THREE

THE POKER NIGHT

There is a picture of Van Gogh's of a billiard-parlor at night. The kitchen now suggests that sort of lurid nocturnal brilliance, the raw colors of childhood's spectrum. Over the yellow linoleum of the kitchen table hangs an electric bulb with a vivid green glass shade. The poker players—Stanley, Steve, Mitch and Pablo—wear colored shirts, solid blues, a purple, a red-and-white check, a light green, and they are men at the peak of their physical manhood, as coarse and direct and powerful as the primary colors. There are vivid slices of watermelon on the table, whiskey bottles and glasses. The bedroom is relatively dim with only the light that spills between the portieres and through the wide window on the street.

For a moment, there is absorbed silence as a hand is dealt.

STEVE:

Anything wild this deal?

PABLO:

One-eyed jacks are wild.

STEVE:

Give me two cards.

PABLO:

You, Mitch?

MITCH:

I'm out.

PABLO:

One.

MITCH:

Anyone want a shot?

STANLEY:

Yeah. Me.

PABLO:

Why don't somebody go to the Chinaman's and bring back a load of chop suey?

STANLEY:

When I'm losing you want to eat! Ante up! Openers? Openers! Get y'r ass off the table, Mitch. Nothing belongs on a poker table but cards, chips and whiskey.

[*He lurches up and tosses some watermelon rinds to the floor.*]

MITCH:

Kind of on your high horse, ain't you?

STANLEY:

How many?

STEVE:

Give me three.

STANLEY:

One.

MITCH:

I'm out again. I oughta go home pretty soon.

STANLEY:

Shut up.

MITCH:

I gotta sick mother. She don't go to sleep until I come in at night.

STANLEY:

Then why don't you stay home with her?

MITCH:

She says to go out, so I go, but I don't enjoy it. All the while I keep wondering how she is.

STANLEY:

Aw, for the sake of Jesus, go home, then!

PABLO:

What've you got?

STEVE:

Spade flush.

MITCH:

You all are married. But I'll be alone when she goes.— I'm going to the bathroom.

STANLEY:

Hurry back and we'll fix you a sugar-tit.

MITCH:

Aw, go rut. [*He crosses through the bedroom into the bathroom.*]

STEVE [*dealing a hand*]:

Seven card stud. [*telling his joke as he deals*] This ole farmer is out in back of his house sittin' down th'owing corn to the chickens when all at once he hears a loud cackle and this young hen comes lickety split around the side of the house with the rooster right behind her and gaining on her fast.

STANLEY [*impatient with the story*]:

Deal!

STEVE:

But when the rooster catches sight of the farmer th'owing the corn he puts on the brakes and lets the hen get away and starts pecking corn. And the old farmer says, "Lord God, I hopes I never gits *that* hongry!"

[*Steve and Pablo laugh. The sisters appear around the corner of the building.*]

STELLA:

The game is still going on.

BLANCHE:

How do I look?

STELLA:

Lovely, Blanche.

BLANCHE:

I feel so hot and frazzled. Wait till I powder before you open the door. Do I look done in?

STELLA:

Why no. You are as fresh as a daisy.

BLANCHE:

One that's been picked a few days.

[*Stella opens the door and they enter.*]

STELLA:

Well, well, well. I see you boys are still at it!

STANLEY:

Where you been?

STELLA:

Blanche and I took in a show. Blanche, this is Mr. Gonzales and Mr. Hubbell.

BLANCHE:

Please don't get up.

STANLEY:

Nobody's going to get up, so don't be worried.

STELLA:

How much longer is this game going to continue?

STANLEY:

Till we get ready to quit.

BLANCHE:

Poker is so fascinating. Could I kibitz?

STANLEY:

You could not. Why don't you women go up and sit with Eunice?

STELLA:

Because it is nearly two-thirty. [*Blanche crosses into the bedroom and partially closes the portieres*] Couldn't you call it quits after one more hand?

[*A chair scrapes. Stanley gives a loud whack of his hand on her thigh.*]

STELLA [*sharply*]:

That's not fun, Stanley.

[*The men laugh. Stella goes into the bedroom.*]

STELLA:

It makes me so mad when he does that in front of people.

BLANCHE:

I think I will bathe.

STELLA:

Again?

BLANCHE:

My nerves are in knots. Is the bathroom occupied?

STELLA:

I don't know.

[*Blanche knocks. Mitch opens the door and comes out, still wiping his hands on a towel.*]

BLANCHE:

Oh!—good evening.

MITCH:

Hello. [*He stares at her.*]

STELLA:

Blanche, this is Harold Mitchell. My sister, Blanche DuBois.

MITCH [*with awkward courtesy*]:

How do you do, Miss DuBois.

STELLA:

How is your mother now, Mitch?

MITCH:

About the same, thanks. She appreciated your sending over that custard.—Excuse me, please.

[*He crosses slowly back into the kitchen, glancing back at Blanche and coughing a little shyly. He realizes he still has the towel in his hands and with an embarrassed laugh hands it to Stella. Blanche looks after him with a certain interest.*]

BLANCHE:

That one seems—superior to the others.

STELLA:

Yes, he is.

BLANCHE:

I thought he had a sort of sensitive look.

STELLA:

His mother is sick.

BLANCHE:

Is he married?

STELLA:

No.

BLANCHE:

Is he a wolf?

STELLA:

Why, Blanche! [*Blanche laughs.*] I don't think he would be.

BLANCHE:

What does—what does he do?

[*She is unbuttoning her blouse.*]

STELLA:

He's on the precision bench in the spare parts department. At the plant Stanley travels for.

BLANCHE:

Is that something much?

STELLA:

No. Stanley's the only one of his crowd that's likely to get anywhere.

BLANCHE:

What makes you think Stanley will?

STELLA:

Look at him.

BLANCHE:

I've looked at him.

STELLA:

Then you should know.

BLANCHE:

I'm sorry, but I haven't noticed the stamp of genius even on Stanley's forehead.

[*She takes off the blouse and stands in her pink silk brassiere and white skirt in the light through the portieres. The game has continued in undertones.*]

STELLA:

It isn't on his forehead and it isn't genius.

BLANCHE:

Oh. Well, what is it, and where? I would like to know.

STELLA:

It's a drive that he has. You're standing in the light, Blanche!

BLANCHE:

Oh, am I!

[*She moves out of the yellow streak of light. Stella has removed her dress and put on a light blue satin kimona.*]

STELLA [*with girlish laughter*]:

You ought to see their wives.

BLANCHE [*laughingly*]:

I can imagine. Big, beefy things, I suppose.

STELLA:

You know that one upstairs? [*more laughter*] One time [*laughing*] the plaster—[*laughing*] cracked—

STANLEY:

You hens cut out that conversation in there!

STELLA:

You can't hear us.

STANLEY:

Well, you can hear me and I said to hush up!

STELLA:

This is my house and I'll talk as much as I want to!

BLANCHE:

Stella, don't start a row.

STELLA:

He's half drunk!—I'll be out in a minute.

[*She goes into the bathroom. Blanche rises and crosses leisurely to a small white radio and turns it on.*]

STANLEY:

Awright, Mitch, you in?

MITCH:

What? Oh!—No, I'm out!

[*Blanche moves back into the streak of light. She raises her arms and stretches, as she moves indolently back to the chair.*

[*Rhumba music comes over the radio. Mitch rises at the table.*]

STANLEY:

Who turned that on in there?

BLANCHE:

I did. Do you mind?

STANLEY:

Turn it off!

STEVE:

Aw, let the girls have their music.

PABLO:

Sure, that's good, leave it on!

STEVE:

Sounds like Xavier Cugat!

[*Stanley jumps up and, crossing to the radio, turns it off. He stops short at the sight of Blanche in the chair. She returns his look without flinching. Then he sits again at the poker table.*

[*Two of the men have started arguing hotly.*]

STEVE:

I didn't hear you name it.

PABLO:

Didn't I name it, Mitch?

MITCH:

I wasn't listenin'.

PABLO:

What were you doing, then?

STANLEY:

He was looking through them drapes. [*He jumps up and jerks roughly at curtains to close them*] Now deal the hand over again and let's play cards or quit. Some people get ants when they win.

[*Mitch rises as Stanley returns to his seat.*]

STANLEY [*yelling*]:

Sit down!

MITCH:

I'm going to the "head." Deal me out.

PABLO:

Sure he's got ants now. Seven five-dollar bills in his pants pocket folded up tight as spitballs.

STEVE:

Tomorrow you'll see him at the cashier's window getting them changed into quarters.

STANLEY:

And when he goes home he'll deposit them one by one in a piggy bank his mother give him for Christmas. [*dealing*] This game is Spit in the Ocean.

[*Mitch laughs uncomfortably and continues through the portieres. He stops just inside.*]

BLANCHE [*softly*]:

Hello! The Little Boys' Room is busy right now.

MITCH:

We've—been drinking beer.

BLANCHE:

I hate beer.

MITCH:

It's—a hot weather drink.

BLANCHE:

Oh, I don't think so; it always makes me warmer. Have you got any cigs? [*She has slipped on the dark red satin wrapper.*]

MITCH:

Sure.

BLANCHE:

What kind are they?

MITCH:

Luckies.

BLANCHE:

Oh, good. What a pretty case. Silver?

MITCH:

Yes. Yes; read the inscription.

BLANCHE:

Oh, is there an inscription? I can't make it out. [*He strikes a match and moves closer*] Oh! [*reading with feigned difficulty*]:

"And if God choose,
I shall but love thee better—after—death!"

Why, that's from my favorite sonnet by Mrs. Browning!

MITCH:

You know it?

BLANCHE:

Certainly I do!

MITCH:

There's a story connected with that inscription.

BLANCHE:

It sounds like a romance.

MITCH:

A pretty sad one.

BLANCHE:

Oh?

MITCH:

The girl's dead now.

BLANCHE [*in a tone of deep sympathy*]:

Oh!

MITCH:

She knew she was dying when she give me this. A very strange girl, very sweet—very!

BLANCHE:

She must have been fond of you. Sick people have such deep, sincere attachments.

MITCH:

That's right, they certainly do.

BLANCHE:

Sorrow makes for sincerity, I think.

MITCH:

It sure brings it out in people.

BLANCHE:

The little there is belongs to people who have experienced some sorrow.

MITCH:

I believe you are right about that.

BLANCHE:

I'm positive that I am. Show me a person who hasn't known any sorrow and I'll show you a shuperficial— Listen to me! My tongue is a little—thick! You boys are responsible for it. The show let out at eleven and we couldn't come home on account of the poker game so we had to go somewhere and drink. I'm not accustomed to having more than one drink. Two is the limit—and *three!* [*She laughs*] Tonight I had three.

STANLEY:

Mitch!

MITCH:

Deal me out. I'm talking to Miss—

BLANCHE:

DuBois.

MITCH:

Miss DuBois?

BLANCHE:

It's a French name. It means woods and Blanche means white, so the two together mean white woods. Like an orchard in spring! You can remember it by that.

MITCH:

You're French?

BLANCHE:

We are French by extraction. Our first American ancestors were French Huguenots.

MITCH:

You are Stella's sister, are you not?

BLANCHE:

Yes, Stella is my precious little sister. I call her little in spite of the fact she's somewhat older than I. Just slightly. Less than a year. Will you do something for me?

MITCH:

Sure. What?

BLANCHE:

I bought this adorable little colored paper lantern at a Chinese shop on Bourbon. Put it over the light bulb! Will you, please?

MITCH:

Be glad to.

BLANCHE:

I can't stand a naked light bulb, any more than I can a rude remark or a vulgar action.

MITCH [*adjusting the lantern*]:

I guess we strike you as being a pretty rough bunch.

BLANCHE:

I'm very adaptable—to circumstances.

MITCH:

Well, that's a good thing to be. You are visiting Stanley and Stella?

BLANCHE:

Stella hasn't been so well lately, and I came down to help her for a while. She's very run down.

MITCH:

You're not—?

BLANCHE:

Married? No, no. I'm an old maid schoolteacher!

MITCH:

You may teach school but you're certainly not an old maid.

BLANCHE:

Thank you, sir! I appreciate your gallantry!

MITCH:

So you are in the teaching profession?

BLANCHE:

Yes. Ah, yes...

MITCH:

Grade school or high school or—

STANLEY [*bellowing*]:

Mitch!

MITCH:

Coming!

BLANCHE:

Gracious, what lung-power! . . . I teach high school. In Laurel.

MITCH:

What do you teach? What subject?

BLANCHE:

Guess!

MITCH:

I bet you teach art or music? [*Blanche laughs delicately*] Of course I could be wrong. You might teach arithmetic.

BLANCHE:

Never arithmetic, sir; never arithmetic! [*with a laugh*] I don't even know my multiplication tables! No, I have the misfortune of being an English instructor. I attempt to instill a bunch of bobby-soxers and drugstore Romeos with reverence for Hawthorne and Whitman and Poe!

MITCH:

I guess that some of them are more interested in other things.

BLANCHE:

How very right you are! Their literary heritage is not what most of them treasure above all else! But they're sweet things! And in the spring, it's touching to notice them making their first discovery of love! As if nobody had ever known it before!

[*The bathroom door opens and Stella comes out. Blanche continues talking to Mitch.*]

Oh! Have you finished? Wait—I'll turn on the radio.

[*She turns the knobs on the radio and it begins to play "Wien, Wien, nur du allein." Blanche waltzes to the music with romantic gestures. Mitch is delighted and moves in awkward imitation like a dancing bear.*

[*Stanley stalks fiercely through the portieres into the bedroom. He crosses to the small white radio and snatches it off the table. With a shouted oath, he tosses the instrument out the window.*]

STELLA:

Drunk — drunk — animal thing, you! [*She rushes through to the poker table*] All of you—please go home! If any of you have one spark of decency in you—

BLANCHE [*wildly*]:

Stella, watch out, he's—

[*Stanley charges after Stella.*]

MEN [*feebly*]:
Take it easy, Stanley. Easy, fellow.—Let's all—

STELLA:
You lay your hands on me and I'll—

[*She backs out of sight. He advances and disappears. There is the sound of a blow. Stella cries out. Blanche screams and runs into the kitchen. The men rush forward and there is grappling and cursing. Something is overturned with a crash.*]

BLANCHE [*shrilly*]:
My sister is going to have a baby!

MITCH:
This is terrible.

BLANCHE:
Lunacy, absolute lunacy!

MITCH:
Get him in here, men.

[*Stanley is forced, pinioned by the two men, into the bedroom. He nearly throws them off. Then all at once he subsides and is limp in their grasp.*

[*They speak quietly and lovingly to him and he leans his face on one of their shoulders.*]

STELLA [*in a high, unnatural voice, out of sight*]:
I want to go away, I want to go away!

MITCH:
Poker shouldn't be played in a house with women.

[*Blanche rushes into the bedroom*]

BLANCHE:
I want my sister's clothes! We'll go to that woman's upstairs!

MITCH:
Where is the clothes?

BLANCHE [*opening the closet*]:
I've got them! [*She rushes through to Stella*] Stella, Stella, precious! Dear, dear little sister, don't be afraid!

[*With her arms around Stella, Blanche guides her to the outside door and upstairs.*]

STANLEY [*dully*]:
What's the matter; what's happened?

MITCH:
You just blew your top, Stan.

PABLO:
He's okay, now.

STEVE:
Sure, my boy's okay!

MITCH:
Put him on the bed and get a wet towel.

PABLO:
I think coffee would do him a world of good, now.

STANLEY [*thickly*]:
I want water.

MITCH.

Put him under the shower!

[*The men talk quietly as they lead him to the bathroom.*]

STANLEY:

Let the rut go of me, you sons of bitches!

[*Sounds of blows are heard. The water goes on full tilt.*]

STEVE:

Let's get quick out of here!

[*They rush to the poker table and sweep up their winings on their way out.*]

MITCH [*sadly but firmly*]:

Poker should not be played in a house with women.

[*The door closes on them and the place is still. The Negro entertainers in the bar around the corner play "Paper Doll" slow and blue. After a moment Stanley comes out of the bathroom dripping water and still in his clinging wet polka dot drawers.*]

STANLEY:

Stella! [*There is a pause*] My baby doll's left me!

[*He breaks into sobs. Then he goes to the phone and dials, still shuddering with sobs.*]

Eunice? I want my baby! [*He waits a moment; then he hangs up and dials again*] Eunice! I'll keep on ringin' until I talk with my baby!

[*An indistinguishable shrill voice is heard. He hurls phone to floor. Dissonant brass and piano sounds as the rooms dim out to darkness and the outer walls appear in the night light. The "blue piano" plays for a brief interval.*

[*Finally, Stanley stumbles half-dressed out to the porch and down the wooden steps to the pavement before the building. There he throws back his head like a baying hound and bellows his wife's name: "Stella! Stella, sweetheart! Stella!"*]

STANLEY:

Stell-*lahhhhh!*

EUNICE [*calling down from the door of her upper apartment*]:

Quit that howling out there an' go back to bed!

STANLEY:

I want my baby down here. Stella, Stella!

EUNICE:

She ain't comin' down so you quit! Or you'll git th' law on you!

STANLEY:

Stella!

EUNICE:

You can't beat on a woman an' then call 'er back! She won't come! And her goin' t' have a baby! . . . You stinker! You whelp of a Polack, you! I hope they do haul you in and turn the fire hose on you, same as the last time!

STANLEY [*humbly*]:

Eunice, I want my girl to come down with me!

EUNICE:

Hah! [*She slams her door.*]

STANLEY [*with heaven-splitting violence*]:

STELL-LAHHHHH!

[*The low-tone clarinet moans. The door upstairs opens again. Stella slips down the rickety stairs in her robe. Her eyes are glistening with tears and her hair loose about her throat and shoulders. They stare at each other. Then they come together with low, animal moans. He falls to his knees on the steps and presses his face to her belly, curving a little with maternity. Her eyes go blind with tenderness as she catches his head and raises him level with her. He snatches the screen door open and lifts her off her feet and bears her into the dark flat.*

[*Blanche comes out on the upper landing in her robe and slips fearfully down the steps.*]

BLANCHE:

Where is my little sister? Stella? Stella?

[*She stops before the dark entrance of her sister's flat. Then catches her breath as if struck. She rushes down to the walk before the house. She looks right and left as if for a sanctuary.*

[*The music fades away. Mitch appears from around the corner.*]

MITCH:

Miss DuBois?

BLANCHE:

Oh!

MITCH:

All quiet on the Potomac now?

BLANCHE:

She ran downstairs and went back in there with him.

MITCH:

Sure she did.

BLANCHE:

I'm terrified!

MITCH:

Ho-ho! There's nothing to be scared of. They're crazy about each other.

BLANCHE:

I'm not used to such—

MITCH:

Naw, it's a shame this had to happen when you just got here. But don't take it serious.

BLANCHE:

Violence! Is so—

MITCH:

Set down on the steps and have a cigarette with me.

BLANCHE:

I'm not properly dressed.

MITCH:

That don't make no difference in the Quarter.

BLANCHE:

Such a pretty silver case.

MITCH:

I showed you the inscription, didn't I?

BLANCHE:

Yes. [*During the pause, she looks up at the sky*] There's so much—so much confusion in the world . . . [*He coughs diffidently*] Thank you for being so kind! I need kindness now.

SCENE FOUR

It is early the following morning. There is a confusion of street cries like a choral chant.

Stella is lying down in the bedroom. Her face is serene in the early morning sunlight. One hand rests on her belly, rounding slightly with new maternity. From the other dangles a book of colored comics. Her eyes and lips have that almost narcotized tranquility that is in the faces of Eastern idols.

The table is sloppy with remains of breakfast and the debris of the preceding night, and Stanley's gaudy pyjamas lie across the threshold of the bathroom. The outside door is slightly ajar on a sky of summer brilliance.

Blanche appears at this door. She has spent a sleepless night and her appearance entirely contrasts with Stella's. She presses her knuckles nervously to her lips as she looks through the door, before entering.

BLANCHE:

Stella?

STELLA [*stirring lazily*]:

Hmmh?

[*Blanche utters a moaning cry and runs into the bedroom, throwing herself down beside Stella in a rush of hysterical tenderness.*]

BLANCHE:

Baby, my baby sister!

STELLA [*drawing away from her*]:
Blanche, what is the matter with you?

[*Blanche straightens up slowly and stands beside the bed looking down at her sister with knuckles pressed to her lips.*]

BLANCHE:
He's left?

STELLA:
Stan? Yes.

BLANCHE:
Will he be back?

STELLA:
He's gone to get the car greased. Why?

BLANCHE:
Why! I've been half crazy, Stella! When I found out you'd been insane enough to come back in here after what happened—I started to rush in after you!

STELLA:
I'm glad you didn't.

BLANCHE:
What were you thinking of? [*Stella makes an indefinite gesture*] Answer me! What? What?

STELLA:
Please, Blanche! Sit down and stop yelling.

BLANCHE:
All right, Stella. I will repeat the question quietly now. How could you come back in this place last night? Why, you must have slept with him!

[*Stella gets up in a calm and leisurely way.*]

STELLA:

Blanche, I'd forgotten how excitable you are. You're making much too much fuss about this.

BLANCHE:

Am I?

STELLA:

Yes, you are, Blanche. I know how it must have seemed to you and I'm awful sorry it had to happen, but it wasn't anything as serious as you seem to take it. In the first place, when men are drinking and playing poker anything can happen. It's always a powder-keg. He didn't know what he was doing.... He was as good as a lamb when I came back and he's really very, very ashamed of himself.

BLANCHE:

And that—that makes it all right?

STELLA:

No, it isn't all right for anybody to make such a terrible row, but — people do sometimes. Stanley's always smashed things. Why, on our wedding night—soon as we came in here—he snatched off one of my slippers and rushed about the place smashing light bulbs with it.

BLANCHE:

He did—*what?*

STELLA:

He smashed all the light bulbs with the heel of my slipper! [*She laughs.*]

BLANCHE:

And you—you *let* him? Didn't *run,* didn't *scream?*

STELLA:

I was—sort of—thrilled by it. [*She waits for a moment*] Eunice and you had breakfast?

BLANCHE:

Do you suppose I wanted any breakfast?

STELLA:

There's some coffee left on the stove.

BLANCHE:

You're so—matter of fact about it, Stella.

STELLA:

What other can I be? He's taken the radio to get it fixed. It didn't land on the pavement so only one tube was smashed.

BLANCHE:

And you are standing there smiling!

STELLA:

What do you want me to do?

BLANCHE:

Pull yourself together and face the facts.

STELLA:

What are they, in your opinion?

BLANCHE:

In my opinion? You're married to a madman!

STELLA:

No!

BLANCHE:

Yes, you are, your fix is worse than mine is! Only you're not being sensible about it. I'm going to *do* something. Get hold of myself and make myself a new life!

STELLA:

Yes?

BLANCHE:

But you've given in. And that isn't right, you're not old! You can get out.

STELLA [*slowly and emphatically*]:

I'm not in anything I want to get out of.

BLANCHE [*incredulously*]:

What—Stella?

STELLA:

I said I am not in anything that I have a desire to get out of. Look at the mess in this room! And those empty bottles! They went through two cases last night! He promised this morning that he was going to quit having these poker parties, but you know how long such a promise is going to keep. Oh, well, it's his pleasure, like mine is movies and bridge. People have got to tolerate each other's habits, I guess.

BLANCHE:

I don't understand you. [*Stella turns toward her*] I don't understand your indifference. Is this a Chinese philosophy you've—cultivated?

STELLA:

Is what—what?

BLANCHE:

This — shuffling about and mumbling — 'One tube smashed—beer bottles—mess in the kitchen!'—as if nothing out of the ordinary has happened! [*Stella laughs uncertainly and picking up the broom, twirls it in her hands.*]

BLANCHE:

Are you deliberately shaking that thing in my face?

STELLA:

No.

BLANCHE:

Stop it. Let go of that broom. I won't have you cleaning up for him!

STELLA:

Then who's going to do it? Are you?

BLANCHE:

I? I!

STELLA:

No, I didn't think so.

BLANCHE:

Oh, let me think, if only my mind would function! We've got to get hold of some money, that's the way out!

STELLA:

I guess that money is always nice to get hold of.

BLANCHE:

Listen to me. I have an idea of some kind. [*Shakily she twists a cigarette into her holder*] Do you remember Shep Huntleigh? [*Stella shakes her head*] Of course you remember Shep Huntleigh. I went out with him at college and wore his pin for a while. Well—

STELLA:

Well?

BLANCHE:

I ran into him last winter. You know I went to Miami during the Christmas holidays?

STELLA:

No.

BLANCHE:

Well, I did. I took the trip as an investment, thinking I'd meet someone with a million dollars.

STELLA:

Did you?

BLANCHE:

Yes. I ran into Shep Huntleigh—I ran into him on Biscayne Boulevard, on Christmas Eve, about dusk . . . getting into his car—Cadillac convertible; must have been a block long!

STELLA:

I should think it would have been—inconvenient in traffic!

BLANCHE:

You've heard of oil wells?

STELLA:

Yes—remotely.

BLANCHE:

He has them, all over Texas. Texas is literally spouting gold in his pockets.

STELLA:

My, my.

BLANCHE:

Y'know how indifferent I am to money. I think of money in terms of what it does for you. But he could do it, he could certainly do it!

STELLA:

Do what, Blanche?

BLANCHE:

Why—set us up in a—shop!

STELLA:

What kind of a shop?

BLANCHE:

Oh, a—shop of some kind! He could do it with half what his wife throws away at the races.

STELLA:

He's married?

BLANCHE:

Honey, would I be here if the man weren't married? [*Stella laughs a little. Blanche suddenly springs up and crosses to phone. She speaks shrilly*] How do I get Western Union?—Operator! Western Union!

STELLA:

That's a dial phone, honey.

BLANCHE:

I can't dial, I'm too—

STELLA:

Just dial O.

BLANCHE:

O?

STELLA:

Yes, "O" for Operator! [*Blanche considers a moment; then she puts the phone down.*]

BLANCHE:

Give me a pencil. Where is a slip of paper? I've got to write it down first—the message, I mean . . .

[*She goes to the dressing table, and grabs up a sheet of Kleenex and an eyebrow pencil for writing equipment.*]

Let me see now . . . [*She bites the pencil*] 'Darling Shep. Sister and I in desperate situation.'

STELLA:

I beg your pardon!

BLANCHE:

'Sister and I in desperate situation. Will explain details later. Would you be interested in—?' [*She bites the pencil again*] 'Would you be—interested—in . . .' [*She smashes the pencil on the table and springs up*] You never get anywhere with direct appeals!

STELLA [*with a laugh*]:

Don't be so ridiculous, darling!

BLANCHE:

But I'll think of something, I've *got* to think of—*something*! Don't, don't laugh at me, Stella! Please, please don't—I—I want you to look at the contents of my purse! Here's what's in it! [*She snatches her purse open*] Sixty-five measly cents in coin of the realm!

STELLA [*crossing to bureau*]:

Stanley doesn't give me a regular allowance, he likes to pay bills himself, but—this morning he gave me ten dollars to smooth things over. You take five of it, Blanche, and I'll keep the rest.

BLANCHE:

Oh, no. No, Stella.

STELLA [*insisting*]:

I know how it helps your morale just having a little pocket-money on you.

BLANCHE:

No, thank you—I'll take to the streets!

STELLA:

Talk sense! How did you happen to get so low on funds?

BLANCHE:

Money just goes—it goes places. [*She rubs her forehead*] Sometime today I've got to get hold of a Bromo!

STELLA:

I'll fix you one now.

BLANCHE:

Not yet—I've got to keep thinking!

STELLA:

I wish you'd just let things go, at least for a—while...

BLANCHE:

Stella, I can't live with him! You can, he's your husband. But how could I stay here with him, after last night, with just those curtains between us?

STELLA:

Blanche, you saw him at his worst last night.

BLANCHE:

On the contrary, I saw him at his best! What such a man has to offer is animal force and he gave a wonderful exhibition of that! But the only way to live with such a man is to—go to bed with him! And that's your job—not mine!

STELLA:

After you've rested a little, you'll see it's going to work out. You don't have to worry about anything while you're here. I mean—expenses...

BLANCHE:

I have to plan for us both, to get us both—out!

STELLA:

You take it for granted that I am in something that I want to get out of.

BLANCHE:

I take it for granted that you still have sufficient memory of Belle Reve to find this place and these poker players impossible to live with.

STELLA:

Well, you're taking entirely too much for granted.

BLANCHE:

I can't believe you're in earnest.

STELLA:

No?

BLANCHE:

I understand how it happened—a little. You saw him in uniform, an officer, not here but—

STELLA:

I'm not sure it would have made any difference where I saw him.

BLANCHE:

Now don't say it was one of those mysterious electric things between people! If you do I'll laugh in your face.

STELLA:

I am not going to say anything more at all about it!

BLANCHE:

All right, then, don't!

STELLA:

But there are things that happen between a man and a woman in the dark—that sort of make everything else seem—unimportant. [*pause*]

BLANCHE:

What you are talking about is brutal desire—just—Desire!—the name of that rattle-trap streetcar that bangs through the Quarter, up one old narrow street and down another . . .

STELLA:

Haven't you ever ridden on that streetcar?

BLANCHE:

It brought me here.—Where I'm not wanted and where I'm ashamed to be . . .

STELLA:

Then don't you think your superior attitude is a bit out of place?

BLANCHE:

I am not being or feeling at all superior, Stella. Believe me I'm not! It's just this. This is how I look at it. A man like that is someone to go out with—once—twice—three times when the devil is in you. But live with? Have a child by?

STELLA:

I have told you I love him.

BLANCHE:

Then I *tremble* for you! I just—*tremble* for you....

STELLA:

I can't help your trembling if you insist on trembling!

[*There is a pause.*]

BLANCHE:

May I—speak—*plainly?*

STELLA:

Yes, do. Go ahead. As plainly as you want to.

[*Outside, a train approaches. They are silent till the noise subsides. They are both in the bedroom.*

[*Under cover of the train's noise Stanley enters from outside. He stands unseen by the women, holding some packages in his arms, and overhears their following conversation. He wears an undershirt and grease-stained seersucker pants.*]

BLANCHE:

Well—if you'll forgive me—he's *common!*

STELLA:

Why, yes, I suppose he is.

BLANCHE:

Suppose! You can't have forgotten that much of our bringing up, Stella, that you just *suppose* that any part of a gentleman's in his nature! *Not one particle, no!* Oh, if he was just—*ordinary!* Just *plain*—but good and wholesome, but—*no.* There's something downright—*bestial*—about him! You're hating me saying this, aren't you?

STELLA [*coldly*]:

Go on and say it all, Blanche.

BLANCHE:

He acts like an animal, has an animal's habits! Eats like one, moves like one, talks like one! There's even something—sub-human—something not quite to the stage of humanity yet! Yes, something—ape-like about him, like one of those pictures I've seen in—anthropological studies! Thousands and thousands of years have passed him right by, and there he is—Stanley Kowalski—survivor of the Stone Age! Bearing the raw meat home from the kill in the jungle! And you—*you* here—*waiting* for him! Maybe he'll strike you or maybe grunt and kiss you! That is, if kisses have been discovered yet! Night falls and the other apes gather! There in the front of the cave, all grunting like him, and swilling and gnawing and hulking! His poker night!—you call it—this party of apes! Somebody growls—some creature snatches at something—the fight is on! *God!* Maybe we are a long way from being made in God's image, but Stella—my sister—there has been *some* progress since then! Such things as art—as poetry and music—such kinds of new light have come into the world since then! In some kinds of people some tenderer feelings have had some little beginning! That we have got to make *grow!* And *cling* to, and hold as our flag! In this dark march toward whatever it is we're approaching.... *Don't—don't hang back with the brutes!*

[*Another train passes outside. Stanley hesitates, licking his lips. Then suddenly he turns stealthily about and withdraws through front door. The women are still unaware of his presence. When the train has passed he calls through the closed front door.*]

STANLEY:

Hey! Hey, Stella!

STELLA [*who has listened gravely to Blanche*]:

Stanley!

BLANCHE:

Stell, I—

[*But Stella has gone to the front door. Stanley enters casually with his packages.*]

STANLEY:

Hiyuh, Stella. Blanche back?

STELLA:

Yes, she's back.

STANLEY:

Hiyuh, Blanche. [*He grins at her.*]

STELLA:

You must've got under the car.

STANLEY:

Them darn mechanics at Fritz's don't know their ass fr'm— *Hey!*

[*Stella has embraced him with both arms, fiercely, and full in the view of Blanche. He laughs and clasps her head to him. Over her head he grins through the curtains at Blanche.*

[*As the lights fade away, with a lingering brightness on their embrace, the music of the "blue piano" and trumpet and drums is heard.*]

SCENE FIVE

Blanche is seated in the bedroom fanning herself with a palm leaf as she reads over a just-completed letter. Suddenly she bursts into a peal of laughter. Stella is dressing in the bedroom.

STELLA:

What are you laughing at, honey?

BLANCHE:

Myself, myself, for being such a liar! I'm writing a letter to Shep. [*She picks up the letter*] "Darling Shep. I am spending the summer on the wing, making flying visits here and there. And who knows, perhaps I shall take a sudden notion to *swoop* down on *Dallas!* How would you feel about that? Ha-ha! [*She laughs nervously and brightly, touching her throat as if actually talking to Shep*] Forewarned is forearmed, as they say!"—How does that sound?

STELLA:

Uh-huh...

BLANCHE [*going on nervously*]:

"Most of my sister's friends go north in the summer but some have homes on the Gulf and there has been a continued round of entertainments, teas, cocktails, and luncheons—"

[*A disturbance is heard upstairs at the Hubbell's apartment.*]

STELLA:

Eunice seems to be having some trouble with Steve.

[*Eunice's voice shouts in terrible wrath.*]

EUNICE:

I heard about you and that blonde!

STEVE:

That's a damn lie!

EUNICE:

You ain't pulling the wool over my eyes! I wouldn't mind if you'd stay down at the Four Deuces, but you always going up.

STEVE:

Who ever seen me up?

EUNICE:

I seen you chasing her 'round the balcony—I'm gonna call the vice squad!

STEVE:

Don't you throw that at me!

EUNICE [*shrieking*]:

You hit me! I'm gonna call the police!

[*A clatter of aluminum striking a wall is heard, followed by a man's angry roar, shouts and overturned furniture. There is a crash; then a relative hush.*]

BLANCHE [*brightly*]:

Did he *kill* her?

[*Eunice appears on the steps in daemonic disorder.*]

STELLA:

No! She's coming downstairs.

EUNICE:

Call the police, I'm going to call the police! [*She rushes around the corner.*]

[*They laugh lightly. Stanley comes around the corner in his green and scarlet silk bowling shirt. He trots up the steps and bangs into the kitchen. Blanche registers his entrance with nervous gestures.*]

STANLEY:

What's a matter with Eun-uss?

STELLA:

She and Steve had a row. Has she got the police?

STANLEY:

Naw. She's gettin' a drink.

STELLA:

That's much more practical!

[*Steve comes down nursing a bruise on his forehead and looks in the door.*]

STEVE:

She here?

STANLEY:

Naw, naw. At the Four Deuces.

STEVE:

That rutting hunk! [*He looks around the corner a bit timidly, then turns with affected boldness and runs after her.*]

BLANCHE:

I must jot that down in my notebook. Ha-ha! I'm compiling a notebook of quaint little words and phrases I've picked up here.

STANLEY:

You won't pick up nothing here you ain't heard before.

BLANCHE:

Can I count on that?

STANLEY:

You can count on it up to five hundred.

BLANCHE:

That's a mighty high number. [*He jerks open the bureau drawer, slams it shut and throws shoes in a corner. At each noise Blanche winces slightly. Finally she speaks*] What sign were you born under?

STANLEY [*while he is dressing*]:

Sign?

BLANCHE:

Astrological sign. I bet you were born under Aries. Aries people are forceful and dynamic. They dote on noise! They love to bang things around! You must have had lots of banging around in the army and now that you're out, you make up for it by treating inanimate objects with such a fury!

[*Stella has been going in and out of closet during this scene. Now she pops her head out of the closet.*]

STELLA:

Stanley was born just five minutes after Christmas.

BLANCHE:

Capricorn—the Goat!

STANLEY:

What sign were *you* born under?

BLANCHE:

Oh, my birthday's next month, the fifteenth of September; that's under Virgo.

STANLEY:

What's Virgo?

BLANCHE:

Virgo is the Virgin.

STANLEY [*contemptuously*]:

Hah! [*He advances a little as he knots his tie*] Say, do you happen to know somebody named Shaw?

[*Her face expresses a faint shock. She reaches for the cologne bottle and dampens her handkerchief as she answers carefully.*]

BLANCHE:

Why, everybody knows somebody named Shaw!

STANLEY:

Well, this somebody named Shaw is under the impression he met you in Laurel, but I figure he must have got you mixed up with some other party because this other party is someone he met at a hotel called the Flamingo.

[*Blanche laughs breathlessly as she touches the cologne-dampened handkerchief to her temples.*]

BLANCHE:

I'm afraid he does have me mixed up with this "other party." The Hotel Flamingo is not the sort of establishment I would dare to be seen in!

STANLEY:

You know of it?

BLANCHE:

Yes, I've seen it and smelled it.

STANLEY:

You must've got pretty close if you could smell it.

BLANCHE:

The odor of cheap perfume is penetrating.

STANLEY:

That stuff you use is expensive?

BLANCHE:

Twenty-five dollars an ounce! I'm nearly out. That's just a hint if you want to remember my birthday! [*She speaks lightly but her voice has a note of fear.*]

STANLEY:

Shaw must've got you mixed up. He goes in and out of Laurel all the time so he can check on it and clear up any mistake.

[*He turns away and crosses to the portieres. Blanche closes her eyes as if faint. Her hand trembles as she lifts the handkerchief again to her forehead.*

[*Steve and Eunice come around corner. Steve's arm is around Eunice's shoulder and she is sobbing luxuriously and he is cooing love-words. There is a murmur of thunder as they go slowly upstairs in a tight embrace.*]

STANLEY [*to Stella*]:

I'll wait for you at the Four Deuces!

STELLA:

Hey! Don't I rate one kiss?

STANLEY:

Not in front of your sister.

[*He goes out. Blanche rises from her chair. She seems faint; looks about her with an expression of almost panic.*]

BLANCHE:

Stella! What have you heard about me?

STELLA:

Huh?

BLANCHE:

What have people been telling you about me?

STELLA:

Telling?

BLANCHE:

You haven't heard any—unkind—gossip about me?

STELLA:

Why, no, Blanche, of course not!

BLANCHE:

Honey, there was—a good deal of talk in Laurel.

STELLA:

About *you,* Blanche?

BLANCHE:

I wasn't so good the last two years or so, after Belle Reve had started to slip through my fingers.

STELLA:

All of us do things we—

BLANCHE:

I never was hard or self-sufficient enough. When people are soft—soft people have got to shimmer and glow—they've got to put on soft colors, the colors of butterfly wings, and put a—paper lantern over the light.... It isn't enough to be soft. You've got to be soft *and attractive.* And I—I'm fading now! I don't know how much longer I can turn the trick.

[*The afternoon has faded to dusk. Stella goes into the bedroom and turns on the light under the paper lantern. She holds a bottled soft drink in her hand.*]

BLANCHE:

Have you been listening to me?

STELLA:

I don't listen to you when you are being morbid! [*She advances with the bottled Coke.*]

BLANCHE [*with abrupt change to gaiety*]:

Is that Coke for me?

STELLA:

Not for anyone else!

BLANCHE:

Why, you precious thing, you! Is it just Coke?

STELLA [*turning*]:

You mean you want a shot in it!

BLANCHE:

Well, honey, a shot never does a Coke any harm! Let me! You mustn't wait on me!

STELLA:

I like to wait on you, Blanche. It makes it seem more like home. [*She goes into the kitchen, finds a glass and pours a shot of whiskey into it.*]

BLANCHE:

I have to admit I love to be waited on . . .

[*She rushes into the bedroom. Stella goes to her with the glass. Blanche suddenly clutches Stella's free hand with a moaning sound and presses the hand to her lips. Stella is embarrassed by her show of emotion. Blanche speaks in a choked voice.*]

You're—you're—so *good* to me! And I—

STELLA:

Blanche.

BLANCHE:

I know, I won't! You hate me to talk sentimental! But honey, *believe* I feel things more than I *tell* you! I *won't* stay long! I won't, I *promise* I—

STELLA:

Blanche!

BLANCHE [*hysterically*]:

I won't, I promise, *I'll* go! Go *soon!* I will *really!* I *won't* hang around until he—throws me out . . .

STELLA:

Now will you stop talking foolish?

BLANCHE:

Yes, honey. Watch how you pour—that fizzy stuff foams over!

[*Blanche laughs shrilly and grabs the glass, but her hand shakes so it almost slips from her grasp. Stella pours the Coke into the glass. It foams over and spills. Blanche gives a piercing cry.*]

STELLA [*shocked by the cry*]:
Heavens!

BLANCHE:
Right on my pretty white skirt!

STELLA:
Oh . . . Use my hanky. Blot gently.

BLANCHE [*slowly recovering*]:
I know—gently—gently . . .

STELLA:
Did it stain?

BLANCHE:
Not a bit. Ha-ha! Isn't that lucky? [*She sits down shakily, taking a grateful drink. She holds the glass in both hands and continues to laugh a little.*]

STELLA:
Why did you scream like that?

BLANCHE:
I don't know why I screamed! [*continuing nervously*] Mitch—Mitch is coming at seven. I guess I am just feeling nervous about our relations. [*She begins to talk rapidly and breathlessly*] He hasn't gotten a thing but a good-night kiss, that's all I have given him, Stella. I want his respect. And men don't want anything they get too easy. But on the other hand men lose interest quickly. Especially when the girl is over—thirty. They think a

girl over thirty ought to—the vulgar term is—"put out." . . . And I—I'm not "putting out." Of course he—he doesn't know—I mean I haven't informed him—of my real age!

STELLA:

Why are you sensitive about your age?

BLANCHE:

Because of hard knocks my vanity's been given. What I mean is—he thinks I'm sort of—prim and proper, you know! [*She laughs out sharply*] I want to *deceive* him enough to make him—want me . . .

STELLA:

Blanche, do you want *him?*

BLANCHE:

I want to *rest!* I want to breathe quietly again! Yes—I *want* Mitch . . . *very badly!* Just think! If it happens! I can leave here and not be anyone's problem . . .

[*Stanley comes around the corner with a drink under his belt.*]

STANLEY [*bawling*]:

Hey, Steve! Hey, Eunice! Hey, Stella!

[*There are joyous calls from above. Trumpet and drums are heard from around the corner.*]

STELLA [*kissing Blanche impulsively*]:

It *will* happen!

BLANCHE [*doubtfully*]:

It will?

STELLA:

It *will!* [*She goes across into the kitchen, looking back at Blanche.*] It will, honey, *it will*. . . . But don't take another drink! [*Her voice catches as she goes out the door to meet her husband.*

[*Blanche sinks faintly back in her chair with her drink. Eunice shrieks with laughter and runs down the steps. Steve bounds after her with goat-like screeches and chases her around corner. Stanley and Stella twine arms as they follow, laughing.*

[*Dusk settles deeper. The music from the Four Deuces is slow and blue.*]

BLANCHE:

Ah, me, ah, me, ah, me . . .

[*Her eyes fall shut and the palm leaf fan drops from her fingers. She slaps her hand on the chair arm a couple of times. There is a little glimmer of lightning about the building.*

[*A Young Man comes along the street and rings the bell.*]

BLANCHE:

Come in.

[*The Young Man appears through the portieres. She regards him with interest.*]

BLANCHE:

Well, well! What can I do for *you?*

YOUNG MAN:

I'm collecting for *The Evening Star.*

BLANCHE:

I didn't know that stars took up collections.

YOUNG MAN:

It's the paper.

BLANCHE:

I know, I was joking—feebly! Will you—have a drink?

YOUNG MAN:

No, ma'am. No, thank you. I can't drink on the job.

BLANCHE:

Oh, well, now, let's see. . . . No, I don't have a dime! I'm not the lady of the house. I'm her sister from Mississippi. I'm one of those poor relations you've heard about.

YOUNG MAN:

That's all right. I'll drop by later. [*He starts to go out. She approaches a little.*]

BLANCHE:

Hey! [*He turns back shyly. She puts a cigarette in a long holder*] Could you give me a light? [*She crosses toward him. They meet at the door between the two rooms.*]

YOUNG MAN:

Sure. [*He takes out a lighter*] This doesn't always work.

BLANCHE:

It's temperamental? [*It flares*] Ah!—thank you. [*He starts away again*] Hey! [*He turns again, still more uncertainly. She goes close to him*] Uh—what time is it?

YOUNG MAN:

Fifteen of seven, ma'am.

BLANCHE:

So late? Don't you just love these long rainy afternoons in New Orleans when an hour isn't just an hour—but a little piece of eternity dropped into your hands—and who knows what to do with it? [*She touches his shoulders.*] You—uh—didn't get wet in the rain?

YOUNG MAN:

No, ma'am. I stepped inside.

BLANCHE:

In a drugstore? And had a soda?

YOUNG MAN:

Uh-huh.

BLANCHE:

Chocolate?

YOUNG MAN:

No, ma'am. Cherry.

BLANCHE [*laughing*]:

Cherry!

YOUNG MAN:

A cherry soda.

BLANCHE:

You make my mouth water. [*She touches his cheek lightly, and smiles. Then she goes to the trunk.*]

YOUNG MAN:

Well, I'd better be going—

BLANCHE [*stopping him*]:

Young man!

[*He turns. She takes a large, gossamer scarf from the trunk and drapes it about her shoulders.*]

[*In the ensuing pause, the "blue piano" is heard. It continues through the rest of this scene and the opening of the next. The young man clears his throat and looks yearningly at the door.*]

Young man! Young, young, young man! Has anyone ever told you that you look like a young Prince out of the Arabian Nights?

[*The Young Man laughs uncomfortably and stands like a bashful kid. Blanche speaks softly to him.*]

Well, you do, honey lamb! Come here. I want to kiss you, just once, softly and sweetly on your mouth!

[*Without waiting for him to accept, she crosses quickly to him and presses her lips to his.*]

Now run along, now, quickly! It would be nice to keep you, but I've got to be good—and keep my hands off children.

[*He stares at her a moment. She opens the door for him and blows a kiss at him as he goes down the steps with a dazed look. She stands there a little dreamily after he has disappeared. Then Mitch appears around the corner with a bunch of roses.*]

BLANCHE [*gaily*]:
Look who's coming! My Rosenkavalier! Bow to me first . . . now present them! *Ahhhh—Merciiii!*

[*She looks at him over them, coquettishly pressing them to her lips. He beams at her self-consciously.*]

SCENE SIX

It is about two A.M. on the same evening. The outer wall of the building is visible. Blanche and Mitch come in. The utter exhaustion which only a neurasthenic personality can know is evident in Blanche's voice and manner. Mitch is stolid but depressed. They have probably been out to the amusement park on Lake Pontchartrain, for Mitch is bearing, upside down, a plaster statuette of Mae West, the sort of prize won at shooting galleries and carnival games of chance.

BLANCHE [*stopping lifelessly at the steps*]:
Well—

[*Mitch laughs uneasily.*]
Well . . .

MITCH:
I guess it must be pretty late—and you're tired.

BLANCHE:
Even the hot tamale man has deserted the street, and he hangs on till the end. [*Mitch laughs uneasily again*] How will you get home?

MITCH:
I'll walk over to Bourbon and catch an owl-car.

BLANCHE [*laughing grimly*]:
Is that streetcar named Desire still grinding along the tracks at this hour?

MITCH [*heavily*]:
I'm afraid you haven't gotten much fun out of this evening, Blanche.

BLANCHE:

I spoiled it for *you.*

MITCH:

No, you didn't, but I felt all the time that I wasn't giving you much—entertainment.

BLANCHE:

I simply couldn't rise to the occasion. That was all. I don't think I've ever tried so hard to be gay and made such a dismal mess of it. I get ten points for trying!—I *did* try.

MITCH:

Why did you try if you didn't feel like it, Blanche?

BLANCHE:

I was just obeying the law of nature.

MITCH:

Which law is that?

BLANCHE:

The one that says the lady must entertain the gentleman—or no dice! See if you can locate my door key in this purse. When I'm so tired my fingers are all thumbs!

MITCH [*rooting in her purse*]:

This it?

BLANCHE:

No, honey, that's the key to my trunk which I must soon be packing.

MITCH:

You mean you are leaving here soon?

BLANCHE:

I've outstayed my welcome.

MITCH:

This it?

[*The music fades away.*]

BLANCHE:

Eureka! Honey, you open the door while I take a last look at the sky. [*She leans on the porch rail. He opens the door and stands awkwardly behind her.*] I'm looking for the Pleiades, the Seven Sisters, but these girls are not out tonight. Oh, yes they are, there they are! God bless them! All in a bunch going home from their little bridge party.... Y' get the door open? Good boy! I guess you—want to go now...

[*He shuffles and coughs a little.*]

MITCH:

Can I—uh—kiss you—good night?

BLANCHE:

Why do you always ask me if you may?

MITCH:

I don't know whether you want me to or not.

BLANCHE:

Why should you be so doubtful?

MITCH:

That night when we parked by the lake and I kissed you, you—

BLANCHE:

Honey, it wasn't the kiss I objected to. I liked the kiss very much. It was the other little—familiarity—that I—felt obliged to—discourage.... I didn't resent it! Not a bit in the world! In fact, I was somewhat flattered that you—desired me! But, honey, you know as well as I do that a single girl, a girl alone in the world, has got to keep a firm hold on her emotions or she'll be lost!

MITCH [*solemnly*]:

Lost?

BLANCHE:

I guess you are used to girls that like to be lost. The kind that get lost immediately, on the first date!

MITCH:

I like you to be exactly the way that you are, because in all my—experience—I have never known anyone like you.

[*Blanche looks at him gravely; then she bursts into laughter and then claps a hand to her mouth.*]

MITCH:

Are you laughing at me?

BLANCHE:

No, honey. The lord and lady of the house have not yet returned, so come in. We'll have a nightcap. Let's leave the lights off. Shall we?

MITCH:

You just—do what you want to.

[*Blanche precedes him into the kitchen. The outer wall of the building disappears and the interiors of the two rooms can be dimly seen.*]

BLANCHE [*remaining in the first room*]:

The other room's more comfortable—go on in. This crashing around in the dark is my search for some liquor.

MITCH:

You want a drink?

BLANCHE:

I want *you* to have a drink! You have been so anxious and solemn all evening, and so have I; we have both been anxious and solemn and now for these few last remaining moments of our lives together—I want to create—*joie de vivre!* I'm lighting a candle.

MITCH:

That's good.

BLANCHE:

We are going to be very Bohemian. We are going to pretend that we are sitting in a little artists' cafe on the Left Bank in Paris! [*She lights a candle stub and puts it in a bottle.*] *Je suis la Dame aux Camellias! Vous êtes—Armand!* Understand French?

MITCH [*heavily*]:

Naw. Naw, I—

BLANCHE:

Voulez-vous couchez avec moi ce soir? Vous ne comprenez pas? Ah, quelle dommage!—I mean it's a damned good thing. . . . I've found some liquor! Just enough for two shots without any dividends, honey . . .

MITCH [*heavily*]:

That's—good.

[*She enters the bedroom with the drinks and the candle.*]

BLANCHE:

Sit down! Why don't you take off your coat and loosen your collar?

MITCH:

I better leave it on.

BLANCHE:

No. I want you to be comfortable.

MITCH:

I am ashamed of the way I perspire. My shirt is sticking to me.

BLANCHE:

Perspiration is healthy. If people didn't perspire they would die in five minutes. [*She takes his coat from him*] This is a nice coat. What kind of material is it?

MITCH:

They call that stuff alpaca.

BLANCHE:

Oh. Alpaca.

MITCH:

It's very light-weight alpaca.

BLANCHE:

Oh. Light weight alpaca.

MITCH:

I don't like to wear a wash-coat even in summer because I sweat through it.

BLANCHE:

Oh.

MITCH:

And it don't look neat on me. A man with a heavy build has got to be careful of what he puts on him so he don't look too clumsy.

BLANCHE:

You are not too heavy.

MITCH:

You don't think I am?

BLANCHE:

You are not the delicate type. You have a massive bone-structure and a very imposing physique.

MITCH:

Thank you. Last Christmas I was given a membership to the New Orleans Athletic Club.

BLANCHE:

Oh, good.

MITCH:

It was the finest present I ever was given. I work out there with the weights and I swim and I keep myself fit. When I started there, I was getting soft in the belly but now my belly is hard. It is so hard now that a man can punch me in the belly and it don't hurt me. Punch me! Go on! See? [*She pokes lightly at him.*]

BLANCHE:

Gracious. [*Her hand touches her chest.*]

MITCH:

Guess how much I weigh, Blanche?

BLANCHE:

Oh, I'd say in the vicinity of—one hundred and eighty?

MITCH:

Guess again.

BLANCHE:

Not that much?

MITCH:

No. More.

BLANCHE:

Well, you're a tall man and you can carry a good deal of weight without looking awkward.

MITCH:

I weigh two hundred and seven pounds and I'm six feet one and one half inches tall in my bare feet—without shoes on. And that is what I weigh stripped.

BLANCHE:

Oh, my goodness, me! It's awe-inspiring.

MITCH [*embarrassed*]:

My weight is not a very interesting subject to talk about. [*He hesitates for a moment*] What's yours?

BLANCHE:

My weight?

MITCH:

Yes.

BLANCHE:

Guess!

MITCH:

Let me lift you.

BLANCHE:

Samson! Go on, lift me. [*He comes behind her and puts his hands on her waist and raises her lightly off the ground*] Well?

MITCH:

You are light as a feather.

BLANCHE:

Ha-ha! [*He lowers her but keeps his hands on her waist. Blanche speaks with an affectation of demureness*] You may release me now.

MITCH:

Huh?

BLANCHE [*gaily*]:

I said unhand me, sir. [*He fumblingly embraces her. Her voice sounds gently reproving*] Now, Mitch. Just because Stanley and Stella aren't at home is no reason why you shouldn't behave like a gentleman.

MITCH:

Just give me a slap whenever I step out of bounds.

BLANCHE:

That won't be necessary. You're a natural gentleman, one of the very few that are left in the world. I don't want you to think that I am severe and old maid schoolteacherish or anything like that. It's just—well—

MITCH:

Huh?

BLANCHE:

I guess it is just that I have—old-fashioned ideals! [*She rolls her eyes, knowing he cannot see her face. Mitch goes to the front door. There is a considerable silence between them. Blanche sighs and Mitch coughs self-consciously.*]

MITCH [*finally*]:

Where's Stanley and Stella tonight?

BLANCHE:

They have gone out. With Mr. and Mrs. Hubbell upstairs.

MITCH:

Where did they go?

BLANCHE:

I think they were planning to go to a midnight prevue at Loew's State.

MITCH:

We should all go out together some night.

BLANCHE:

No. That wouldn't be a good plan.

MITCH:

Why not?

BLANCHE:

You are an old friend of Stanley's?

MITCH:

We was together in the Two-forty-first.

BLANCHE:

I guess he talks to you frankly?

MITCH:

Sure.

BLANCHE:

Has he talked to you about me?

MITCH:

Oh—not very much.

BLANCHE:

The way you say that, I suspect that he has.

MITCH:

No, he hasn't said much.

BLANCHE:

But what he *has* said. What would you say his attitude toward me was?

MITCH:

Why do you want to ask that?

BLANCHE:

Well—

MITCH:

Don't you get along with him?

BLANCHE:

What do you think?

MITCH:

I don't think he understands you.

BLANCHE:

That is putting it mildly. If it weren't for Stella about to have a baby, I wouldn't be able to endure things here.

MITCH:

He isn't—nice to you?

BLANCHE:

He is insufferably rude. Goes out of his way to offend me.

MITCH:

In what way, Blanche?

BLANCHE:

Why, in every conceivable way.

MITCH:

I'm surprised to hear that.

BLANCHE:

Are you?

MITCH:

Well, I—don't see how anybody could be rude to you.

BLANCHE:

It's really a pretty frightful situation. You see, there's no privacy here. There's just these portieres between the two rooms at night. He stalks through the rooms in his underwear at night. And I have to ask him to close the bathroom door. That sort of commonness isn't necessary. You probably wonder why I don't move out. Well, I'll tell you frankly. A teacher's salary is barely sufficient for her living expenses. I didn't save a penny last year and so I had to come here for the summer. That's why I have to put up with my sister's husband. And he has to put up with me, apparently so much against his wishes. ... Surely he must have told you how much he hates me!

MITCH:

I don't think he hates you.

BLANCHE:

He hates me. Or why would he insult me? The first time I laid eyes on him I thought to myself, that man is my executioner! That man will destroy me, unless ——

MITCH:

Blanche—

BLANCHE:

Yes, honey?

MITCH:

Can I ask you a question?

BLANCHE:

Yes. What?

MITCH:

How old are you?

[*She makes a nervous gesture.*]

BLANCHE:

Why do you want to know?

MITCH:

I talked to my mother about you and she said, "How old is Blanche?" And I wasn't able to tell her. [*There is another pause.*]

BLANCHE:

You talked to your mother about me?

MITCH:

Yes.

BLANCHE:

Why?

MITCH:

I told my mother how nice you were, and I liked you.

BLANCHE:

Were you sincere about that?

MITCH:

You know I was.

BLANCHE:

Why did your mother want to know my age?

MITCH:

Mother is sick.

BLANCHE:

I'm sorry to hear it. Badly?

MITCH:

She won't live long. Maybe just a few months.

BLANCHE:

Oh.

MITCH:

She worries because I'm not settled.

BLANCHE:

Oh.

MITCH:

She wants me to be settled down before she— [*His voice is hoarse and he clears his throat twice, shuffling nervously around with his hands in and out of his pockets.*]

BLANCHE:

You love her very much, don't you?

MITCH:

Yes.

BLANCHE:

I think you have a great capacity for devotion. You will be lonely when she passes on, won't you? [*Mitch clears his throat and nods.*] I understand what that is.

MITCH:

To be lonely?

BLANCHE:

I loved someone, too, and the person I loved I lost.

MITCH:

Dead? [*She crosses to the window and sits on the sill, looking out. She pours herself another drink.*] A man?

BLANCHE:

He was a boy, just a boy, when I was a very young girl. When I was sixteen, I made the discovery—love. All at once and much, much too completely. It was like you suddenly turned a blinding light on something that had always been half in shadow, that's how it struck the world for me. But I was unlucky. Deluded. There was something different about the boy, a nervousness, a softness and tenderness which wasn't like a man's, although he wasn't the least bit effeminate looking—still —that thing was there. . . . He came to me for help. I didn't know that. I didn't find out anything till after our marriage when we'd run away and come back and all I knew was I'd failed him in some mysterious way and wasn't able to give the help he needed but couldn't speak of! He was in the quicksands and clutching at me—but I wasn't holding him out, I was slipping in with him! I didn't know that. I didn't know anything except I loved him unendurably but without being able to help him or help myself. Then I found out. In the worst of all possible ways. By coming suddenly into a room that I thought was empty—which wasn't empty, but had two people in it . . . the boy I had married and an older man who had been his friend for years . . .

[*A locomotive is heard approaching outside. She claps her hands to her ears and crouches over. The headlight of the locomotive glares into the room as it thunders past. As the noise recedes she straightens slowly and continues speaking.*]

Afterward we pretended that nothing had been discovered. Yes, the three of us drove out to Moon Lake Casino, very drunk and laughing all the way.

[*Polka music sounds, in a minor key faint with distance.*]

We danced the Varsouviana! Suddenly in the middle of the dance the boy I had married broke away from me and ran out of the casino. A few moments later—a shot!

[*The polka stops abruptly.*

[*Blanche rises stiffly. Then, the polka resumes in a major key.*]

I ran out—all did!—all ran and gathered about the terrible thing at the edge of the lake! I couldn't get near for the crowding. Then somebody caught my arm. "Don't go any closer! Come back! You don't want to see!" See? See what! Then I heard voices say—Allan! Allan! The Grey boy! He'd stuck the revolver into his mouth, and fired—so that the back of his head had been—blown away!

[*She sways and covers her face.*]

It was because—on the dance floor—unable to stop myself—I'd suddenly said—"I saw! I know! You disgust me..." And then the searchlight which had been turned on the world was turned off again and never for one moment since has there been any light that's stronger than this—kitchen—candle...

[*Mitch gets up awkwardly and moves toward her a little. The polka music increases. Mitch stands beside her.*]

MITCH [*drawing her slowly into his arms*]:
You need somebody. And I need somebody, too. Could it be—you and me, Blanche?

[*She stares at him vacantly for a moment. Then with a soft cry huddles in his embrace. She makes a sobbing effort to speak but the words won't come. He kisses her forehead and her eyes and finally her lips. The Polka tune fades out. Her breath is drawn and released in long, grateful sobs.*]

BLANCHE:
Sometimes—there's God—so quickly!

SCENE SEVEN

It is late afternoon in mid-September.

The portieres are open and a table is set for a birthday supper, with cake and flowers.

Stella is completing the decorations as Stanley comes in.

STANLEY:
What's all this stuff for?

STELLA:
Honey, it's Blanche's birthday.

STANLEY:
She here?

STELLA:
In the bathroom.

STANLEY [*mimicking*]:
"Washing out some things"?

STELLA:
I reckon so.

STANLEY:
How long she been in there?

STELLA:
All afternoon.

STANLEY [*mimicking*]:
"Soaking in a hot tub"?

STELLA:
Yes.

STANLEY:

Temperature 100 on the nose, and she soaks herself in a hot tub.

STELLA:

She says it cools her off for the evening.

STANLEY:

And you run out an' get her cokes, I suppose? And serve 'em to Her Majesty in the tub? [*Stella shrugs*] Set down here a minute.

STELLA:

Stanley, I've got things to do.

STANLEY:

Set down! I've got th' dope on your big sister, Stella.

STELLA:

Stanley, stop picking on Blanche.

STANLEY:

That girl calls *me* common!

STELLA:

Lately you been doing all you can think of to rub her the wrong way, Stanley, and Blanche is sensitive and you've got to realize that Blanche and I grew up under very different circumstances than you did.

STANLEY:

So I been told. And told and told and told! You know she's been feeding us a pack of lies here?

STELLA:

No, I don't, and—

STANLEY:

Well, she has, however. But now the cat's out of the bag! I found out some things!

STELLA:

What—things?

STANLEY:

Things I already suspected. But now I got proof from the most reliable sources—which I have checked on!

[*Blanche is singing in the bathroom a saccharine popular ballad which is used contrapuntally with Stanley's speech.*]

STELLA [*to Stanley*]:

Lower your voice!

STANLEY:

Some canary bird, huh!

STELLA:

Now please tell me quietly what you think you've found out about my sister.

STANLEY:

Lie Number One: All this squeamishness she puts on! You should just know the line she's been feeding to Mitch. He thought she had never been more than kissed by a fellow! But Sister Blanche is no lily! Ha-ha! Some lily she is!

STELLA:

What have you heard and who from?

STANLEY:

Our supply-man down at the plant has been going through Laurel for years and he knows all about her and everybody else in the town of Laurel knows all about her. She is as famous in Laurel as if she was the President of the United States, only she is not respected by any party! This supply-man stops at a hotel called the Flamingo.

BLANCHE [*singing blithely*]:

"Say, it's only a paper moon, Sailing over a cardboard sea —But it wouldn't be make-believe If you believed in me!"

STELLA:

What about the—Flamingo?

STANLEY:

She stayed there, too.

STELLA:

My sister lived at Belle Reve.

STANLEY:

This is after the home-place had slipped through her lily-white fingers! She moved to the Flamingo! A second-class hotel which has the advantage of not interfering in the private social life of the personalities there! The Flamingo is used to all kinds of goings-on. But even the management of the Flamingo was impressed by Dame Blanche! In fact they was so impressed by Dame Blanche that they requested her to turn in her room key—for permanently! This happened a couple of weeks before she showed here.

BLANCHE [*singing*]:

"It's a Barnum and Bailey world, Just as phony as it can be—
But it wouldn't be make-believe If you believed in me!"

STELLA:

What—contemptible—lies!

STANLEY:

Sure, I can see how you would be upset by this. She pulled the wool over your eyes as much as Mitch's!

STELLA:

It's pure invention! There's not a word of truth in it and if I were a man and this creature had dared to invent such things in my presence—

BLANCHE [*singing*]:

"Without your love,
It's a honky-tonk parade!
Without your love,
It's a melody played In a penny arcade..."

STANLEY:

Honey, I told you I thoroughly checked on these stories! Now wait till I finished. The trouble with Dame Blanche was that she couldn't put on her act any more in Laurel! They got wised up after two or three dates with her and then they quit, and she goes on to another, the same old line, same old act, same old hooey! But the town was too small for this to go on forever! And as time went by she became a town character. Regarded as not just different but downright loco—nuts.

[*Stella draws back.*]

And for the last year or two she has been washed up like poison. That's why she's here this summer, visiting royalty, putting on all this act—because she's practically told by the mayor to get out of town! Yes, did you know there was an army camp near Laurel and your sister's was one of the places called "Out-of-Bounds"?

BLANCHE:

"It's only a paper moon, Just as phony as it can be—
But it wouldn't be make-believe If you believed in me!"

STANLEY:

Well, so much for her being such a refined and particular type of girl. Which brings us to Lie Number Two.

STELLA:

I don't want to hear any more!

STANLEY:

She's not going back to teach school! In fact I am willing to bet you that she never had no idea of returning to Laurel! She didn't resign temporarily from the high school because of her nerves! No, siree, Bob! She didn't. They kicked her out of that high school before the spring term ended—and I hate to tell you the reason that step was taken! A seventeen-year-old boy—she'd gotten mixed up with!

BLANCHE:

"It's a Barnum and Bailey world, Just as phony as it
can be—"

[*In the bathroom the water goes on loud; little breathless cries and peals of laughter are heard as if a child were frolicking in the tub.*]

STELLA:

This is making me—sick!

STANLEY:

The boy's dad learned about it and got in touch with the high school superintendent. Boy, oh, boy, I'd like to have been in that office when Dame Blanche was called on the carpet! I'd like to have seen her trying to squirm out of that one! But they had her on the hook good and proper that time and she knew that the jig was all up! They told her she better move on to some fresh territory. Yep, it was practickly a town ordinance passed against her!

[*The bathroom door is opened and Blanche thrusts her head out, holding a towel about her hair.*]

BLANCHE:

Stella!

STELLA [*faintly*]:

Yes, Blanche?

BLANCHE:

Give me another bath-towel to dry my hair with. I've just washed it.

STELLA:

Yes, Blanche. [*She crosses in a dazed way from the kitchen to the bathroom door with a towel.*]

BLANCHE:

What's the matter, honey?

STELLA:

Matter? Why?

BLANCHE:

You have such a strange expression on your face!

STELLA:

Oh— [*She tries to laugh*] I guess I'm a little tired!

BLANCHE:

Why don't you bathe, too, soon as I get out?

STANLEY [*calling from the kitchen*]:

How soon is that going to be?

BLANCHE:

Not so terribly long! Possess your soul in patience!

STANLEY:

It's not my soul, it's my kidneys I'm worried about!

[*Blanche slams the door. Stanley laughs harshly. Stella comes slowly back into the kitchen.*]

STANLEY:

Well, what do you think of it?

STELLA:

I don't believe all of those stories and I think your supply-man was mean and rotten to tell them. It's possible that some of the things he said are partly true. There are things about my sister I don't approve of—things that caused sorrow at home. She was always—flighty!

STANLEY:

Flighty!

STELLA:

But when she was young, very young, she married a boy who wrote poetry. . . . He was extremely good-looking. I think Blanche didn't just love him but worshipped the ground he walked on! Adored him and thought him almost too fine to be human! But then she found out—

STANLEY:

What?

STELLA:

This beautiful and talented young man was a degenerate. Didn't your supply-man give you that information?

STANLEY:

All we discussed was recent history. That must have been a pretty long time ago.

STELLA:

Yes, it was—a pretty long time ago...

[*Stanley comes up and takes her by the shoulders rather gently. She gently withdraws from him. Automatically she starts sticking little pink candles in the birthday cake.*]

STANLEY:

How many candles you putting in that cake?

STELLA:

I'll stop at twenty-five.

STANLEY:

Is company expected?

STELLA:

We asked Mitch to come over for cake and ice-cream.

[*Stanley looks a little uncomfortable. He lights a cigarette from the one he has just finished.*]

STANLEY:

I wouldn't be expecting Mitch over tonight.

[*Stella pauses in her occupation with candles and looks slowly around at Stanley.*]

STELLA:

Why?

STANLEY:

Mitch is a buddy of mine. We were in the same outfit together—Two-forty-first Engineers. We work in the same plant and now on the same bowling team. You think I could face him if—

STELLA:

Stanley Kowalski, did you—did you repeat what that—?

STANLEY:

You're goddam right I told him! I'd have that on my conscience the rest of my life if I knew all that stuff and let my best friend get caught!

STELLA:

Is Mitch through with her?

STANLEY:

Wouldn't you be if—?

STELLA:

I said, *Is Mitch through with her?*

[*Blanche's voice is lifted again, serenely as a bell. She sings "But it wouldn't be make-believe If you believed in me."*]

STANLEY:

No, I don't think he's necessarily through with her—just wised up!

STELLA:

Stanley, she thought Mitch was—going to—going to marry her. I was hoping so, too.

STANLEY:

Well, he's not going to marry her. Maybe he *was,* but he's not going to jump in a tank with a school of sharks—now! [*He rises*] Blanche! Oh, Blanche! Can I please get in my bathroom? [*There is a pause.*]

BLANCHE:

Yes, indeed, sir! Can you wait one second while I dry?

STANLEY:

Having waited one hour I guess one second ought to pass in a hurry.

STELLA:

And she hasn't got her job? Well, what will she do!

STANLEY:

She's not stayin' here after Tuesday. You know that, don't you? Just to make sure I bought her ticket myself. A bus ticket?

STELLA:

In the first place, Blanche wouldn't go on a bus.

STANLEY:

She'll go on a bus and like it.

STELLA:

No, she won't, no, she won't, Stanley!

STANLEY:

She'll go! Period. P.S. She'll go *Tuesday!*

STELLA [*slowly*]:

What'll—she—do? What on earth will she—*do!*

STANLEY:

Her future is mapped out for her.

STELLA:

What do you mean?

[*Blanche sings.*]

STANLEY:

Hey, canary bird! Toots! Get *OUT* of the *BATHROOM!*

[*The bathroom door flies open and Blanche emerges with a gay peal of laughter, but as Stanley crosses past her, a frightened look appears in her face, almost a look of panic. He doesn't look at her but slams the bathroom door shut as he goes in.*]

BLANCHE [*snatching up a hair-brush*]:
Oh, I feel so good after my long, hot bath, I feel so good and cool and—rested!

STELLA [*sadly and doubtfully from the kitchen*]:
Do you, Blanche?

BLANCHE [*snatching up a hairbrush*]:
Yes, I do, so refreshed! [*She tinkles her highball glass.*] A hot bath and a long, cold drink always give me a brand new outlook on life! [*She looks through the portieres at Stella, standing between them, and slowly stops brushing*] Something has happened!—What is it?

STELLA [*turning away quickly*]:
Why, nothing has happened, Blanche.

BLANCHE:
You're lying! Something has!

[*She stares fearfully at Stella, who pretends to be busy at the table. The distant piano goes into a hectic breakdown.*]

SCENE EIGHT

Three quarters of an hour later.

The view through the big windows is fading gradually into a still-golden dusk. A torch of sunlight blazes on the side of a big water-tank or oil-drum across the empty lot toward the business district which is now pierced by pin-points of lighted windows or windows reflecting the sunset.

The three people are completing a dismal birthday supper. Stanley looks sullen. Stella is embarrassed and sad.

Blanche has a tight, artificial smile on her drawn face. There is a fourth place at the table which is left vacant.

BLANCHE [*suddenly*]:
Stanley, tell us a joke, tell us a funny story to make us all laugh. I don't know what's the matter, we're all so solemn. Is it because I've been stood up by my beau?

[*Stella laughs feebly.*]

It's the first time in my entire experience with men, and I've had a good deal of all sorts, that I've actually been stood up by anybody! Ha-ha! I don't know how to take it. . . . Tell us a funny little story, Stanley! Something to help us out.

STANLEY:
I didn't think you liked my stories, Blanche.

BLANCHE:
I like them when they're amusing but not indecent.

STANLEY:
I don't know any refined enough for your taste.

BLANCHE:

Then let me tell one.

STELLA:

Yes, you tell one, Blanche. You used to know lots of good stories.

[*The music fades.*]

BLANCHE:

Let me see, now. . . . I must run through my repertoire! Oh, yes—I love parrot stories! Do you all like parrot stories? Well, this one's about the old maid and the parrot. This old maid, she had a parrot that cursed a blue streak and knew more vulgar expressions than Mr. Kowalski!

STANLEY:

Huh.

BLANCHE:

And the only way to hush the parrot up was to put the cover back on its cage so it would think it was night and go back to sleep. Well, one morning the old maid had just uncovered the parrot for the day—when who should she see coming up the front walk but the preacher! Well, she rushed back to the parrot and slipped the cover back on the cage and then she let in the preacher. And the parrot was perfectly still, just as quiet as a mouse, but just as she was asking the preacher how much sugar he wanted in his coffee—the parrot broke the silence with a loud—[*She whistles*]—and said—"God *damn,* but that was a short day!"

[*She throws back her head and laughs. Stella also makes an ineffectual effort to seem amused. Stanley pays no attention to the story but reaches way over the table to spear his fork into the remaining chop which he eats with his fingers.*]

BLANCHE:

Apparently Mr. Kowalski was not amused.

STELLA:

Mr. Kowalski is too busy making a pig of himself to think of anything else!

STANLEY:

That's right, baby.

STELLA:

Your face and your fingers are disgustingly greasy. Go and wash up and then help me clear the table.

[*He hurls a plate to the floor.*]

STANLEY:

That's how I'll clear the table! [*He seizes her arm*] Don't ever talk that way to me! "Pig—Polack—disgusting—vulgar—greasy!"—them kind of words have been on your tongue and your sister's too much around here! What do you two think you are? A pair of queens? Remember what Huey Long said—"Every Man is a King!" And I am the king around here, so don't forget it! [*He hurls a cup and saucer to the floor*] My place is cleared! You want me to clear your places?

[*Stella begins to cry weakly. Stanley stalks out on the porch and lights a cigarette.*

[*The Negro entertainers around the corner are heard.*]

BLANCHE:

What happened while I was bathing? What did he tell you, Stella?

STELLA:

Nothing, nothing, nothing!

BLANCHE:

I think he told you something about Mitch and me! You know why Mitch didn't come but you won't tell me! [*Stella shakes her head helplessly*] I'm going to call him!

STELLA:

I wouldn't call him, Blanche.

BLANCHE:

I am, I'm going to call him on the phone.

STELLA [*miserably*]:

I wish you wouldn't.

BLANCHE:

I intend to be given some explanation from someone!

[*She rushes to the phone in the bedroom. Stella goes out on the porch and stares reproachfully at her husband. He grunts and turns away from her.*]

STELLA:

I hope you're pleased with your doings. I never had so much trouble swallowing food in my life, looking at that girl's face and the empty chair! [*She cries quietly.*]

BLANCHE [*at the phone*]:

Hello. Mr. Mitchell, please. . . . Oh. . . . I would like to leave a number if I may. Magnolia 9047. And say it's important to call. . . . Yes, very important. . . . Thank you. [*She remains by the phone with a lost, frightened look.*]

[*Stanley turns slowly back toward his wife and takes her clumsily in his arms.*]

STANLEY:

Stell, it's gonna be all right after she goes and after you've had the baby. It's gonna be all right again between you and me the way that it was. You remember that way that it was? Them nights we had together? God, honey, it's gonna be sweet when we can make noise in the night the way that we used to and get the colored lights going with nobody's sister behind the curtains to hear us!

[*Their upstairs neighbors are heard in bellowing laughter at something. Stanley chuckles.*]

Steve an' Eunice...

STELLA:

Come on back in. [*She returns to the kitchen and starts lighting the candles on the white cake.*] Blanche?

BLANCHE:

Yes. [*She returns from the bedroom to the table in the kitchen.*] Oh, those pretty, pretty little candles! Oh, don't burn them, Stella.

STELLA:

I certainly will.

[*Stanley comes back in.*]

BLANCHE:

You ought to save them for baby's birthdays. Oh, I hope candles are going to glow in his life and I hope that his eyes are going to be like candles, like two blue candles lighted in a white cake!

STANLEY [*sitting down*]:
What poetry!

BLANCHE [*she pauses reflectively for a moment*]:
I shouldn't have called him.

STELLA:
There's lots of things could have happened.

BLANCHE:
There's no excuse for it, Stella. I don't have to put up with insults. I won't be taken for granted.

STANLEY:
Goddamn, it's hot in here with the steam from the bathroom.

BLANCHE:
I've said I was sorry three times. [*The piano fades out.*] I take hot baths for my nerves. Hydrotherapy, they call it. You healthy Polack, without a nerve in your body, of course you don't know what anxiety feels like!

STANLEY:
I am not a Polack. People from Poland are Poles, not Polacks. But what I am is a one-hundred-per-cent American, born and raised in the greatest country on earth and proud as hell of it, so don't ever call me a Polack.

[*The phone rings. Blanche rises expectantly.*]

BLANCHE:
Oh, that's for me, I'm sure.

STANLEY:

I'm not sure. Keep your seat. [*He crosses leisurely to phone.*] H'lo. Aw, yeh, hello, Mac.

[*He leans against wall, staring insultingly in at Blanche. She sinks back in her chair with a frightened look. Stella leans over and touches her shoulder.*]

BLANCHE:

Oh, keep your hands off me, Stella. What is the matter with you? Why do you look at me with that pitying look?

STANLEY [*bawling*]:

QUIET IN THERE!—We've got a noisy woman on the place.—Go on, Mac. At Riley's? No, I don't wanta bowl at Riley's. I had a little trouble with Riley last week. I'm the team captain, ain't I? All right, then, we're not gonna bowl at Riley's, we're gonna bowl at the West Side or the Gala! All right, Mac. See you!

[*He hangs up and returns to the table. Blanche fiercely controls herself, drinking quickly from her tumbler of water. He doesn't look at her but reaches in a pocket. Then he speaks slowly and with false amiability.*]

Sister Blanche, I've got a little birthday remembrance for you.

BLANCHE:

Oh, have you, Stanley? I wasn't expecting any, I—I don't know why Stella wants to observe my birthday! I'd much rather forget it—when you—reach twenty-seven! Well—age is a subject that you'd prefer to—ignore!

STANLEY:

Twenty-seven?

BLANCHE [*quickly*]:
What is it? Is it for *me?*

[*He is holding a little envelope toward her.*]

STANLEY:
Yes, I hope you like it!

BLANCHE:
Why, why—Why, it's a—

STANLEY:
Ticket! Back to Laurel! On the Greyhound! Tuesday!

[*The Varsouviana music steals in softly and continues playing. Stella rises abruptly and turns her back. Blanches tries to smile. Then she tries to laugh. Then she gives both up and springs from the table and runs into the next room. She clutches her throat and then runs into the bathroom. Coughing, gagging sounds are heard.*]

Well!

STELLA:
You didn't need to do that.

STANLEY:
Don't forget all that I took off her.

STELLA:
You needn't have been so cruel to someone alone as she is.

STANLEY:
Delicate piece she is.

STELLA:
She is. She was. You didn't know Blanche as a girl. Nobody, nobody, was tender and trusting as she was. But people like you abused her, and forced her to change.

[*He crosses into the bedroom, ripping off his shirt, and changes into a brilliant silk bowling shirt. She follows him.*]

Do you think you're going bowling now?

STANLEY:

Sure.

STELLA:

You're not going bowling. [*She catches hold of his shirt*] Why did you do this to her?

STANLEY:

I done nothing to no one. Let go of my shirt. You've torn it.

STELLA:

I want to know why. Tell me why.

STANLEY:

When we first met, me and you, you thought I was common. How right you was, baby. I was common as dirt. You showed me the snapshot of the place with the columns. I pulled you down off them columns and how you loved it, having them colored lights going! And wasn't we happy together, wasn't it all okay till she showed here?

[*Stella makes a slight movement. Her look goes suddenly inward as if some interior voice had called her name. She begins a slow, shuffling progress from the bedroom to the kitchen, leaning and resting on the back of the chair and then on the edge of a table with a blind look and listening expression. Stanley, finishing with his shirt, is unaware of her reaction.*]

And wasn't we happy together? Wasn't it all okay? Till

she showed here. Hoity-toity, describing me as an ape. [*He suddenly notices the change in Stella*] Hey, what is it, Stell? [*He crosses to her.*]

STELLA [*quietly*]:
Take me to the hospital.

[*He is with her now, supporting her with his arm, murmuring indistinguishably as they go outside.*]

SCENE NINE

A while later that evening. Blanche is seated in a tense hunched position in a bedroom chair that she has re-covered with diagonal green and white stripes. She has on her scarlet satin robe. On the table beside chair is a bottle of liquor and a glass. The rapid, feverish polka tune, the "Varsouviana," is heard. The music is in her mind; she is drinking to escape it and the sense of disaster closing in on her, and she seems to whisper the words of the song. An electric fan is turning back and forth across her.

Mitch comes around the corner in work clothes: blue denim shirt and pants. He is unshaven. He climbs the steps to the door and rings. Blanche is startled.

BLANCHE:

Who is it, please?

MITCH [*hoarsely*]:

Me. Mitch.

[*The polka tune stops.*]

BLANCHE:

Mitch!—Just a minute.

[*She rushes about frantically, hiding the bottle in a closet, crouching at the mirror and dabbing her face with cologne and powder. She is so excited that her breath is audible as she dashes about. At last she rushes to the door in the kitchen and lets him in.*]

Mitch!—Y'know, I really shouldn't let you in after the treatment I have received from you this evening! So utterly uncavalier! But hello, beautiful!

[*She offers him her lips. He ignores it and pushes past her into the flat. She looks fearfully after him as he stalks into the bedroom.*]

My, my, what a cold shoulder! And such uncouth apparel! Why, you haven't even shaved! The unforgivable insult to a lady! But I forgive you. I forgive you because it's such a relief to see you. You've stopped that polka tune that I had caught in my head. Have you ever had anything caught in your head? No, of course you haven't, you dumb angel-puss, you'd never get anything awful caught in your head!

[*He stares at her while she follows him while she talks. It is obvious that he has had a few drinks on the way over.*]

MITCH:

Do we have to have that fan on?

BLANCHE:

No!

MITCH:

I don't like fans.

BLANCHE:

Then let's turn it off, honey. I'm not partial to them!

[*She presses the switch and the fan nods slowly off. She clears her throat uneasily as Mitch plumps himself down on the bed in the bedroom and lights a cigarette.*]

I don't know what there is to drink. I—haven't investigated.

MITCH:

I don't want Stan's liquor.

BLANCHE:

It isn't Stan's. Everything here isn't Stan's. Some things on the premises are actually mine! How is your mother? Isn't your mother well?

MITCH:

Why?

BLANCHE:

Something's the matter tonight, but never mind. I won't cross-examine the witness. I'll just— [*She touches her forehead vaguely. The polka tune starts up again.*] —pretend I don't notice anything different about you! That— music again...

MITCH:

What music?

BLANCHE:

The "Varsouviana"! The polka tune they were playing when Allan— Wait!

[*A distant revolver shot is heard. Blanche seems relieved.*]

There now, the shot! It always stops after that.

[*The polka music dies out again.*]

Yes, now it's stopped.

MITCH:

Are you boxed out of your mind?

BLANCHE:

I'll go and see what I can find in the way of— [*She crosses into the closet, pretending to search for the bottle.*]

Oh, by the way, excuse me for not being dressed. But I'd practically given you up! Had you forgotten your invitation to supper?

MITCH:

I wasn't going to see you any more.

BLANCHE:

Wait a minute. I can't hear what you're saying and you talk so little that when you do say something, I don't want to miss a single syllable of it.... What am I looking around here for? Oh, yes—liquor! We've had so much excitement around here this evening that I *am* boxed out of my mind! [*She pretends suddenly to find the bottle. He draws his foot up on the bed and stares at her contemptuously.*] Here's something. Southern Comfort! What is that, I wonder?

MITCH:

If you don't know, it must belong to Stan.

BLANCHE:

Take your foot off the bed. It has a light cover on it. Of course you boys don't notice things like that. I've done so much with this place since I've been here.

MITCH:

I bet you have.

BLANCHE:

You saw it before I came. Well, look at it now! This room is almost—dainty! I want to keep it that way. I wonder if this stuff ought to be mixed with something? Ummm, it's sweet, so sweet! It's terribly, terribly sweet!

Why, it's a *liqueur,* I believe! Yes, that's what it *is,* a liqueur! [*Mitch grunts.*] I'm afraid you won't like it, but try it, and maybe you will.

MITCH:

I told you already I don't want none of his liquor and I mean it. You ought to lay off his liquor. He says you been lapping it up all summer like a wild cat!

BLANCHE:

What a fantastic statement! Fantastic of him to say it, fantastic of you to repeat it! I won't descend to the level of such cheap accusations to answer them, even!

MITCH:

Huh.

BLANCHE:

What's in your mind? I see something in your eyes!

MITCH [*getting up*]:

It's dark in here.

BLANCHE:

I like it dark. The dark is comforting to me.

MITCH:

I don't think I ever seen you in the light. [*Blanche laughs breathlessly*] That's a fact!

BLANCHE:

Is it?

MITCH:

I've never seen you in the afternoon.

BLANCHE:

Whose fault is that?

MITCH:

You never want to go out in the afternoon.

BLANCHE:

Why, Mitch, you're at the plant in the afternoon!

MITCH:

Not Sunday afternoon. I've asked you to go out with me sometimes on Sundays but you always make an excuse. You never want to go out till after six and then it's always some place that's not lighted much.

BLANCHE:

There is some obscure meaning in this but I fail to catch it.

MITCH:

What it means is I've never had a real good look at you, Blanche. Let's turn the light on here.

BLANCHE [*fearfully*]:

Light? Which light? What for?

MITCH:

This one with the paper thing on it. [*He tears the paper lantern off the light bulb. She utters a frightened gasp.*]

BLANCHE:

What did you do that for?

MITCH:

So I can take a look at you good and plain!

BLANCHE:

Of course you don't really mean to be insulting!

MITCH:

No, just realistic.

BLANCHE:

I don't want realism. I want magic! [*Mitch laughs*] Yes, yes, magic! I try to give that to people. I misrepresent things to them. I don't tell truth, I tell what *ought* to be truth. And if that is sinful, then let me be damned for it!—*Don't turn the light on!*

[*Mitch crosses to the switch. He turns the light on and stares at her. She cries out and covers her face. He turns the light off again.*]

MITCH [*slowly and bitterly*]:

I don't mind you being older than what I thought. But all the rest of it—Christ! That pitch about your ideals being so old-fashioned and all the malarkey that you've dished out all summer. Oh, I knew you weren't sixteen any more. But I was a fool enough to believe you was straight.

BLANCHE:

Who told you I wasn't—"straight"? My loving brother-in-law. And you believed him.

MITCH:

I called him a liar at first. And then I checked on the story. First I asked our supply-man who travels through Laurel. And then I talked directly over long-distance to this merchant.

BLANCHE:

Who is this merchant?

MITCH:

Kiefaber.

BLANCHE:

The merchant Kiefaber of Laurel! I know the man. He whistled at me. I put him in his place. So now for revenge he makes up stories about me.

MITCH:

Three people, Kiefaber, Stanley and Shaw, swore to them!

BLANCHE:

Rub-a-dub-dub, three men in a tub! And such a filthy tub!

MITCH:

Didn't you stay at a hotel called The Flamingo?

BLANCHE:

Flamingo? No! Tarantula was the name of it! I stayed at a hotel called The Tarantula Arms!

MITCH [*stupidly*]:

Tarantula?

BLANCHE:

Yes, a big spider! That's where I brought my victims. [*She pours herself another drink*] Yes, I had many intimacies with strangers. After the death of Allan—intimacies with strangers was all I seemed able to fill my empty heart with. . . . I think it was panic, just panic, that drove me from one to another, hunting for some protection—here and there, in the most—unlikely places—even, at last, in a seventeen-year-old boy but—somebody wrote the superintendent about it—"This woman is morally unfit for her position!"

[*She throws back her head with convulsive, sobbing laughter. Then she repeats the statement, gasps, and drinks.*]

True? Yes, I suppose—unfit somehow—anyway. . . . So I came here. There was nowhere else I could go. I was played out. You know what played out is? My youth was suddenly gone up the water-spout, and—I met you. You said you needed somebody. Well, I needed somebody, too. I thanked God for you, because you seemed to be gentle—a cleft in the rock of the world that I could hide in! But I guess I was asking, hoping—too much! Kiefaber, Stanley and Shaw have tied an old tin can to the tail of the kite.

[*There is a pause. Mitch stares at her dumbly.*]

MITCH:

You lied to me, Blanche.

BLANCHE:

Don't say I lied to you.

MITCH:

Lies, lies, inside and out, all lies.

BLANCHE:

Never inside, I didn't lie in my heart . . .

[*A Vendor comes around the corner. She is a blind Mexican woman in a dark shawl, carrying bunches of those gaudy tin flowers that lower-class Mexicans display at funerals and other festive occasions. She is calling barely audibly. Her figure is only faintly visible outside the building.*]

MEXICAN WOMAN:

Flores. Flores. Flores para los muertos. Flores. Flores.

BLANCHE:

What? Oh! Somebody outside . . . [*She goes to the door, opens it and stares at the Mexican Woman.*]

MEXICAN WOMAN [*she is at the door and offers Blanche some of her flowers*]:

Flores? Flores para los muertos?

BLANCHE [*frightened*]:

No, no! Not now! Not now!

[*She darts back into the apartment, slamming the door.*]

MEXICAN WOMAN [*she turns away and starts to move down the street*]:

Flores para los muertos.

[*The polka tune fades in.*]

BLANCHE [*as if to herself*]:

Crumble and fade and—regrets—recriminations. . . "If you'd done this, it wouldn't've cost me that!"

MEXICAN WOMAN:

Corones para los muertos. Corones . . .

BLANCHE:

Legacies! Huh. . . . And other things such as bloodstained pillow-slips—"Her linen needs changing"—"Yes, Mother. But couldn't we get a colored girl to do it?" No, we couldn't of course. Everything gone but the—

MEXICAN WOMAN:

Flores.

BLANCHE:

Death—I used to sit here and she used to sit over there

and death was as close as you are.... We didn't dare even admit we had ever heard of it!

MEXICAN WOMAN:

Flores para los muertos, flores—flores...

BLANCHE:

The opposite is desire. So do you wonder? How could you possibly wonder! Not far from Belle Reve, before we had lost Belle Reve, was a camp where they trained young soldiers. On Saturday nights they would go in town to get drunk—

MEXICAN WOMAN [*softly*]:

Corones...

BLANCHE:

—and on the way back they would stagger onto my lawn and call—"Blanche! Blanche!"—the deaf old lady remaining suspected nothing. But sometimes I slipped outside to answer their calls.... Later the paddy-wagon would gather them up like daisies . . . the long way home...

[*The Mexican Woman turns slowly and drifts back off with her soft mournful cries. Blanche goes to the dresser and leans forward on it. After a moment, Mitch rises and follows her purposefully. The polka music fades away. He places his hands on her waist and tries to turn her about.*]

BLANCHE:

What do you want?

MITCH [*fumbling to embrace her*]:

What I been missing all summer.

BLANCHE:

Then marry me, Mitch!

MITCH:

I don't think I want to marry you any more.

BLANCHE:

No?

MITCH [*dropping his hands from her waist*]:

You're not clean enough to bring in the house with my mother.

BLANCHE:

Go away, then. [*He stares at her*] Get out of here quick before I start screaming fire! [*Her throat is tightening with hysteria*] Get out of here quick before I start screaming fire.

[*He still remains staring. She suddenly rushes to the big window with its pale blue square of the soft summer light and cries wildly.*]

Fire! Fire! Fire!

[*With a startled gasp, Mitch turns and goes out the outer door, clatters awkwardly down the steps and around the corner of the building. Blanche staggers back from the window and falls to her knees. The distant piano is slow and blue.*]

SCENE TEN

It is a few hours later that night.

Blanche has been drinking fairly steadily since Mitch left. She has dragged her wardrobe trunk into the center of the bedroom. It hangs open with flowery dresses thrown across it. As the drinking and packing went on, a mood of hysterical exhilaration came into her and she has decked herself out in a somewhat soiled and crumpled white satin evening gown and a pair of scuffed silver slippers with brilliants set in their heels.

Now she is placing the rhinestone tiara on her head before the mirror of the dressing-table and murmuring excitedly as if to a group of spectral admirers.

BLANCHE:

How about taking a swim, a moonlight swim at the old rock-quarry? If anyone's sober enough to drive a car! Ha-ha! Best way in the world to stop your head buzzing! Only you've got to be careful to dive where the deep pool is—if you hit a rock you don't come up till tomorrow...

[*Tremblingly she lifts the hand mirror for a closer inspection. She catches her breath and slams the mirror face down with such violence that the glass cracks. She moans a little and attempts to rise.*

[*Stanley appears around the corner of the building. He still has on the vivid green silk bowling shirt. As he rounds the corner the honky-tonk music is heard. It continues softly throughout the scene.*

[*He enters the kitchen, slamming the door. As he peers in at Blanche, he gives a low whistle. He has had a few drinks on the way and has brought some quart beer bottles home with him.*]

BLANCHE:

How is my sister?

STANLEY:

She is doing okay.

BLANCHE:

And how is the baby?

STANLEY [*grinning amiably*]:

The baby won't come before morning so they told me to go home and get a little shut-eye.

BLANCHE:

Does that mean we are to be alone in here?

STANLEY:

Yep. Just me and you, Blanche. Unless you got somebody hid under the bed. What've you got on those fine feathers for?

BLANCHE:

Oh, that's right. You left before my wire came.

STANLEY:

You got a wire?

BLANCHE:

I received a telegram from an old admirer of mine

STANLEY:

Anything good?

BLANCHE:

I think so. An invitation.

STANLEY:

What to? A fireman's ball?

BLANCHE [*throwing back her head*]:
A cruise of the Caribbean on a yacht!

STANLEY:
Well, well. What do you know?

BLANCHE:
I have never been so surprised in my life.

STANLEY:
I guess not.

BLANCHE:
It came like a bolt from the blue!

STANLEY:
Who did you say it was from?

BLANCHE:
An old beau of mine.

STANLEY:
The one that give you the white fox-pieces?

BLANCHE:
Mr. Shep Huntleigh. I wore his ATO pin my last year at college. I hadn't seen him again until last Christmas. I ran in to him on Biscayne Boulevard. Then—just now—this wire—inviting me on a cruise of the Caribbean! The problem is clothes. I tore into my trunk to see what I have that's suitable for the tropics!

STANLEY:
And come up with that—gorgeous—diamond—tiara?

BLANCHE:
This old relic? Ha-ha! It's only rhinestones.

STANLEY:

Gosh. I thought it was Tiffany diamonds. [*He unbuttons his shirt.*]

BLANCHE:

Well, anyhow, I shall be entertained in style.

STANLEY:

Uh-huh. It goes to show, you never know what is coming.

BLANCHE:

Just when I thought my luck had begun to fail me—

STANLEY:

Into the picture pops this Miami millionaire.

BLANCHE:

This man is not from Miami. This man is from Dallas.

STANLEY:

This man is from Dallas?

BLANCHE:

Yes, this man is from Dallas where gold spouts out of the ground!

STANLEY:

Well, just so he's from somewhere! [*He starts removing his shirt.*]

BLANCHE:

Close the curtains before you undress any further.

STANLEY [*amiably*]:

This is all I'm going to undress right now. [*He rips the sack off a quart beer bottle*] Seen a bottle-opener?

[*She moves slowly toward the dresser, where she stands with her hands knotted together.*]

I used to have a cousin who could open a beer bottle with his teeth. [*Pounding the bottle cap on the corner of table*] That was his only accomplishment, all he could do—he was just a human bottle-opener. And then one time, at a wedding party, he broke his front teeth off! After that he was so ashamed of himself he used t' sneak out of the house when company came . . .

[*The bottle cap pops off and a geyser of foam shoots up. Stanley laughs happily, holding up the bottle over his head.*]

Ha-ha! Rain from heaven! [*He extends the bottle toward her*] Shall we bury the hatchet and make it a loving-cup? Huh?

BLANCHE:

No, thank you.

STANLEY:

Well, it's a red-letter night for us both. You having an oil millionaire and me having a baby.

[*He goes to the bureau in the bedroom and crouches to remove something from the bottom drawer.*]

BLANCHE [*drawing back*]:

What are you doing in here?

STANLEY:

Here's something I always break out on special occasions like this. The silk pyjamas I wore on my wedding night!

BLANCHE:

Oh.

STANLEY:

When the telephone rings and they say, "You've got a son!" I'll tear this off and wave it like a flag! [*He shakes out a brilliant pyjama coat*] I guess we are both entitled to put on the dog. [*He goes back to the kitchen with the coat over his arm.*]

BLANCHE:

When I think of how divine it is going to be to have such a thing as privacy once more—I could weep with joy!

STANLEY:

This millionaire from Dallas is not going to interfere with your privacy any?

BLANCHE:

It won't be the sort of thing you have in mind. This man is a gentleman and he respects me. [*improvising feverishly*] What he wants is my companionship. Having great wealth sometimes makes people lonely! A cultivated woman, a woman of intelligence and breeding, can enrich a man's life—immeasurably! I have those things to offer, and this doesn't take them away. Physical beauty is passing. A transitory possession. But beauty of the mind and richness of the spirit and tenderness of the heart—and I have all of those things—aren't taken away, but grow! Increase with the years! How strange that I should be called a destitute woman! When I have all of these treasures locked in my heart. [*A choked sob comes from her*] I think of myself as a very, very rich woman! But I have been foolish—casting my pearls before swine!

STANLEY:

Swine, huh?

BLANCHE:

Yes, swine! Swine! And I'm thinking not only of you but of your friend, Mr. Mitchell. He came to see me tonight. He dared to come here in his work clothes! And to repeat slander to me, vicious stories that he had gotten from you! I gave him his walking papers . . .

STANLEY:

You did, huh?

BLANCHE:

But then he came back. He returned with a box of roses to beg my forgiveness! He implored my forgiveness. But some things are not forgivable. Deliberate cruelty is not forgivable. It is the one unforgivable thing in my opinion and it is the one thing of which I have never, never been guilty. And so I told him, I said to him, "Thank you," but it was foolish of me to think that we could ever adapt ourselves to each other. Our ways of life are too different. Our attitudes and our backgrounds are incompatible. We have to be realistic about such things. So farewell, my friend! And let there be no hard feelings . . .

STANLEY:

Was this before or after the telegram came from the Texas oil millionaire?

BLANCHE:

What telegram? No! No, after! As a matter of fact, the wire came just as—

STANLEY:

As a matter of fact there wasn't no wire at all!

BLANCHE:

Oh, oh!

STANLEY:

There isn't no millionaire! And Mitch didn't come back with roses 'cause I know where he is—

BLANCHE:

Oh!

STANLEY:

There isn't a goddam thing but imagination!

BLANCHE:

Oh!

STANLEY:

And lies and conceit and tricks!

BLANCHE:

Oh!

STANLEY:

And look at yourself! Take a look at yourself in that worn-out Mardi Gras outfit, rented for fifty cents from some rag-picker! And with the crazy crown on! What queen do you think you are?

BLANCHE:

Oh—God . . .

STANLEY:

I've been on to you from the start! Not once did you pull any wool over this boy's eyes! You come in here and sprinkle the place with powder and spray perfume and cover the light-bulb with a paper lantern, and lo and behold the place has turned into Egypt and you are the Queen of the Nile! Sitting on your throne and swilling down my liquor! I say—*Ha!—Ha!* Do you hear me? *Ha—ha—ha!* [*He walks into the bedroom.*]

BLANCHE:

Don't come in here!

[*Lurid reflections appear on the walls around Blanche.*

The shadows are of a grotesque and menacing form. She catches her breath, crosses to the phone and jiggles the hook. Stanley goes into the bathroom and closes the door.]

Operator, operator! Give me long-distance, please. . . . I want to get in touch with Mr. Shep Huntleigh of Dallas. He's so well known he doesn't require any address. Just ask anybody who—Wait!!—No, I couldn't find it right now. . . . Please understand, I—No! No, wait! . . . One moment! Someone is—Nothing! Hold on, please!

[*She sets the phone down and crosses warily into the kitchen. The night is filled with inhuman voices like cries in a jungle.*

[*The shadows and lurid reflections move sinuously as flames along the wall spaces.*

[*Through the back wall of the rooms, which have become transparent, can be seen the sidewalk. A prostitute has rolled a drunkard. He pursues her along the walk, overtakes her and there is a struggle. A policeman's whistle breaks it up. The figures disappear.*

[*Some moments later the Negro Woman appears around the corner with a sequined bag which the prostitute had dropped on the walk. She is rooting excitedly through it.*

[*Blanche presses her knuckles to her lips and returns slowly to the phone. She speaks in a hoarse whisper.*]

BLANCHE:

Operator! Operator! Never mind long-distance. Get Western Union. There isn't time to be—Western—Western Union!

[*She waits anxiously.*]

Western Union? Yes! I—want to—Take down this message! "In desperate, desperate circumstances! Help me! Caught in a trap. Caught in—" *Oh!*

[*The bathroom door is thrown open and Stanley comes out in the brilliant silk pyjamas. He grins at her as he knots the tasseled sash about his waist. She gasps and backs away from the phone. He stares at her for a count of ten. Then a clicking becomes audible from the telephone, steady and rasping.*]

STANLEY:

You left th' phone off th' hook.

[*He crosses to it deliberately and sets it back on the hook. After he has replaced it, he stares at her again, his mouth slowly curving into a grin, as he weaves between Blanche and the outer door.*

[*The barely audible "blue piano" begins to drum up louder. The sound of it turns into the roar of an approaching locomotive. Blanche crouches, pressing her fists to her ears until it has gone by.*]

BLANCHE [*finally straightening*]:

Let me—let me get by you!

STANLEY:

Get by me? Sure. Go ahead. [*He moves back a pace in the doorway.*]

BLANCHE:

You—you stand over there! [*She indicates a further position.*]

STANLEY [*grinning*]:
You got plenty of room to walk by me now.

BLANCHE:
Not with you there! But I've got to get out somehow!

STANLEY:
You think I'll interfere with you? Ha-ha!

[*The "blue piano" goes softly. She turns confusedly and makes a faint gesture. The inhuman jungle voices rise up. He takes a step toward her, biting his tongue which protrudes between his lips.*]

STANLEY [*softly*]:
Come to think of it—maybe you wouldn't be bad to—interfere with . . .

[*Blanche moves backward through the door into the bedroom.*]

BLANCHE:
Stay back! Don't you come toward me another step or I'll—

STANLEY:
What?

BLANCHE:
Some awful thing will happen! It will!

STANLEY:
What are you putting on now?

[*They are now both inside the bedroom.*]

BLANCHE:
I warn you, don't, I'm in danger!

[He takes another step. She smashes a bottle on the table and faces him, clutching the broken top.]

STANLEY:

What did you do that for?

BLANCHE:

So I could twist the broken end in your face!

STANLEY:

I bet you would do that!

BLANCHE:

I would! I will if you—

STANLEY:

Oh! So you want some roughhouse! All right, let's have some roughhouse!

[He springs toward her, overturning the table. She cries out and strikes at him with the bottle top but he catches her wrist.]

Tiger—tiger! Drop the bottle-top! Drop it! We've had this date with each other from the beginning!

[She moans. The bottle-top falls. She sinks to her knees: He picks up her inert figure and carries her to the bed. The hot trumpet and drums from the Four Deuces sound loudly.]

SCENE ELEVEN

It is some weeks later. Stella is packing Blanche's things. Sound of water can be heard running in the bathroom.

The portieres are partly open on the poker players—Stanley, Steve, Mitch and Pablo—who sit around the table in the kitchen. The atmosphere of the kitchen is now the same raw, lurid one of the disastrous poker night.

The building is framed by the sky of turquoise. Stella has been crying as she arranges the flowery dresses in the open trunk.

Eunice comes down the steps from her flat above and enters the kitchen. There is an outburst from the poker table.

STANLEY:

Drew to an inside straight and made it, by God.

PABLO:

Maldita sea tu suerto!

STANLEY:

Put it in English, greaseball.

PABLO:

I am cursing your rutting luck.

STANLEY [*prodigiously elated*]:

You know what luck is? Luck is believing you're lucky. Take at Salerno. I believed I was lucky. I figured that 4 out of 5 would not come through but I would . . . and I did. I put that down as a rule. To hold front position in this rat-race you've got to believe you are lucky.

MITCH:

You . . . you . . . you. . . . Brag . . . brag . . . bull . . . bull.

[*Stella goes into the bedroom and starts folding a dress.*]

STANLEY:

What's the matter with him?

EUNICE [*walking past the table*]:

I always did say that men are callous things with no feelings, but this does beat anything. Making pigs of yourselves. [*She comes through the portieres into the bedroom.*]

STANLEY:

What's the matter with her?

STELLA:

How is my baby?

EUNICE:

Sleeping like a little angel. Brought you some grapes. [*She puts them on a stool and lowers her voice.*] Blanche?

STELLA:

Bathing.

EUNICE:

How is she?

STELLA:

She wouldn't eat anything but asked for a drink.

EUNICE:

What did you tell her?

STELLA:

I—just told her that—we'd made arrangements for her

to rest in the country. She's got it mixed in her mind with Shep Huntleigh.

[*Blanche opens the bathroom door slightly.*]

BLANCHE:

Stella.

STELLA:

Yes, Blanche?

BLANCHE:

If anyone calls while I'm bathing take the number and tell them I'll call right back.

STELLA:

Yes.

BLANCHE:

That cool yellow silk—the bouclé. See if it's crushed. If it's not too crushed I'll wear it and on the lapel that silver and turquoise pin in the shape of a seahorse. You will find them in the heart-shaped box I keep my accessories in. And Stella . . . Try and locate a bunch of artificial violets in that box, too, to pin with the seahorse on the lapel of the jacket.

[*She closes the door. Stella turns to Eunice.*]

STELLA:

I don't know if I did the right thing.

EUNICE:

What else could you do?

STELLA:

I couldn't believe her story and go on living with Stanley.

EUNICE:

Don't ever believe it. Life has got to go on. No matter what happens, you've got to keep on going.

[*The bathroom door opens a little.*]

BLANCHE [*looking out*]:

Is the coast clear?

STELLA:

Yes, Blanche. [*to Eunice*] Tell her how well she's looking.

BLANCHE:

Please close the curtains before I come out.

STELLA:

They're closed.

STANLEY:

—How many for you?

PABLO:

—Two.

STEVE:

—Three.

[*Blanche appears in the amber light of the door. She has a tragic radiance in her red satin robe following the sculptural lines of her body. The "Varsouviana" rises audibly as Blanche enters the bedroom.*]

BLANCHE [*with faintly hysterical vivacity*]:

I have just washed my hair.

STELLA:

Did you?

BLANCHE:

I'm not sure I got the soap out.

EUNICE:

Such fine hair!

BLANCHE: [*accepting the compliment*]:

It's a problem. Didn't I get a call?

STELLA:

Who from, Blanche?

BLANCHE:

Shep Huntleigh . . .

STELLA:

Why, not yet, honey!

BLANCHE:

How strange! I—

[*At the sound of Blanche's voice Mitch's arm supporting his cards has sagged and his gaze is dissolved into space. Stanley slaps him on the shoulder.*]

STANLEY:

Hey, Mitch, come to!

[*The sound of this new voice shocks Blanche. She makes a shocked gesture, forming his name with her lips. Stella nods and looks quickly away. Blanche stands quite still for some moments—the silver-backed mirror in her hand and a look of sorrowful perplexity as though all human experience shows on her face. Blanche finally speaks but with sudden hysteria.*]

BLANCHE:

What's going on here?

[*She turns from Stella to Eunice and back to Stella. Her rising voice penetrates the concentration of the game. Mitch ducks his head lower but Stanley shoves back his chair as if about to rise. Steve places a restraining hand on his arm.*]

BLANCHE [*continuing*]:
What's happened here? I want an explanation of what's happened here.

STELLA [*agonizingly*]:
Hush! Hush!

EUNICE:
Hush! Hush! Honey.

STELLA:
Please, Blanche.

BLANCHE:
Why are you looking at me like that? Is something wrong with me?

EUNICE:
You look wonderful, Blanche. Don't she look wonderful?

STELLA:
Yes.

EUNICE:
I understand you are going on a trip.

STELLA:
Yes, Blanche *is*. She's going on a vacation.

EUNICE:

I'm green with envy.

BLANCHE:

Help me, help me get dressed!

STELLA [*handing her dress*]:

Is this what you—

BLANCHE:

Yes, it will do! I'm anxious to get out of here—this place is a trap!

EUNICE:

What a pretty blue jacket.

STELLA:

It's lilac colored.

BLANCHE:

You're both mistaken. It's Della Robbia blue. The blue of the robe in the old Madonna pictures. Are these grapes washed?

[*She fingers the bunch of grapes which Eunice had brought in.*]

EUNICE:

Huh?

BLANCHE:

Washed, I said. Are they washed?

EUNICE:

They're from the French Market.

BLANCHE:

That doesn't mean they've been washed. [*The cathedral*

bells chime] Those cathedral bells—they're the only clean thing in the Quarter. Well, I'm going now. I'm ready to go.

EUNICE [*whispering*]:

She's going to walk out before they get here.

STELLA:

Wait, Blanche.

BLANCHE:

I don't want to pass in front of those men.

EUNICE:

Then wait'll the game breaks up.

STELLA:

Sit down and ...

[*Blanche turns weakly, hesitantly about. She lets them push her into a chair.*]

BLANCHE:

I can smell the sea air. The rest of my time I'm going to spend on the sea. And when I die, I'm going to die on the sea. You know what I shall die of? [*She plucks a grape*] I shall die of eating an unwashed grape one day out on the ocean. I will die—with my hand in the hand of some nice-looking ship's doctor, a very young one with a small blond mustache and a big silver watch. "Poor lady," they'll say, "the quinine did her no good. That unwashed grape has transported her soul to heaven." [*The cathedral chimes are heard*] And I'll be buried at sea sewn up in a clean white sack and dropped overboard—at noon—in the blaze of summer—and into an ocean as blue as [*chimes again*] my first lover's eyes!

[*A Doctor and a Matron have appeared around the corner of the building and climbed the steps to the porch. The gravity of their profession is exaggerated—the unmistakable aura of the state institution with its cynical detachment. The Doctor rings the doorbell. The murmur of the game is interrupted.*]

EUNICE [*whispering to Stella*]:
That must be them.

[*Stella presses her fists to her lips.*]

BLANCHE [*rising slowly*]:
What is it?

EUNICE [*affectedly casual*]:
Excuse me while I see who's at the door.

STELLA:
Yes.

[*Eunice goes into the kitchen.*]

BLANCHE [*tensely*]:
I wonder if it's for me.

[*A whispered colloquy takes place at the door.*]

EUNICE [*returning, brightly*]:
Someone is calling for Blanche.

BLANCHE:
It *is* for me, then! [*She looks fearfully from one to the other and then to the portieres. The "Varsouviana" faintly plays*] Is it the gentleman I was expecting from Dallas?

EUNICE:
I think it is, Blanche.

BLANCHE:

I'm not quite ready.

STELLA:

Ask him to wait outside.

BLANCHE:

I . . .

[*Eunice goes back to the portieres. Drums sound very softly.*]

STELLA:

Everything packed?

BLANCHE:

My silver toilet articles are still out.

STELLA:

Ah!

EUNICE [*returning*]:

They're waiting in front of the house.

BLANCHE:

They! Who's "they"?

EUNICE:

There's a lady with him.

BLANCHE:

I cannot imagine who this "lady" could be! How is she dressed?

EUNICE:

Just—just a sort of a—plain-tailored outfit.

BLANCHE:

Possibly she's—[*Her voice dies out nervously.*]

STELLA:

Shall we go, Blanche?

BLANCHE:

Must we go through that room?

STELLA:

I will go with you.

BLANCHE:

How do I look?

STELLA:

Lovely.

EUNICE [*echoing*]:

Lovely.

[*Blanche moves fearfully to the portieres. Eunice draws them open for her. Blanche goes into the kitchen.*]

BLANCHE [*to the men*]:

Please don't get up. I'm only passing through.

[*She crosses quickly to outside door. Stella and Eunice follow. The poker players stand awkwardly at the table—all except Mitch, who remains seated, looking down at the table. Blanche steps out on a small porch at the side of the door. She stops short and catches her breath.*]

DOCTOR:

How do you do?

BLANCHE:

You are not the gentleman I was expecting. [*She suddenly gasps and starts back up the steps. She stops by*

Stella, who stands just outside the door, and speaks in a frightening whisper] That man isn't Shep Huntleigh.

[*The "Varsouviana" is playing distantly.*

[*Stella stares back at Blanche. Eunice is holding Stella's arm. There is a moment of silence—no sound but that of Stanley steadily shuffling the cards.*

[*Blanche catches her breath again and slips back into the flat. She enters the flat with a peculiar smile, her eyes wide and brilliant. As soon as her sister goes past her, Stella closes her eyes and clenches her hands. Eunice throws her arms comfortingly about her. Then she starts up to her flat. Blanche stops just inside the door. Mitch keeps staring down at his hands on the table, but the other men look at her curiously. At last she starts around the table toward the bedroom. As she does, Stanley suddenly pushes back his chair and rises as if to block her way. The Matron follows her into the flat.*]

STANLEY:

Did you forget something?

BLANCHE [*shrilly*]:

Yes! Yes, I forgot something!

[*She rushes past him into the bedroom. Lurid reflections appear on the walls in odd, sinuous shapes. The "Varsouviana" is filtered into a weird distortion, accompanied by the cries and noises of the jungle. Blanche seizes the back of a chair as if to defend herself.*]

STANLEY [*sotto voce*]:

Doc, you better go in.

DOCTOR [*sotto voce, motioning to the Matron*]:
Nurse, bring her out.

[*The Matron advances on one side, Stanley on the other. Divested of all the softer properties of womanhood, the Matron is a peculiarly sinister figure in her severe dress. Her voice is bold and toneless as a firebell.*]

MATRON:
Hello, Blanche.

[*The greeting is echoed and re-echoed by other mysterious voices behind the walls, as if reverberated through a canyon of rock.*]

STANLEY:
She says that she forgot something.

[*The echo sounds in threatening whispers.*]

MATRON:
That's all right.

STANLEY:
What did you forget, Blanche?

BLANCHE:
I— I—

MATRON:
It don't matter. We can pick it up later.

STANLEY:
Sure. We can send it along with the trunk.

BLANCHE [*retreating in panic*]:
I don't know you—I don't know you. I want to be—left alone—please!

MATRON:

Now, Blanche!

ECHOES [*rising and falling*]:

Now, Blanche—now, Blanche—now, Blanche!

STANLEY:

You left nothing here but spilt talcum and old empty perfume bottles—unless it's the paper lantern you want to take with you. You want the lantern?

[*He crosses to dressing table and seizes the paper lantern, tearing it off the light bulb, and extends it toward her. She cries out as if the lantern was herself. The Matron steps boldly toward her. She screams and tries to break past the Matron. All the men spring to their feet. Stella runs out to the porch, with Eunice following to comfort her, simultaneously with the confused voices of the men in the kitchen. Stella rushes into Eunice's embrace on the porch.*]

STELLA:

Oh, my God, Eunice help me! Don't let them do that to her, don't let them hurt her! Oh, God, oh, please God, don't hurt her! What are they doing to her? What are they doing? [*She tries to break from Eunice's arms.*]

EUNICE:

No, honey, no, no, honey. Stay here. Don't go back in there. Stay with me and don't look.

STELLA:

What have I done to my sister? Oh, God, what have I done to my sister?

EUNICE:

You done the right thing, the only thing you could do.

She couldn't stay here; there wasn't no other place for her to go.

[*While Stella and Eunice are speaking on the porch the voices of the men in the kitchen overlap them. Mitch has started toward the bedroom. Stanley crosses to block him. Stanley pushes him aside. Mitch lunges and strikes at Stanley. Stanley pushes Mitch back. Mitch collapses at the table, sobbing.*

[*During the preceding scenes, the Matron catches hold of Blanche's arm and prevents her flight. Blanche turns wildly and scratches at the Matron. The heavy woman pinions her arms. Blanche cries out hoarsely and slips to her knees.*]

MATRON:

These fingernails have to be trimmed. [*The Doctor comes into the room and she looks at him.*] Jacket, Doctor?

DOCTOR:

Not unless necessary.

[*He takes off his hat and now he becomes personalized. The unhuman quality goes. His voice is gentle and reassuring as he crosses to Blanche and crouches in front of her. As he speaks her name, her terror subsides a little. The lurid reflections fade from the walls, the inhuman cries and noises die out and her own hoarse crying is calmed.*]

DOCTOR:

Miss DuBois.

[*She turns her face to him and stares at him with des-*

perate pleading. He smiles; then he speaks to the Matron.]

It won't be necessary.

BLANCHE [*faintly*]:

Ask her to let go of me.

DOCTOR [*to the Matron*]:

Let go.

[*The Matron releases her. Blanche extends her hands toward the Doctor. He draws her up gently and supports her with his arm and leads her through the portieres.*]

BLANCHE [*holding tight to his arm*]:

Whoever you are—I have always depended on the kindness of strangers.

[*The poker players stand back as Blanche and the Doctor cross the kitchen to the front door. She allows him to lead her as if she were blind. As they go out on the porch, Stella cries out her sister's name from where she is crouched a few steps up on the stairs.*]

STELLA:

Blanche! Blanche, Blanche!

[*Blanche walks on without turning, followed by the Doctor and the Matron. They go around the corner of the building.*

[*Eunice descends to Stella and places the child in her arms. It is wrapped in a pale blue blanket. Stella accepts the child, sobbingly. Eunice continues downstairs and enters the kitchen where the men, except for*

Stanley, are returning silently to their places about the table. Stanley has gone out on the porch and stands at the foot of the steps looking at Stella.]

STANLEY [*a bit uncertainly*]:

Stella?

[*She sobs with inhuman abandon. There is something luxurious in her complete surrender to crying now that her sister is gone.*]

STANLEY [*voluptuously, soothingly*]:

Now, honey. Now, love. Now, now, love. [*He kneels beside her and his fingers find the opening of her blouse*] Now, now, love. Now, love. . . .

[*The luxurious sobbing, the sensual murmur fade away under the swelling music of the "blue piano" and the muted trumpet.*]

STEVE:

This game is seven-card stud.

CURTAIN